# Review of Research and Practice

# Volume 3

Edited by

Virgina Gonzalez
*University of Cincinnati*

Josefina Tinajero
*University of Texas at El Paso*

 LAWRENCE ERLBAUM ASSOCIATES, PUBLISHERS

2005   Mahwah, New Jersey                    London

Lawrence Erlbaum Associates, Inc., Publishers
10 Industrial Avenue
Mahwah, New Jersey 07430

**ISBN 0-8058-5275-1 (hardcover)**
**ISBN 0-8058-5276-X (paperback)**

Books published by Lawrence Erlbaum Associates are printed on
acid-free paper, and their bindings are chosen for strength and
durability.

Printed in the United States of America
10 9 8 7 6 5 4 3 2 1

# NABE Review of Research & Practice (NRRP) Volume 3

## 2004

## NRRP SECTIONS

The *NABE Review of Research & Practice* (NRRP) Volume 3 has **3 sections** for fulfilling its goals.

The Research section is edited by Dr. Virginia Gonzalez.

The Applied Education/Action Research section is overseen by Dr. Evangeline Harris Stefanakis, Associate Editor of this section.

The Position Papers and Reflections section is overseen by Dr. Liliana Minaya-Rowe, Associate Editor of this section.

In addition, Dr. Beverly Irby, Dr. Rafael Lara-Alecio, and Dr. Martha Galloway offer support as Technical Associate Editors.

# Contents

## II  APPLIED EDUCATION/ACTION RESEARCH

## III  POSITION PAPERS AND REFLECTIONS

# Editor's Note
# NABE Review of Research
# and Practice (NRRP) Volume 3

## OVERVIEW OF CONTENT AND MISSION
## OF THE NRRP VOLUME 3

It is a pleasure for me to unveil the National Association for Bilingual Education (NABE) *Review of Research and Practice* (NRRP) Volume 3 that appears for the first time in hard copy as an archival record of NABE 2004 Conference. Volumes 1 and 2 appeared online (under its former name *NABE Journal of Research & Practice*—NJRP) and served as an outlet to establish an archival record for NABE 2002 and 2003 Conferences. Our team effort is now crystallized with the valuable support of Lawrence Erlbaum Associates (LEA) for publishing a hard copy of the NRRP Volume 3 serving as an archival record for NABE 2004 Conference. The appearance of this paper copy establishes the NRRP as a formal publication of articles written by bilingual education and English as a second language (ESL) education experts who presented at the NABE 2004 Conference. The collection of eight articles presented as chapters in the NRRP Volume 3 represents valuable information linking research and practice that helps to increase the knowledge base of scholars and practitioners in the field of bilingual and ESL education.

I am especially pleased with the valuable contributions of articles by recognized and prolific scholars and educators such as (1) Stephen Krashen; (2) a team of collaborators including Beverly Irby and Rafael Lara-Alecio with Linda Rodriguez, Genevieve Brown, and Martha Galloway for a research article contribution; and with Rick Bruhn, Mei Lou, and W. Tom Thweatt III for a second action research article contribution; and (3) co-authors Jaime Castellano and Margarita Pinkos. Together this group of experts brings valuable knowledge that advances the field of bilingual and ESL education. The publication of these articles in the First Research Section fulfills one of the most important missions of NABE and the *NRRP*. As one of NABE's sponsored publications, the NRRP has as a central mission to help advance the research-based knowledge of the field of bilingual and ESL education. More specifically, by disseminating research-based knowledge, one of the central missions of the NRRP is fulfilled: To advocate for the use of research-based knowledge for developing and implementing high-quality educational programs for bilingual, ESL, and *all* learners.

Another important set of articles in the *NRRP* come from presentations at NABE 2004 Conference by junior scholars as single authors or co-authors with senior scholars. Volume 4 brings articles co-authored by Iliana Alanis and her mentor, Josefina Villamil Tinajero; and an article single authored by Afra Ahmed Hersi. The publication of articles authored and co-authored by junior scholars helps accomplish another central *NRRP* mission: to serve as an outlet of publication for junior scholars who need mentoring for finding jobs and achieving tenure in universities and colleges. The *NRRP* also has as a mission to support educators working as action researchers in schools, by publishing their presentations at NABE Conferences. The publication of junior scholars' and educators' valuable articles provides an important professional development service as members of the NRRP Editorial Board and Expert Reviewers function as role models and mentors in order to support the scholarly work of junior academic peers and educators. The *NRRP* offers much needed support for junior scholars and educators working in the field of bilingual and ESL education for achieving tenure in a timely manner, and by doing so to secure the next generation of leaders and mentors who will continue developing NABE's mission.

## Sections and Central Theme of the NRRP, Volume 3

The *NRRP* has three sections that cluster articles into a **First Research Section**, a **Second Applied Education and Action Research Section**, and a **Third Position Papers and Reflections Section.**

Volume 3 features a **First Research Section of four articles**. The central *theme* emerging centers on a timely issue: The valuable role of research-based knowledge for supporting the acquisition of academic English proficiency, and related reading abilities, within the context of two-way bilingual education programs. Stephen Krashen masterfully present a critique of the still scarce existing research evidence of one aspect of two-way bilingual programs: Their impact and effectiveness on increasing academic English proficiency in language-minority students, as reflected by performance on tests of English reading comprehension. Krashen grabs the attention of the reader by presenting a compelling methodological analysis of the research literature pointing to inadequate research-based evidence for a demonstration of two-way bilingual programs as the best option, although promising based on available scarce data. However, Krashen as an avid supporter of bilingual education makes a case for educators to continue conducting research on this area. He calls attention to the need for conducting larger scale studies, and having better control of methodological flaws in order to discover the promising value of two-way bilingual programs on the English academic language proficiency of language-minority students.

Iliana Alanis and Josefina Villamil Tinajero continue exploring *the central theme for Volume 4* by presenting research on the effect of early reading intervention on first-Grade Spanish-speaking students attending a bilingual Spanish /English education program. Using a research design that combined quantitative and qualitative methods, their data revealed varying levels of achievement in reading comprehension and literacy, which intersected with multiple cognitive development, instructional, and background factors. Their study revealed that the use of the native language and culturally relevant texts, the inclusion of family and culture, and high teacher expectations facilitate language-minority children's literacy development within the context of two-way bilingual programs. Their study helps bilingual and ESL educators to better understand the complexity of multiple educational factors explaining English academic language development in young children, and the value of high-quality instruction for bilingual literacy (or biliteracy) development.

Linda Rodriguez, Beverly Irby, Genevieve Brown, Rafael Lara-Alecio, and Martha Galloway represent a team of collaborators that skillfully demonstrate the effectiveness of bilingual education for English and Spanish reading achievement in young learners. Their study also connects to *the central theme for Volume 4* and contributes to the research literature by presenting longitudinal data supporting the effectiveness of a Montessori bilingual education program over a traditional transitional bilingual education program.

Virginia Gonzalez studied the effect of developmental, socioeconomic status (SES), and linguistic factors affecting the assessment of cognition and language in monolingual and bilingual young children. This study also connects to *the central theme for Volume 4* by presenting qualitative and quantitative data demonstrating that the performance of bilingual low SES students on an alternative cognitive assessment is affected by language of administration and response and cultural attributes. Thus, the fact that most language-minority children come from disadvantaged SES backgrounds, rather than they speak Spanish or are limited-English proficient, is the most important variable influencing their performance in cognitive developmental measures.

**There are three articles featured in the Second Applied Education/Action Research Section.** The first article is co-authored by Jaime Castellano and Margarita Pinkos and illustrates *the central theme of Volume 4* by making a case for connecting dual language (or two-way bilingual) education programs with gifted education. They skillfully present a rationale for the reader to consider the cost effectiveness of intersecting bilingual and gifted programs, in light of research evidence and an analysis of its successful implementation in the School District of Palm Beach County, Florida.

The second article is authored by Afra Ahmed Hersi, and presents a sociocultural case study using in-depth interviews with three Somali high school students. Hersi examines Somali high school students' sociocultural experiences and educational challenges emerging from their need to develop literacy in their native language and English for increasing academic achievement. A significant practical implication suggested by the study was the importance of creating extra academic and psychosocial support for Somali students by offering professional development for teachers, and working collaboratively with organizations and institutions within the Somali community.

The third article contributed by a team of collaborators including Rick Bruhn, Beverly Irby, Mei Lou, W. Tom Thweatt, III, and Rafael Lara-Alecio presents a training model for bilingual school counselors. They skillfully provide a model master program with collaborative curriculum between the school, ESL parents and community, and university professors to mentor and train effectively counselors that can serve as bridges and committed advocates for ESL Spanish-speaking students and their families.

The **Third Section brings one Position Paper**. Stephen Krashen presents a compelling argument and suggestions for improving the public relations and dissemination of information about reasons to support bilingual education programs in the public schools. This position paper also relates to *the central theme of Volume 4*: To support the acquisition of academic English proficiency, and related reading abilities, within the context of bilingual education programs. Krashen suggests to "tell the public the truth about bilingual education." That is, to dispel myths about bilingual education and to make an effort to present compelling evidence and arguments that inform the public about how and why bilingual education helps children acquire English more effectively than other education programs. He also proposes that researchers and scholars concentrate their efforts in gathering compelling information about the instructional effectiveness of bilingual education for teaching English to language-minority students. Finally, he strongly recommends that a good start to achieve this goal is to increase the instructional resources of good bilingual programs, and to concentrate on providing good reading materials to increase English and native-language development.

## A COMMENT ON TERMINOLOGY USED BY AUTHORS

Finally, I would like to make a comment on the terminology used by invited and contributing authors for referring to ESL students. It was very interesting to me to find a variety of terms used by different authors, reflecting the transitions that we are presently experiencing in the field of bilingual and ESL education. The labels for the students whose first language (L1) is other than English have historically been through a number of stages since the inception of the bilingual and ESL education areas; and has evolve through the decades of the 1960s, 1970s, 1980s, 1990s, and presently in the 2000 years.

Some of the authors refer to "culturally and linguistically diverse" students, which is abbreviated by the acronym CLD or CLDS, a term that entered our field during the early 1990s. During the 1990s we also coined the term "language-minority students," abbreviated by LMS, which was the label of choice for some authors. Other authors refer to English language learners, abbreviated by ELLs, which is the most recent term coined. The onset of the No Child Left Behind (NCLB) policy in December 2001 made the ELLs terms widely spread. Authors using the label ELLs also refer to the need to include *all* learners within high-quality education programs. The "education for all" has also become a common phrase in the terminology used by bilingual and ESL educators since the onset of the NCLB policy.

What is interesting to acknowledge is that throughout the years, since the 1960s until today, the most traditional terminology of ESL and bilingual education is still widely used by educators to refer to our field and students. Some authors selected ESL as their label for educators and students. As bilingual and ESL educators, and member of NABE, we all embrace the celebration of diversity, and acknowledge that diverse students are becoming the "new majority" or the "new mainstream" students, comprised in the term *all* students.

In closing, I must state that I celebrate and appreciate the contributions of *all* authors to the NRRP Volume 3. This Volume celebrates the powerful effect of high-quality bilingual education for increasing developmental and academic achievement outcomes and progress among our ESL students; and makes the case for the importance of research for ESL and bilingual, and *all*, educators to better serve English language learners.

Happy readings!

*—Virginia Gonzalez, Ph. D.*
*Co-Editor-in-Chief*
*NRRP*

# I

# RESEARCH

# 1

# The Acquisition of Academic English by Children in Two-Way Programs: What Does the Research Say?

Stephen Krashen
*University of Southern California*

## ABSTRACT

This paper focuses on one aspect of two-way bilingual programs: Progress in acquiring academic English, as reflected by performance on tests of English reading comprehension by language-minority students. A review of studies reveals that two-way students do indeed progress in English and results are promising, but the research has not yet demonstrated that two-way programs are the best possible alternative.

## INTRODUCTION

Two-way bilingual programs are those in which majority language children and minority language children attend the same classes at the same time. The idea being that majority language children will acquire the minority language and minority language children will acquire the majority language. There has been a great deal of excitement about these programs. Claims have been made that two-way has been shown to be the most effective form of bilingual education, and the best possible program for language-minority children in general. It is important that we take a careful look at the research to see if these claims are supported.

The purpose of this paper is to examine one aspect of the research on two-way programs, specifically to examine the progress of language-minority students in acquiring academic English. The focus here is on performance on tests of reading comprehension, a measure considered to be the gold standard for academic English. The questions to be discussed are these: (1) Do English learners in two-way programs show evidence of significant acquisition of English? (2) Do they outperform children in non-bilingual (all-English) options? (3) Do they outperform children participating in other forms of bilingual education? Some data is also available comparing two-way children with native speakers of English.

I will review the studies in ascending order of their ability to answer these three questions. First, I briefly discuss studies that had to be excluded from this analysis. Then, we look at studies that lacked comparison groups. These studies are able to provide us with some information regarding the first question. The third group consists of studies in which two-way students are compared to similar students in mainstream or submersion classes, an attempt to answer question (2). The fourth group consists of studies comparing two-way students to those in other Kinds of bilingual education programs, an attempt to answer question (3). Finally, I include a section on studies in which two-way children are compared to native speakers of English.

## GROUP ONE: EXCLUDED STUDIES

I begin this review by excluding a number of studies from the analysis, reports in which few details are reported (Thomas & Collier, 1997), reports in which it is not possible to determine how well English learners did because their scores are combined with those of native speakers of English (Christian, Montone, Lindholm, & Carranza, 1997; Lindholm & Fairchild, 1990; Rhodes, Crandell, & Christian, 1990; Sensec, 2002),[1] and reports in which two-way students were not tested in English (Coy & Litherland, 2000). In addition, in several of these studies, a substantial percentage of language-minority speakers appear to have already acquired a considerable amount of English before beginning the program. These studies do not shed light on any of the three issues to be discussed. Finally, two studies labeled "dual language" comparisons were excluded because comparisons were not monolingual speakers of English but were bilingual English-dominant (Oller & Eilers, 2002; Perez & Flores, 2002).

## GROUP TWO: STUDIES
## WITHOUT COMPARISON GROUPS

Sugarman and Howard (2002) studied eleven two-way programs, and reported that Spanish speakers in these programs improved on different tests of English from Grade three to five. There was, however, no comparison group and the measures used were not standardized. Thus, there was no way to compare the progress of children in two-way with counterparts in other programs. Sugarman and Howard's results, however, provide a positive answer to the first of the three questions posed in the introduction; they show that children in two-way programs make progress in acquiring English.

Several studies provide data using standardized tests without comparison groups. Before proceeding with a discussion of these studies, it should be noted that results in these studies are reported as Normal Curve Equivalent (NCE) scores, which are very useful when making comparisons across studies. NCE scores are constructed so that the mean is 50 and the standard deviation is 21.06.

NCE scores are not the same as ordinary percentiles, except at 1, 50, and 99. Of special interest is the fact that when scores are below the 50th percentile, NCE scores are higher than percentiles. A percentile rank of 29, for example, is equivalent to an NCE score of 38. Above the 50th percentile, NCE scores are lower than percentiles. A percentile rank of 76 is equivalent to an NCE score of about 65. Thus, in discussing the studies to follow, both NCE and percentiles will be included. (I thank Jim Crawford for pointing out the necessity of doing this.)

De Jong (2002) reported that different cohorts of Spanish-dominant children in a two-way program consistently attained NCE scores between 38 (29th percentile) and 43 (37th percentile) on the Stanford Reading Test in Grade five between 1995 and 2000. Sample sizes were small, however, ranging from 13 to 18 students. A possible problem with this study is that "Spanish-dominant" does not necessarily mean limited English proficient; no information was provided on subjects' initial English proficiency.

In Lindholm (2002), on tests of English reading, English learners in three two-way programs achieved NCE scores of 34 (23rd percentile), 35 (24th percentile) and 39 (30th percentile) by Grade 6, with one group achieving an NCE score of 43 (37th percentile) by Grade 7 (see Table 10.6, p. 217). (However, one group attained only the 9th percentile in Grade 5, see discussion below.) A subgroup studied longitudinally (n = 149) attained an NCE score of 41 in Grade 7 (34th percentile). Because few subjects were classified as orally proficient in English in Kindergarten (Lindholm, 2002, p. 190) we can be confident that most subjects in this group were in fact limited in English when they began the program (see footnote 1 for studies in which this was not the case).

Thomas and Collier (2002) reported that a larger percentage of Spanish-speaking children at a two-way program at the Grant School in Oregon exceeded state norms than did students state and district-wide. This is impressive, but it was only true for one of the two groups tested, consisting of 12 students in Grade 3. In Grade 5, Grant students do not do well, scoring lower than district and state norms, but Thomas and Collier note that the Grant group (only 17 children) included latecomers. The Grant school has a very high mobility rate (71% annual). There was no separate analysis of those who have been in the program since Kindergarten.

A multiple regression analysis, however, revealed a positive and statistically significant relationship between years in the program and scores on the English reading test, controlling for socioeconomic status (SES), which can be considered an index of poverty level. Moreover, the effect of years in the program was larger than the effect of SES.

It is difficult to determine whether children at Grant began Kindergarten with no English. It is unlikely. At Grade 1, Grant students in scored 13.81 on the

SOLOM measure of oral English, a test with a range of 5 to 25; a score of 19 is considered "proficient." By way of comparison, English speakers in the two-way program did not reach this level in Spanish until Grade 4 in Spanish.

## GROUP THREE: COMPARISON TO ENGLISH LEARNERS IN THE MAINSTREAM

We would expect English learners in properly organized two-way programs to out-perform comparison children in the mainstream, especially those in "submersion" programs. In Ajuira (1994), "Hispanic" two-way students in Grade 1 did better than comparison students in a mainstream class on a modified version of the Iowa Test of Basic Skills. Ajuria modified the test herself, making it shorter, and including only items of "average difficulty" and items rated "fairly easy" (p. 139). The scores ranged from zero to six, but Ajuira does not tell us how this scale was constructed.

The two-way students scored 3.7 on a 0–6 scale and the mainstream students scored 2.4. Native speakers in the mainstream scored 3.4, below the level of the two-way Hispanic children. Before calling this a victory for two-way, however, there are problems:

1. Two-way students were given the same test the previous semester and scores were identical. There were, therefore, no gains.

2. Only 11 students were tested in the two-way program and only seven in the mainstream program.

3. We do not know if the Hispanic students were ever limited in English.

4. The mainstream classroom was an inferior pedagogical environment: "Mate-rials were painfully lacking in the mainstream classroom, to the extent that there was only one Big Book in the entire room, and the other few books there were occu-pied less than a quarter of one bookshelf. The readers the students used in the small reading groups were kept by the teacher, and were only available to the students during reading time . . . In both classrooms of the bilingual program, in contrast, there were well over twenty Big Books in Spanish and in English . . ." (p. 88). Na-tive speakers of English in the two-way program did much better than those in the mainstream program (4.4 versus 3.4). This could be because of the value of the two-way program or the impoverished print environment of the mainstream classroom (or both). Perhaps the correct generalization is that two-way students did better than those who were in submersion in a print-deprived environment.

Castillo (2001) reported that "native Spanish speakers" ages 5 to 8 (K–2) in two-way did far better than comparisons in a "regular classroom" (41st versus 11th percentile on ITBS Reading), but only four children were in the comparison group. (Refer to Table 1.1.) We do not know if the "native Spanish speakers" were limited in English (although it appears that those in the submersion class

TABLE 1.1
Years in Program and ITBS Scores (Percentiles)

| Years in Program | n | Mean |
|---|---|---|
| 1 | 21 | 57 |
| 2 | 20 | 26 |
| 3 | 20 | 34 |

From: Castillo (2001)

were). Results were also quite variable: the standard deviation for the two-way group was 26. The two-way students also did better than the full group of comparison students (mean = 34, *sd* = 27); 30 out of 34 of the comparison children were native speakers of English.

Castillo examined the impact of years in the two-way program, reporting very high scores the first year, and lower scores for those in the program longer. The very high score after Grade 1 is unusual, and suggests that not all the children were limited in English.

The results of this study are difficult to interpret. To be sure, two-way children did better than comparisons, both Spanish and English native speakers. But there were only four children in the Spanish-dominant comparison group, and scores were very high at the beginning but lower for those in the program two and three years. The data could mean that two-way is highly successful, and it could mean the opposite, that children begin the program with high levels of English proficiency and then get worse. In addition, the lower scores could also be a result of high-scoring children exiting the program.

Collier and Thomas (2002) provided some additional data. Two-way children in Houston appeared to be well ahead of children acquiring English whose families refused special help for their children. These "refusers" scored at the 20th percentile level at Grade 5 (NCE = 32). Children in English as a second language (ESL) only programs, however, reached the 66th percentile in Grade 5 (NCE = 59), doing better than two-way children. Two-way children in Houston scored at the 52nd percentile in Grade 5 (NCE = 541.3). It is possible, however, that those assigned to ESL had higher levels of English when entering school, and the data are not controlled for poverty and neighborhood, as are students in Collier and Thomas' other Houston comparisons (see below).

## GROUP THREE: COMPARISON WITH OTHER BILINGUAL EDUCATION PROGRAMS

### Comparison to Transitional Bilingual Education

In Clayton (1993), "Spanish-speaking" students who had participated in transitional bilingual education outperformed "Spanish-speaking" students who had been in a two-way program on English reading. The two-way students had been in

TABLE 1.2
Comparison of Two-Way and Transitional
Bilingual Education (TBE) Graduates, Grades 3–8

|            | 1991 n/mean | 1992 n/mean |
|------------|-------------|-------------|
| Two-way    | 83/662.23   | 83/690.41   |
| TBE        | 59/686.61   | 59/708.8    |

From: Clayton (1993)

the program for at least four years. The results were similar when parental education was controlled, but the difference was greater when parents in both groups had no education. Two-way students outperformed Native American students from similar SES status. Students were in Grades 3 through 8. We do not know if "Spanish-speaking" meant limited in English, however. Clayton suggests that the two-way program had an inferior reading program (p. 155) and was a newer program (p. 157). Table 1.2 presents data from two successive years of testing.

Cazabon, Lambert and Hall (1993) report on the English proficiency of Spanish-speaking children in a two way program in Massachusetts, as compared to children "in a standard bilingual program" (p. 5). Two-way and comparison children were similar in social class and intellectual ability, as measured by the Raven Matrices test.

It is not clear that all children classified as Spanish speakers ("Spanish amigos") were Spanish dominant. In Grade 1, for two cohorts combined, seven out of 47 were considered English-dominant (Lau classification score of 4 or 5 out of 5), and none were classified as completely Spanish-dominant. This measure was not applied at the beginning of the program, but seven months into Grade 1; it is quite possible that the children had acquired considerable English conversational competence by then.

Table 1.3 presents scores on the California Achievement Test for two cohorts. The results are impressive: two-way children outperform comparisons in all Grade levels for both cohorts, and achieve above the expected (grade level) score in Grade 3 in one cohort. There are, however, reasons to be somewhat cautious:

1. The sample sizes are very small.
2. The study only goes up to Grade 3.
3. There is unusual variability in the Grade 3 1989–90 score (standard deviation = 2.6). (The *sd* of 7.3 for comparisons in Grade 1 appears to be an error; more likely, it was .73).
4. The 1990–91 cohort shows a decline from Grades 2 to 3, making less than one year progress in one academic year.

It is noteworthy that "Spanish amigos" children were behind comparisons on a measure of "communication skills" (done in an interview) in Grade 1 but

TABLE 1.3
"Spanish Amigos" English Competence (Grade Level Equivalents)

| Grade | n | Score | Comp n | Comparison Score | Expected |
|---|---|---|---|---|---|
| | | | *1989–1990 Cohort* | | |
| 1 | 8 | 1.38  (.17) | 8 | .95 (7.3) | 1.7 |
| 2 | 10 | 2.07  (.71) | 9 | 1.92  (.53) | 2.7 |
| 3 | 6 | 4.65 (2.6) | 6 | 1.48  (.26) | 3.7 |
| | | | *1990–91 Cohort* | | |
| 1 | 12 | 1.29  (.43) | 12 | .69  (.49) | 1.7 |
| 2 | 10 | 3.11 (1.16) | 10 | 1.56  (.52) | 2.7 |
| 3 | 7 | 2.87 (1.44) | 7 | 2.14  (.47) | 3.7 |

From: Cazabon, Lambert, and Hall (1993)

performed better than comparisons in Grades 2 and 3, increasing their lead in Grade 3.

In their Houston report, Thomas and Collier go a long way toward controlling for pre-existing differences among the groups. In their report, data is provided for two-way bilingual education as well as two alternative programs: transitional bilingual education (TBE) and "developmental bilingual education." All three provide equivalent amounts of Spanish and English up to the end of Grade 3. In Grade 4, the transitional program contains more English, while the other two maintain 50–50 Spanish–English.

Table 1.4 presents NCE scores and percentiles for English reading. Note that TBE groups appear twice in the Table: Each type of "enriched" bilingual education program had its own comparison group, matching it in neighborhood and socioeconomic status.

Cross-sectional comparisons pit TBE comparison groups against each of the enriched bilingual options. There appears to be no difference in the TBE-developmental comparison, but two-way students do better than TBE compari-

TABLE 1.4
Comparison of Bilingual Programs/Cross-Sectional
(NCE/Percentiles)

| Grade | TBE | Developmental | TBE | Two-Way |
|---|---|---|---|---|
| 1 | 51.5/53 | 50.1/50 | 51.9/54 | 59.8/68 |
| 2 | 47.3/45 | 47.9/46 | 44.7/40 | 54.9/59 |
| 3 | 46.8/44 | 46.9/44 | 48.9/48 | 54/58 |
| 4 | 44.7/40 | 43.9/39 | 44.4/40 | 52.6/55 |
| 5 | 41.4/34 | 41.4/34 | 38.9/30 | 51.3/52 |

From: Thomas and Collier (2002)

sons. Also, two-way students clearly do better than the developmental students. Although this was not a "planned" comparison with control for socio-economic status, the result is noteworthy because two-way students performed better than TBE students, but developmental students did not.

### Houston: Potential Confounds

Before concluding that these data demonstrate the superiority of two-way programs, we need to discuss some unusual aspects of the Houston data.

1. Scores for all groups are high in Grade 1. In fact, they are higher than the level typically required for reclassification. This suggests that a significant percentage of the children had considerable English knowledge before starting school.

2. Scores then decline for all groups, as we saw before in Castillo (2001). By Grade 5, in fact, scores for some groups are below typical reclassification levels. This suggests that higher scoring children are being exited and lower scoring children are entering the program late. (Note that if this were true, it would exaggerate the effectiveness of a program that kept all its students and did not allow new ones to enter late, e.g. two-way bilingual education.)

3. The two-way advantage was present early, in Grade 1. This suggests that a selection bias was present, that the two-way students were exceptional from the beginning.

Thomas and Collier (personal communication) have pointed out that that children tested at the end of Grade 1 could have been in school and receiving the benefits of bilingual education for three years before testing. Houston offers bilingual Pre-Kindergarten and Kindergarten. It is thus possible that first Grade scores do not represent beginning scores.

Thomas and Collier's (2002) Table C-8 (see Table 1.5 in this article) provides some helpful information: It is a quasi-longitudinal analysis of children who have been in the Houston system for several years. It is not a pure longitudinal analysis, because different numbers of children were tested at each level; thus, the same cohorts were followed, but precisely the same children were not tested each year. Sometimes, in fact, the numbers vary quite a bit; there was a large increase in the number tested in Grade 4 (see Table 1.5). A valuable aspect of this data is the fact that separate scores are presented for children who began school in Pre-K, Kindergarten, and Grade 1.

Table 1.5, from Thomas and Collier's (2002) Table C-8 (see Table 1.5 in this article), presents scores of children who began in school in Grade 1, who did not have Pre-Kindergarten or Kindergarten. When tested at the end of Grade 1, they had had only one year of schooling. In all cases I present the sample size in parentheses, followed by the NCE score given in Thomas and Collier (2002), followed

TABLE 1.5
Children Beginning School at Grade 1 (NCE/Percentiles)

| Grade | TBE | DEV | TBE | Two-way |
|---|---|---|---|---|
| 1 | (25) 48.9/48 | (15) 44.5/40 | (9) 46.3/44 | (11) 51.3/53 |
| 2 | (24) 56.9/63 | (18) 51.5/53 | (8) 39.5/31 | (8) 51.4/53 |
| 3 | (34) 54.3/58 | (20) 49.5/49 | (14) 54/58 | (15) 55.9/61 |
| 4 | (169) 51.5/53 | (169) 45.3/41 | (40) 48.8/48 | (18) 42/35 |

From: Thomas and Collier, 2002, Table C-8.

by the corresponding percentile. Note that scores are quite high even when children start school at Grade 1.

With respect to concern (2), the decline, Thomas and Collier (personal communication) point out that declines are a common occurrence as students move toward middle school and a more demanding curriculum.

Thomas and Collier (personal communication) also pointed out that children are offered bilingual education in Texas from Pre-Kindergarten to Grade 5. Exit is not automatic when a certain level is reached. If this is so, if most students stay in the program, the exiting of high scorers is not a factor in the decline and two-way does not have an unfair advantage in this regard.

Interestingly, these drops appear to coincide with a reduction of the amount of instruction provided in the first language. They may also be related to a problem nearly all language-minority children suffer from. Because they also tend to be of low socio-economic class, they tend to live in neighborhoods and attend schools with little access to books (Neuman & Celano, 2001). Recreational reading may make a particularly strong contribution to reading tests at the upper grade levels.

With respect to concern (3), the early advantage of the two-way group, Thomas and Collier noted that this group had the advantage of having two-way bilingual education in Pre-Kindergarten and Kindergarten. Table 1.5, however, shows that their advantage was present even for those starting in Grade 1.

As Thomas and Collier pointed out, the sample sizes in the longitudinal study are small, and one must be cautious in generalizing from them. Also, as noted earlier, the data is not strictly longitudinal. These concerns are, of course, an invitation for additional research.

## Comparison with Developmental Bilingual Education

De Jong (2004) compared a two-way and a developmental bilingual program, focusing on children who stayed in the program continuously from Kindergarten to Grade 5. The sample size was modest (26 in the two-way and 19 in the developmental program), but results were similar for children in other cohorts not (yet) followed to Grade five. On the Language Assessment Scales (LAS, Duncan & DeAvila, 1986) reading test, two-way children did better than those in the devel-

TABLE 1.6
Two-Way Versus Developmental Bilingual Education

| | READING | | WRITING | |
| --- | --- | --- | --- | --- |
| | *2-way* | *develop.* | *2-way* | *develop.* |
| 2 | 82 | 68 | 69 | 52 |
| 3 | 94 | 82 | 88 | 72 |
| 4 | 92 | 88 | 83 | 72 |
| 5 | 97 | 95 | 87 | 82 |

| | ORAL COMP. | |
| --- | --- | --- |
| | *2-way* | *develop.* |
| K | 2.2 | 3.4 |
| 1 | 3.8 | 3.8 |
| 2 | 4.3 | 4.6 |
| 3 | 4.2 | 4 |
| 4 | 4.3 | 4.8 |
| 5 | 5 | 4.8 |

From: de Jong (2004)

opmental program, but the latter group appeared to be closing the gap. Scores are also quite high, but the test used was designed for English Learners, not native speakers of English. Because of the small sample and the presence of a ceiling effect (all scores very high), Table 1.6 includes results of the LAS writing test as well. Again the two-way children do somewhat better.

The results probably underestimate the advantage of the two-way group: It appears that the developmental children Knew more English when they came to school (Table 1.6). On a measure of oral English comprehension, they scored very close to the proficient level after Kindergarten (3.4 on a 5 point scale, when 4 and 5 = proficient in English).

## GROUP FOUR: COMPARISONS
## TO NATIVE SPEAKERS OF ENGLISH

According to Alanis (2000), Spanish-dominant students in two schools in Grades 3, 4, and 5 in a two-way program did as well as English-dominant students in the same program and as well as monolingual English speakers on the Texas Learning Index test of English reading. The sample size was small: in one school, only seven Spanish-dominant children were tested, in the other, only 27. In addition, it was clear that the Spanish-dominant children did not begin school with zero English: Of 18 students tested in oral English, only two were considered "non-proficient" in Grade 1. Thirteen were classified as "limited," two as "proficient" and one was at the "mastery" level in English.

The most serious problem with this study, however, was that it does not really qualify as a two-way bilingual program. Both English and Spanish-dominant children were in the same classroom, but the program had much more emphasis on English than Spanish. It appeared to be an English immersion program with some support in the primary language: it was supposed to be 50/50, but "it was clear from classroom observations and interviews that the 50/50 split was not implemented . . . teachers . . . utilized more Spanish than English and lacked Spanish resources in all content areas" (p. 16). Even though the schools were on the border (Brownsville), "most students had a strong preference for English" and "teachers stressed the English Texas Assessment of Academic Skills [TAAS] for their students" (p. 16). Alanis also noted that there was no emphasis placed on Spanish literacy: "the original goal of the program was only Spanish oral proficiency as opposed to equal levels of bilingualism and biliteracy" (p. 16).[2]

Some of the studies discussed previously also compared two-way students to English dominant and native speakers of English. Recall that Castillo (2001) found that two-ways did better than a group of native English speakers (n = 30), but only 11 two-way students were tested and there was no information on their initial level of English. Ajuria (1994)'s two-way students also did better than native speakers of English in the mainstream (n = 20), but recall that the mainstream classroom was severely lacking in many essentials and a modified version of a standardized test was used. Clayton (1993) reported that two-way students did better than a group of Native American children with similar backgrounds, but it is not clear whether the "two-way" children were in two-way programs or whether it was a combined sample of children in two-way and TBE programs. The sample size for the comparison with Native American children suggests it was a combined group. There were 83 children in the two-way group and 59 in the TBE group in the two-way versus TBE comparison, but 150 in the two-way vs. Native American comparison. Also not explained is the fact that the "two-way" scores in the Native American comparison are much lower than those for either bilingual group.

Thomas and Collier (2002) also provided a comparison with native speakers of English in their Houston sample. All native speakers performed around the 50th percentile in English reading; two-way students scored above this level at all Grade levels tested, an impressive result even though there was no control for variables such as neighborhood or poverty.

## DISCUSSION

With respect to question (1), "Do they acquire significant amounts of English?," several studies reassure us and show that children in two-way programs improve in English. Table 1.7 presents Grade five results in NCE's and percentiles for the three studies using standardized tests, including all groups tested. Even discount-

TABLE 1.7
Attainment by Grade 5

| Study | Scores: NRC (Percentiles) at Grade 5 |
|---|---|
| de Jong (2002) | 38 (29); 38 (29); 40 (30); 42 (35); 43 (37) |
| Lindholm (2002) | 20 (9); 34 (22); 40 (30) |
| Collier & Thomas (2002) | 51 (53) |

ing the lowest score as an outlier (9th percentile in Lindholm, 2002), the results are variable, and not always high enough for reclassification, and the Thomas and Collier score is much higher than the others.

With respect to question (2), whether two-way students do better than English learners in the mainstream, two studies suffer from very small samples, short durations, and lack of measures for initial competence. In another, Thomas and Collier's Houston data, two-way students do better than those in submersion but not as well as those in ESL-only. These data, however, are uncontrolled for a number of important factors.

With respect to question (3), two-way children outperform children in transitional bilingual education in two studies, but do worse in another. None of the studies provides us assurance that the children were at similar levels when starting school. One study, the Amigos project, ends at Grade 2 and has a small sample size, and in the Houston study scores for all children were very high at Grade 1, and are lower in subsequent years. In addition, children in two-way in Houston were superior and had high scores after only one year of school, suggesting a selection bias and considerable previous English competence. The only direct comparison of two-way with a developmental program showed evidence that two-way children did better, but sample sizes were modest and the developmental children appeared to be closing the gap between the two programs (note that Thomas and Collier, 2002, contains an indirect comparison of two-way programs with developmental bilingual education, with two-way programs doing better.)

Two-way children do as well or better than native speakers of English in five studies. In three of the five, the sample sizes were small or modest, one of the "two-way" programs was really immersion with some oral first language support, and durations were short in two studies.

The results are thus encouraging but they are not the overwhelming and massive support we sometimes read about in the popular press. It should be pointed out that supporters of bilingual education have criticized studies claiming to support immersion for similar flaws. In Krashen (1996) I faulted Gersten (1985) for a small sample size and a short duration (up to the end of Grade 2). I also noted that Rossell's (1990) analysis was suspect because scores were very high long before reclassification.

Rossell and Baker (1966) criticized many studies for not controlling for individual differences at the outset of the program, which is also a problem in the studies discussed here. I argued (Krashen, 1996) that with large numbers of studies, this is not a problem if there is no reason to suspect differences; large numbers of studies provides quasi-randomization. This is clearly what is called for in the case of two-way bilingual education.

This review has obvious limitations. I have limited this analysis to performance of English learners on tests of academic English. While we need to be reassured that English language development is satisfactory, we also need to consider several other factors: (1) long term cognitive development, (2) social and attitudinal factors, (3) the ease of implementation and efficacy of different versions of two-way bilingual education, and (4) the effect on the heritage language and the effect on language-majority students, especially those from low-income families who may have little opportunity for first language development outside of school because of print-poor environments.

One could argue that one need not show superiority in English language development: If children are clearly showing substantial growth in English, enough to access the regular curriculum in a reasonable amount of time, small differences among programs are clearly unimportant. If all students eventually acquire English very well, if in fact it turns out that students in one program reach a certain level of English a few months faster than children in another clearly does not matter. But thus far, the attainment of children in two-way programs in academic English is not consistently overwhelming. (Refer to Table 1.8.)

In addition, I have ignored the variants among two-way programs in design. Lindolm (2001), for example, presented two different models. With more studies, we will be able to consider design as a predictor.

## CONCLUSIONS

Only a handful of studies exist, and they report generally positive but variable attainment in academic English among English learners. In studies comparing two-way children with those in other options, sample sizes are often small, there is usually no control for initial differences, and scores are sometimes high at the beginning and then decline. Supporters of bilingual education, such as this writer, have critiqued studies claiming to support immersion on similar grounds.

Thus, a close look at the data shows that two-way programs show some promising results, but research has not yet demonstrated that they are the best possible program.

## ACKNOWLEDGMENTS

I thank Wayne Thomas, Virginia Collier, James Crawford, and Giselle Waters for comments on earlier versions of this paper.

TABLE 1.8
Summary of Studies

| Study | Results | Commentary |
|---|---|---|
| NO COMP. GROUP | | |
| Sugarman & Howard (2001) | Gains in English proficiency | Tests unstandardized, no comparison group<br>No measure of initial competence |
| de Jong (2002) | Two-way achieve 29 to 37 percentile by Grade 5 | Small n, no comparison group<br>No measure of initial competence |
| Lindholm (2002) | Two-way achieve 23 to 30 percentile by Grade 6<br>One group only at 9 percentile in Grade 5 | No comparison group |
| Thomas/Collier (Oregon) | Two-way better than state, district norms | Small n (12), initial competence not clear |
| COMP. W. MAINSTREAM | | |
| Ajuria (1994) | Two-way better than comparisons in mainstream | Small n (11,7), only 1 year, no gains<br>Second semester, comparisons in print-<br>Deprived environment, modified test<br>No measure of initial competence |
| Castillo (2001) | Two-way much better than comparisons in mainstream | Small n (4 comparisons!), up to Grade 2<br>Only, 2-way scores very high after Grade<br>One, then decline, no measure of initial<br>Competence |
| Thomas/Collier (Houston) | ESL only > TBE > submersion | Uncontrolled |

16

| | | |
|---|---|---|
| **COMP. W. TBE** | | |
| Clayton (1993) | TBE graduates do better than 2-way graduates | No measure of initial competence<br>Two-way had "inferior" reading program |
| Cazabon et al. (1993) | Two-way do better than TBE | Small n, up to Grade 2 only, initial English competence unclear<br>Grade 1 scores very high, then decline |
| Thomas/Collier (Houston) | Two-way better than TBE | No measure of initial competence<br>Two-way advantage present very early |
| **COMP. W. DEVELOPMENTAL** | | |
| de Jong (2004) | Two-way better than developmental | Small n, ceiling on reading test<br>Dev. have better oral comprehension at K |
| **COMP. W. Non-speakers of Eng** | | |
| Alanis (2000) | Two-way = English dominant | Small n, 2-way did not begin with zero English; 2-way not really 2-way |
| Ajuria (1994) | Two-way better than English native speakers | Test modified, mainstream class print-deprived<br>One year only |
| Castillo (2001) | Two-way better than English native speakers | Up to Grade 2 only; no measure of initial Competence; small n (11 2-way children) |
| Clayton (1983) | Two-way better than Native American children | Not clear if 2-way group alone was<br>Included or entire 2-way + TBE group |
| Thomas/Collier (Houston) | Two-way better than English native speakers | Uncontrolled (see also above) |

## ENDNOTES

1. In Christian, Montone, Lindholm, and Carranza (1997), test scores were combined for minority and majority language children. In addition, many of the Spanish speakers entered school with signifi- cant English competence; 45% of entering students at one school (Inter-American) were consid- ered "bilingual" and half of the Spanish speakers at another (River Glen) were classified as fluent in English in Grade one. Lindholm and Fairchild (1990) cover progress only to Grade one and the comparison group included English and Spanish dominant children. Senesac (2002) reported that Spanish speakers in a two-way program performed at Grade level in Grades three through eight, but approximately half the sample were never classified as limited English proficient (Senesac, 2002, p. 4).

2. Stipek, Ryan, and Alarcon (2001) is another "two-way" program that had tremendous emphasis on English : For children in Pre-K and K, teacher talk was in English 57% of the time to Spanish- dominant children, mixed 19%, and in Spanish 24% of the time. For Grades 1 and 2, teacher input was in English 77% of the time, 9% mixed, and 14% in Spanish. Pre-K and K Spanish-speaking children responded in Spanish (with no mixing) only 11% of time, and those in Grades 1 and 2, only 12%

## REFERENCES

Ajuria, A. (1994). *An exploration of classroom activity and student success in a two-way bilingual and a mainstream program.* Ph Dissertation, Boston College.

Alanis, I. (2000). A Texas two-way bilingual program: Its effects on linguistic and academic achieve- ment. *Bilingual Research Journal, 24*(3).

Castillo, C. (2001). *The effects of dual language education program on student achievement and de- velopment of leadership abilities.* Ph. D dissertation, Our Lady of the Lake University.

Cazabon, M., Lambert, W., & Hall, G. (1993). *Two-way bilingual education: A progress report on the Amigos program.* Santa Cruz, CA and Washington, DC: National Center for Research on Cultural Diversity and Second Language Learning.

Clayton, S.(1993). *Language policy and equal status: A change from monolingualism to bilingualism in a small district in California.* PhD dissertation, Claremont Graduate School and San Diego State University

Christian, D., Montone, C., Lindholm, K., & Carranza, I. (1997). *Profiles in two-way immersion edu- cation.* McHenry, IL: Delta Systems.

Coy, S., & Litherland, L. (2000). From a foreign language perspective: A snapshot view of a dual lan- guage program in two inner-city high poverty elementary schools. *ERIC Document ED 446 450.*

de Jong, E. (2002). Effective bilingual education: From theory to academic achievement in a two-way bilingual program. *Bilingual Research Journal, 26*(1), 1–20. http://brj.asu.edu/content/vol26_no1/ abstracts.html

de Jong, E. (2004). L2 proficiency development in a two-way and a developmental bilingual program. *NABE Journal of Research and Practice, 2*(1), 1–21. http://njrp.tamu.edu

Duncan, S. E., & De Avila, E. A. (1986). *Language Assessment Scales (LAS).* Monterey, CA: CTB/ McGraw-Hill.

Gersten, R. (1985). Structured immersion for language-minority students: Results of a longitudinal evaluation. *Educational Evaluation and Policy Analysis, 7,* 187–196.

Krashen, S. (1996). *Under attack: The case against bilingual education.* Culver City, CA: Language Education Associates.

Lindholm, K. (2002). *Dual language education.* Clevedon, UK: Multilingual Matters

Lindholm, K., & Fairchild, H. (1990). Evaluation of an elementary school bilingual immersion program. In A. Padilla, H. Fairchild, & C. Valadez (Eds.) *Bilingual education: Issues and strategies* (pp. 126–136). Beverly Hills: Sage.

Neuman, S., & Celano, D. (2001). Access to print in low-income and middle-income communities. *Reading Research Quarterly, 36*(1), 8–26.

Oller, D. K., & Eilers, R. (2002) *Language and literacy in bilingual children*. Clevedon, UK: Multilingual Matters.

Perez. B. & Flores, B. (2002). Biliteracy development in two-way immersion classrooms: Analysis of third Grade Spanish and English reading. In D. Schallert, C. Fairbanks, J. Worthy, B. Maloch, & J. Hoffman (Eds.). *51st Yearbook of the National Reading Conference* (pp. 357–367). Oak Creek, WI: National Reading Conference

Rossell, C. (1990). The effectiveness of educational alternatives for limited-English-proficient children. In G. Imhoff (Ed.) *Learning in two languages* (pp. 71–121). New Brunswick, NJ: Transaction Publishers.

Rossell, C., & Baker, K., (1996). The educational effectiveness of bilingual education. *Research in the Teaching of English, 30*, 7–74.

Senesac, B. (2002). Two-way bilingual immersion: A portrait of quality schooling. *Bilingual Research Journal, 26*(1), 1–17.

Sugarman, J., & Howard, L. (2001). *Two-way immersion shows promising results: Findings from a new study*. Washington, DC: Center for Applied Linguistics.

Thomas, W. P., & Collier, V. (1997). *School effectiveness for language-minority students*. Washington, DC: NCBE. http://www.ncela.gwu.edu/ncbepubs/resource/effectiveness/thomas-collier97.pdf.

Thomas, W. P., & Collier, V. (2002). *A national study of school effectiveness for language-minority students' long-term academic achievement*. Final Report: Project 1.1. University of California, Santa Cruz: Center for Research, Education, Diversity and Excellence. http://www.crede. ucsc. edu/research/llaa/1.1_final.html

# 2

# Early Reading Strategies for First-Grade Spanish-Speaking Students Attending a Bilingual Spanish/English Education Program

Iliana Alanís
*University of Texas at Brownsville*

Josefina Villamil Tinajero
*University of Texas at El Paso*

## ABSTRACT

Research on mainstream students beginning reading instruction reveals a clearer and deeper understanding of the abilities that lead to success with reading and writing in English. There is a gap however, in the research related to the instruction of language-minority children. The purpose of this paper is to describe strategies used in early reading intervention for Spanish-speaking students attending Grade 1 in a bilingual Spanish /English education program. A research design that combined quantitative and qualitative methods revealed varying levels of achievement for each area tested. Although many elements known to prevent reading difficulties among monolingual students have much in common with the cognitive development of language-minority children, many factors intersect to aid in the development of reading comprehension and literacy development for this population of students. The use of the native language, the inclusion of family and culture, high teacher expectations and the use of culturally relevant texts all serve to facilitate children's literacy development.

## INTRODUCTION

Reading is the most important skill for success in school and society. In order to participate fully in society, literacy is essential. Illiteracy has a negative effect on quality of life as children who fail to learn to read will surely fail to reach their full potential. Although reading is the cornerstone of all school-based learning, reading failure is pervasive. The results of the 1998 National Assessment of Educational Progress showed 38% of fourth-grade students and 26% of eighth-grade students reading at a "below basic" level of achievement (National Center for Education Statistics, 1999). Results of the 2003 National Assessment of Educational Progress showed scores settling back to the same level as in 1992, with a 1-point dip. These numbers indicate that a significant number of students exhibit little mastery of the knowledge necessary to perform work at each grade level. And while minority students showed some improvements, they are still struggling to catch up with their white peers (National Center for Education Statistics, 2004). Therefore, a major responsibility among educators is to provide the best reading instruction possible for children who are at risk of reading failure while meeting quantifiable standards of achievement. At the same time, schools face serious challenges brought on by changes in our societies. U. S. Census figures indicate a 60,000 increase in the Hispanic population alone over the next fifty years (U. S. Census Bureau, 2004). Nationally, the school-age population is growing more and more diverse with dramatic increases in language-minority children expected.

Of great concern to educators is the number of language-minority children who are failing at literacy. Unacceptable gaps in reading performance exist between children in different demographic groups. The "reading gap" describes the difference between the target level of reading proficiency, which should be possible for students to achieve, and the actual level of reading proficiency. With proper instruction, about 85–90% of students should be able to read grade-level texts independently (Honig, Diamond & Gutlohn, 2000). Unfortunately, however, few classrooms attain this goal. The growing diversity of the U. S. will likely widen the "reading gap" even further. Texas for example, reports state achievement passing scores for English reading in the third grade as 96% for Whites and 85% for Hispanics. Scores drop at the fifth grade with White students' scores at an 89% passing rate and Hispanic scores at a 73% passing rate reflecting the increasing level of curriculum difficulty as students progress in grade levels (Texas Education Agency, 2003). To compound the issue many language-minority children are totally immersed in a second-language reading curriculum with minimal attention to their native-language literacy. These children are confronted with the task of learning to read in a language that they have yet to master orally. Because reading instruction strongly builds on oral language proficiency, second-language speaking children may experience a considerable gap in reading performance.

During the past several decades, research on beginning reading instruction reveals a clearer and deeper understanding of the abilities that lead to improving success with reading and writing in English for native-English speakers. This knowledge is useful to teachers, parents, and ultimately to the children and has direct implications for the primary grades, programs of reading instruction and most particularly for those children who have trouble learning to read. There remains however, a paucity of research related to the instruction of language-minority children who are struggling with reading in their native language.

## OVERVIEW OF THE STUDY

The purpose of this paper is to describe concrete strategies used in an early reading intervention for first-grade language-minority children. These strategies, based on the essential components of research-based programs for beginning reading instruction, are described as it provides practical strategies that support the development of reading and writing in Spanish. Interventions used at both school sites were based on the researchers' ongoing review of the research-based evidence that identifies critical elements of reading instruction for monolingual English speakers at-risk of reading failure (Allington & Walmsley, 1995; National Reading Panel, 2000; Snow, Burns, & Griffin, 1998) in combination with reflective analysis on the experiential context of the schools and classrooms in question. Although specific interventions that language-minority children would benefit from have yet to be more fully investigated, the notion was explored that elements known to prevent reading difficulties among monolingual students have much in common with the cognitive development of language-minority children.

This study used an action research approach, arguably one of the most powerful approaches to scholarly writing on school improvement today (McLaughlin, Watts, & Beard, 2000). Action research can be defined as the process of studying a real school or classroom situation to understand and improve the quality of actions or instruction (Hensen, 1996; McTaggart, 1997). Through action research teachers and pre-service teachers can observe their practice to explore a problem and a possible course of action.

Research-based programs for beginning reading instruction provide comprehensive, well-organized instructional plans and practice opportunities that permit all children to make sense of reading. Intervention efforts therefore, focused on early literacy skills through systematic and explicit instruction related to breaking spoken words into sounds, blending sounds to form words, and relating letters and sounds. The researchers' intent was to teach first-grade language-minority children strategies to aid in comprehending what they read while developing their literacy skills. Instruction was adapted to the needs of individual students based on assessment. It included alphabetic knowledge, phonemic awareness, vocabulary development and the reading of texts, as well as systematic phonics instruction. Explicit Spanish phonics instruction has been shown to improve Spanish-speaking students' reading achievement in both Spanish and English (Carillo, 1994). This systematic phonics instruction however, was seen as a means to an end. Rather than focusing primarily on teaching children a large number of letter–sound relationships, students were provided ample reading and writing activities that allowed them to practice their new knowledge in context. In the case of language-minority children, additional components considered included contextual factors, such as the school personnel's use of native language, family involvement, and appreciation of cultural diversity.

## CRITICAL FEATURES OF LITERACY DEVELOPMENT

The intervention represents two efforts in schools along the Texas–Mexico border. School A utilized university-based tutors and school B tapped into classroom teacher expertise. Critical to student success was the design and implementation of reading strategies that would lead to improvements in achievement levels for students in "at-risk" situations. These strategies centered on the critical features of literacy development for monolingual children as identified in the literature (e.g., Begorary, 2001; Burns, Griffin, Snow, 1999; Homan, King, & Hogarty, 2001). Critical features included emphasis on essential reading skills, comprehension, vocabulary development, and writing. A brief review of the literacy research is presented below.

### Emphasis on Essential Reading Skills

In early literacy three key features are phonological awareness, alphabetic principle, and print concepts (Ehri, 1998; Snow et al., 1998). An important element of phonological awareness is phonemic awareness. Phonemic awareness is the ability to manipulate the individual sounds, or phonemes, in spoken words. Before children learn to read print, they need to become aware of how the sounds in words work. They must understand that words are made up of speech sounds or phonemes. Effective phonemic awareness instruction teaches children to notice, think about, and work with sounds in spoken language. This understanding facilitates acquisition of the alphabetic principle and involves learning the letter–sound correspondences as well as spelling patterns and applying this knowledge in reading text. The term "print concepts" is used as an umbrella concept about printed text that students need to grasp in order to learn to read. Some of these concepts relate to the features of written language, while others relate to directionality, or the way that printed text is organized (Honig, Diamond, & Gutlohn, 2000). Knowledge of print concepts is fundamental to beginning reading. Because all children are not exposed to the same range of print-related experiences, they come to school with varying levels of print awareness and knowledge.

### Listening and Reading Comprehension

The long-term goal of reading instruction is comprehension. Reading comprehension is influenced by a broad range of factors, such as vocabulary knowledge, appreciation for text structure, thinking and reasoning skills, world experiences, ability to apply reading comprehension strategies and word reading ability (Pinnell & Scharer, 2003). In order to achieve this goal, students need to become fluent readers able to: (1) recognize words automatically; (2) group individual words into meaningful phrases; and (3) apply rapid phonic, morphemic, and contextual analyses to identify unknown words. Rapid and accurate word reading allows children to focus their attention on the meaning of what they read. According to Allington (1983), one of the reasons children fail to read fluently is that they have never been exposed to fluent reading models. Auditory modeling may be the most powerful technique for developing prosodic reading (Dowhower, 1991). There are many forms of auditory modeling, including having students simply follow along in the text as they listen to a live model and having students do choral and paired reading. Fluency with connected text represents a level of expertise beyond the alphabetic code.

Effective comprehension instruction is instruction that helps students become independent, strategic, and metacognitive readers who are able to develop, control, and use a variety of comprehension strategies to ensure that they understand what they read. To achieve this goal, comprehension instruction must begin as soon as students begin to read and it must be explicit, intensive, and persistent (Pearson & Gallagher, 1983).

## Vocabulary Development

Language and literacy skills in the primary grades are directly related to later academic success (Cunningham & Stanovich, 1997). With regard to the role of children's vocabulary knowledge in learning to read, a strong relation has been observed between the size of their vocabularies and their reading comprehension scores (Anderson & Freebody, 1981; Daneman, 1991). Children's reading comprehension levels are affected by the types of opportunities for building an extensive lexicon, which, in turn, is dependent on exposure to a language-rich environment. As beginning readers, children use the words they have heard to make sense of the words they see in print. As such, learners with extensive vocabularies are likely to achieve reading success (Anderson & Freebody, 1981).

In order to facilitate vocabulary development, intentional vocabulary instruction in specific concepts and word meanings is necessary (Baumann & Kameenui, 1991) particularly for those words that are conceptually difficult or that represent complex concepts that are not part of students' everyday experience. Specific word instruction provides students with a more complete, in-depth knowledge of word meanings. It is necessary because students who have in-depth word knowledge are more likely to read with fluency, accuracy, and comprehension than are students who have more limited word knowledge. In addition, students with in-depth word knowledge are more likely to use these words in their own speaking or writing (Graves, Juel, & Graves, 1998).

## Writing Development

Although reading and writing development is discussed in different sections, they are interrelated processes. A strong program of literacy development connects reading and writing. Teachers should provide experiences that lead naturally to writing as well as help students with the different aspects of the writing process. The best writing comes when students choose topics that tap into their own experiences and interests (Freeman & Freeman, 1997). Students also get ideas for writing from their reading. In the early stages of writing teachers can encourage emergent writers to invent spellings and punctuation to represent their thoughts. Writing should then be shared and social. In classrooms, where students share their writing with others in a supportive environment, they become more aware of the need for using conventional writing forms that classmates can understand. Control over standard forms takes time, but when students write for authentic purposes they gradually refine their inventions and move toward writing that others can read.

## Language and Literacy

The ability to read provides social, academic, and economic benefits. As children learn to read, they learn how spoken and written language relates to each other. Children's concepts about literacy are formed from the earliest years by observing and interacting with readers and writers as well as through their own attempts to read and write (Sulzby & Teale, 1991). Literacy is no longer regarded as simply a cognitive skill to be learned. Rather, it is viewed as a complex interactive and interpretative process where development is determined by the social and cultural context (Bruner 1967; Vygotsky, 1978). Literacy is both broader and more specific than reading. Literate behaviors include writing and other creative or analytical acts and at the same time invoke very particular bits of knowledge and skill in specific subject matter domain (Anderson & Pearson, 1984). Language experiences are a central component of effective literacy instruction. Children learn about themselves, each other, and the world around them from spoken language. Young children gain functional knowledge of the parts, products, and uses of the writing system from their ability to attend to and analyze the external sound structure of spoken words.

The connection between language and literacy is crucial for language-minority children. Teaching children to read and write first in their native language has long been a cornerstone of effective bilingual instruction programs. There is a high correlation between learning to read in the native language and subsequent reading achievement in a second language (August & Hakuta, 1997; Greene, 1998; Thomas & Collier, 1997). Research indicates that literacy strategies learned in one language transfer to reading and writing situations in a second language without having to be relearned. In addition, texts that contain language that sounds most like spoken language support beginning readers. As the data was analyzed over time, inquiry focused increasingly on the role of systematic intervention, applied in a culturally responsive context, for language-minority children.

## METHODOLOGY

### Research Design

In order to develop analytical schemes grounded in empirical data, the researchers used a research design that combined quantitative methods (e.g., t-test, chi-square) and qualitative methods (i.e., journals, questionnaires, interviews, running records) collected systematically over a period of 12 months.

### Research Questions

At the initial stages in the design of the research project, the following research questions were stated:

1. What are the immediate effects of supplemental reading instruction for first-grade Spanish-speaking readers in bilingual programs?
2. What are the instructional components critical for developing reading skills in language-minority children?

### Participants

#### Tutors

Participants for school A included 5 pre-service teachers in their junior year of college enrolled in an instructional methods course that served as tutors for 25 first-grade Spanish-speaking students on one elementary campus. In January 2002, 2 tutors dropped from the project due to other course work and matriculation. The remaining 3 tutors worked with 13 of the original 25 first-grade students. All three were female, of Mexican American descent and bilingual speakers with varying levels of English proficiency. All were in the first year of their teacher preparation program enrolled in an instructional planning and curriculum development course.

In school B, a fully certified bilingual classroom teacher with over 20 years of experience participated as a tutor. This teacher had extensive preparation in the use of the Reading Recovery Program.

## Students

Students at both sites identified as Mexican-American and indicated Spanish as their native language. Their classroom teachers identified these students as considerably below level readers through scores on the first-grade assessment, *Tejas LEE*.

The neighborhood schools are Title I campuses where all students qualify for free and reduced lunch. In these border community schools, the student ethnic distribution is more than 80% Mexican-American and over 50% of the student population is designated as limited English proficient by state standards.

## Measures

Formative evaluation data was gathered throughout the year to evaluate and refine the project efforts. Information was gathered regarding student progress, tutor participation and teacher reflections. Standardized test scores, running records, and informal classroom observations were collected to monitor student progress.

Students' early reading skills were assessed using a variety of evaluation procedures, such as Reading Recovery instruments (i.e., pre and post testing, observations, and survey instruments). Students' were assessed using the *Tejas LEE*, the Spanish version of the Texas Primary Reading Inventory. The intent of the *Tejas LEE* is to capture specific skills and steps in the development of Spanish reading and comprehension development that can be used to plan individual reading instruction for early intervention and prevention of reading problems.

## Procedures

Based on the common elements of successful early intervention programs for monolingual children (Gaskins, 1999; Gullatt & Lofton, 1998; Zelasko & Antunez, 2000) it was concluded that the intervention model should consist of structured, fast-paced lessons delivered in addition to the classroom instruction as a small-group tutoring program with 3–4 students. The intervention was done as a pullout in addition to classroom instruction. The intervention was conducted in classrooms or occasionally in the library.

Intervention for school A consisted of 66 sessions three times a week implemented over 23 weeks due to campus and university holidays. A one–three teacher–student ratio was utilized to provide a focused opportunity for instruction based on research that investigated the effect of group size during supplemental reading instruction. See Appendix A for a sample of a lesson plan guide used by university tutors in school A.

Procedures in school B consisted of a one-to-one teacher–student ratio, intensive tutoring implemented over a period of 15 weeks. Classroom teachers used 'Descrubiendo la Lectura' (Escamilla & Andrade, 1992) as a framework for developing procedures and principles of the intervention. Some of the important principles of this program included teaching for independent strategic processing within the zone of proximal development, providing frequent and intensive opportunities to read, exposure to frequent, regular spelling–sound relationships, and using reading to obtain meaning form print (Clay, 1995; Sensenbaugh, 1995). Follow-up procedures were implemented after 4 months. In both sites each session was approximately 20 minutes in length and conducted in the students' primary language, Spanish. See Appendix B for a list of parts of a lesson guide used by Reading Recovery implementation in school B.

A systematic, structured intervention plan was developed around the critical features of reading for both sites (Appendices A & B). Much of the time was spent on explicit skill instruction coordinated with opportunities to practice skills in context. Students were provided with many opportunities to practice skills, with assistance from the tutor as well as independently. Project participants kept a record of the number of days taught and results of on-going assessments. Tutors in school A consulted with their University Supervisor on a weekly basis for support, feedback, and guidance. Tutors received weekly site visits and observations by the University Supervisor. Classroom teachers consulted and received regular visits from project directors to receive ongoing supervision and feedback.

Preliminary research findings drawn from the two schools in this study indicate that the instructional components and their respective strategies most critical for the development of reading skills for monolingual children lead to effective development of literacy for language-minority children as well. These will be discussed in the following section. It is important to note in addition to the instructional components critical attention to the role of native language, context, and culture must not be dismissed in the case of language-minority children.

## Instructional Components Used to Develop Phonemic Awareness Strategies

### Identifying and Working with Syllables in Spoken Words

Spanish is in many respects a syllabic language—the spoken language is built upon a relatively small collection of distinctive syllables, and the printed language is easily decoded syllable by syllable (Moran & Calfee, 1993). Students began by clapping the syllables in their name e.g., /An/dre/u/. Using a student's name is a very powerful tool. It is after all the most important word in their lexicon. They would also clap vocabulary words and key words in their stories as the tutor/ teacher read them. Students would also tap out the syllables with a pencil on their desk or would place their hand under their chin to feel the downward movement of the chin with each new syllable.

### Identifying and Working with Onsets and Rhymes in Spoken Syllables

As students developed their syllable recognition they worked on listening for initial, medial, and final syllables e.g., **ga**-to, el-e-**fan**-te, pi-za-**ron**. Tutors/teachers would then focus on changing the initial syllable to form a new word, for example, *ga-to* became the word *pa-to*. Students would then work in pairs to create their own words. Students would also add syllables to words to create new words, for example, *pa-to, za-pá-to*. To aid in development tutors/teachers created syllable cards that students could manipulate to form words. These words were later used in their writing activities.

### Identifying and Making Oral Rhymes

Tutors/teachers introduced rhymes by reading stories to children that contained rhymes or creating their own oral stories. Students would then identify rhyming words through games or through the creation of their own sentences. One activity was to give each child a set of cards. One card would read *rima* (rhymes) and the other card would read *no rima*. (does not rhyme) As the tutor/teacher would call out a pair of words the student would raise the card that indicated whether the pair of words rhymed or not. This activity allowed students to be active versus passive learners.

### Identifying and Working with Individual Phonemes in Spoken Words

Although Spanish is a syllabic language and identifying individual phonemes may not be as natural in the reading process for Spanish speakers as it is for English speakers, students did work on isolating and saying the first or last sound in a word e.g., *perro /p/, lion /n/* as well as blending phonemes e.g., */m/ /a/ /n/ /o/—mano*.

This strategy however, is particularly important in helping children learn to spell. The explanation for this may be that children who have phonemic awareness understand that sounds and letters are related in a predictable way. Thus, they are able to relate the sounds to letters as they spell words. Phonemic awareness instruction improves children's ability to read words thus improving their reading comprehension. Phonemic awareness instruction aids reading comprehension primarily through its influence on word reading (Armbruster, Lehr, & Osborn, 2001).

## Comprehension

Studies on good readers have identified a number of comprehension strategies to be highly useful. From the array of strategies examined, the following were especially helpful in the intervention.

### Listening Comprehension

A strategy used in each session included listening to a tutor/teacher read from patterned and predictable text related to the students' language arts theme. Story reading introduced children to new words, new sentences, and new ideas. In addition, they heard the kinds of vocabulary, sentences, and text structures they would find in their academic books and were expected to read and understand.

### Story Read Alouds

Reading aloud to children everyday and talking about books and stories supported and extended oral language development and helped students connect oral to written language. Before and during the readings tutors/teachers would provide opportunities for students to gain meaning from text by making informed predictions. Reading to children allowed students the opportunity to listen to good models of fluent reading-models that read effortlessly and with expression. Developing fluency played a major role in reading comprehension.

### Fluency

Fluency provides a bridge between word recognition and comprehension. Students were encouraged to make connections among the ideas in the text and between the text and their background knowledge. Research has established that readers' existing knowledge is critical in determining their ability to comprehend what they read (Snow et. al., 1998). In addition, tutors/teachers focused on words in texts versus in isolation. Instant or automatic word recognition is a necessary, but not sufficient, reading skill. Students who can read words in isolation quickly may not be able to automatically transfer this speed and accuracy. It was therefore important in the intervention to provide students with instruction and practice in fluency as they read connected text.

Students began with text that was relatively short and easy for them. This allowed students to feel success early on in the intervention without experiencing frustration. As part of this strategy students were encouraged to engage in repeated oral reading as they received feedback from the tutor/teacher related to decoding strategies. Three rereadings were sufficient for most students. Often readings were conducted through choral reading and partner reading.

### Choral and Partner Reading

Choral reading was practiced through the use of patterned or predictable books that were not too long and were at the students' independent reading level. For partner reading students were paired by reading levels. More fluent reads were paired with less fluent readers. The stronger reader would read a paragraph first, providing a model of fluent reading. Then the less fluent reader would read the same text aloud. The stronger reader would help his/her partner with word recognition when necessary.

## Vocabulary Development

Students in this study learned most vocabulary indirectly with some vocabulary learned directly.

## Indirect Vocabulary

Children learned word meanings indirectly in three ways. First, the use of small group instruction allowed children to learn word meanings through conversations with other peers and tutors/teachers. Second, vocabulary developed as children listened to the tutors/teachers read to them. As tutors/teachers read the selection aloud they discussed new vocabulary and concepts while helping them relate the words to their prior knowledge and experience. And finally, children learned many new words by reading on their own. Part of helping children read on their own was by selecting books for emergent readers that had the following characteristics (Fornshell, 2003):

- Familiar concepts.
- A small amount of easy-to-see print.
- Print that was clearly separated from the pictures.
- Pictures that clearly illustrated the text message.

## Direct Vocabulary

Direct vocabulary instruction included providing students with specific word instruction (i.e., teaching important words before reading) and teaching students word-learning strategies such as context clues. Pictures or realia were used for students to have multiple ways of understanding the new vocabulary. Tutors/teachers and students would discuss the new vocabulary word and whenever possible relate it to their prior experiences or background knowledge. Vocabulary words were taught and extended through oral language activities. Students were encouraged to used varied words in sessions that included varied vocabulary. Interestingly, what mattered was not just the variety of words that the adults used, but also the variety of words that the children used as they spoke with the adults and listened to others (Dickinson & Tabors, 2002).

## Writing Development

Emergent readers and writers are just beginning to grasp the concept that oral language can be written down and others can then read and derive meaning from the written word. As children engage in shared reading activities and as they develop writing skills, they begin to discover relationships between the sounds of the language and the symbols that represent those sounds. Opportunities were provided at each session for students to analyze new words by saying them slowly and predicting the sequence of sounds as they wrote them down. The intervention presented explicit models that provided high-quality instruction and strategies. The use of Cunningham's Making Words (1994) enabled children to achieve high standards in their writing as they practiced making words related to their readings.

Letter cubes and word boxes were used to help students create new words. Through independent writing, students had numerous opportunities to apply newly learned techniques and strategies in context. Classroom teachers were also encouraged to display student writing. Student work displayed in the native or second language encourages writing, develops self-esteem, and promotes a community of learners engaged in supportive interactions.

## Language and Literacy

Tutors encouraged students to develop the language and culture they brought from home and build on their prior experiences, challenging the perception in the broader society that these children arrived to school with deficits. Children were asked to share their experiences with their neighbor and/or the tutor. Some students would then be asked to share what their friend said, or share an idea of their own. This brief activity is different from the traditional approach in which the teacher poses the discussion questions, and then calls on individual children to respond by taking turns. In this activity all children had the opportunity to talk and share experiences. The small group setting lowered the anxiety level for many children thus increasing their native language vocabulary. Using oral language to relate personal experiences to new learning is after all the basis of comprehension.

## RESULTS AND DISCUSSION

Data from school A were analyzed using raw scores on the *Tejas LEE* subtests and conducting a compared means paired *t*-test. In Table 2.1 the means and standard deviations for all of the tests are presented. Subtests for the *Tejas LEE* in-

TABLE 2.1
Paired *t*-test Results for Tejas Lee Subtests Mean Percent Correct

| Subtest Name | Pre-test | | Post-test | | |
| --- | --- | --- | --- | --- | --- |
| | M | SD | M | SD | t(12) |
| *Reconocimiento de Palabras* | 28 | .32 | 91 | .10 | 7.3*** |
| *Comprensión de Oraciones* | 11 | .29 | 85 | .25 | 7.7*** |
| *Conocimiento de Sonidos* | | | | | |
| *Difícil* | 50 | .33 | 90 | .17 | 4.7*** |
| *Fácil* | 74 | .27 | 99 | .03 | 3.2* |
| *Conocimiento de Fonológico* | | | | | |
| *Unión de* | | | | | |
| *Silabas* | 63 | .44 | 100 | .00 | 2.9* |
| *Sonidos* | 40 | .34 | 100 | .00 | 6.2*** |
| *Omisión de Sonidos* | 26 | .38 | 94 | .10 | 6.7*** |

*p < .05. ***p < .001.

cluded *Reconocimiento de Palabras* (Word recognition), *Comprensión de Oraciones* (Sentence Comprehension), *Conocimiento de Sonidos, Difícil Y Fácil* (Sound Recognition, Difficult and Easy), and *Conocimiento de Fonológico* (Phoneme Awareness) which includes *Unión de Sonidos y Omision de Sonidos* (Blending of Syllables and Sounds and Omitting Sounds).

Pretests were administered in September with posttests administered in May. A clear increase in the scores for all 13 children can be seen with varying levels of achievement for each area at the minimum statistical significance level of .05. The largest gains appear to be in the areas of *Reconocimiento de Palabras* (Word recognition) and *Comprensión de Oraciones* (Sentence Comprehension). The smallest gains resulted in the areas of *Conocimiento de Sonidos, Fácil* (Sound Recognition, Easy) and *Unión de Silabas* (Blending of Syllables). In both areas of *Conocimiento de Fonológico* (Phoneme Awareness) which includes *Unión de Sonidos y Omision de Sonidos* (Blending of Syllables and Sounds and Omitting Sounds) the students appear to have reached a ceiling indicated by high means and low standard deviations. Based on student results it was concluded the tutoring model should be tested more carefully to see if similar gains would be obtained in a more controlled situation.

The results from school B, reported through running records, weekly logs, interviews and observation field notes indicated similar gains in student performance.

Based on Table 2.2 of the 13 children tested, seven indicate a gain in both areas of Sound Recognition and four children indicate a change in the area of Sound Recognition: Difficult. Table 2.3 indicates varying levels of achievement in each area. However, the greater reliance on qualitative methodology at this school site

TABLE 2.2
Tejas Lee Results: Sound Recognition (Reconocimiento de Sonidos)

| Name | Difficult | | Easy | |
|---|---|---|---|---|
| | Pre | Post | Pre | Post |
| Child A | 0/13 | 13/13 | 8/14 | 14/14 |
| Child B | 12/13 | 13/13 | 14/14 | 14/14 |
| Child C | 0/15 | 5/13 | 3/14 | 14/14 |
| Child D | 7/13 | 13/13 | 12/14 | 14/14 |
| Child E | 12/13 | 12/13 | 12/14 | 14/14 |
| Child F | 13/13 | 13/13 | 14/14 | 14/14 |
| Child G | 1/13 | 11/13 | 4/14 | 14/14 |
| Child H | 5/13 | 12/13 | 8/14 | 14/14 |
| Child I | 10/13 | 13/13 | 14/14 | 14/14 |
| Child J | 7/13 | 13/13 | 14/14 | 14/14 |
| Child K | 7/13 | 9/13 | 14/14 | 14/14 |
| Child L | 7/13 | 13/13 | 10/14 | 14/14 |
| Child M | 5/13 | 12/13 | 8/14 | 12/14 |

TABLE 2.3
Reading Recovery Results: Observation Test in Spanish
(Examen de Observacion en Español)

|  | Child A (pre-test) | Child A (post-test) | Child B (pre-test) | Child B (post-test) |
|---|---|---|---|---|
| Letter ID | 60 | 61 | 59 | 61 |
| Word Test | 18 | 25 | 9 | 20 |
| Concepts | 20 | 20 | 16 | 25 |
| Vocabulary | 24 | 27 | ¿ | ¿ |
| Dictation | 37 | 39 | 21 | 39 |
| Total Level | — | 3 | — | 1 |

created sets of data that provide information about the impacts of the intervention on other central stakeholders in the reading intervention process, including teachers, tutors, and program policy makers (i.e., administrators and supervisors).

In the sections that follow, we discuss these results in detail. Because our second research question focused on the instructional components critical for developing reading skills in language-minority children, we begin by describing the characteristics most positively associated with developing literacy skills and conclude with additional characteristics that may have had an impact on students' overall success.

## The Effects of Supplemental Reading Instruction for Grade 1 Spanish-Speaking Children

### Emphasis on Essential Reading Skills

For the past 25 years researchers have studied the role of phoneme awareness in learning to read. Myriad correlation studies have established a strong positive relationship between phoneme awareness and success in early reading and several training studies have suggested a possible causal connection (see reviews by Adams, 1990; Blachman, 2000; National Institute of Child Health and Human Development, 2000). The understanding that words are made up of speech sounds or phonemes leads to the ability to read connected text. The prevalent view is that there is a reciprocal or interactive relationship between phoneme awareness and early reading skill (Ehri, 1992; Stahl & Murray, 1994). The high means in the areas of sound recognition and sound and syllable blending may be due to the focused opportunities spent on phonological awareness. Tutors taught children to notice, think about, and work with sounds in their native language. Their scores may suggest that Spanish-speaking students have a relatively easier time developing these skills given the shallow orthography and syllabic nature of the Spanish language.

## Listening and Reading Comprehension

Children who are able to read text without struggling with the decoding aspect are better able to comprehend what they have read. At each session students would listen to a story read by the teacher. This task provided for a strong model that children could follow and imitate. Tutors also allowed children time to share reading through the practice of paired reading of repeated text and familiar literature. This practice may have led to fluency which allowed children to focus their attention on the meaning of what they read. This may explain the gains in the areas of word recognition and sentence comprehension. A further explanation may be the time tutors spent reading to children from authentic literature to develop listening comprehension as well as the opportunities for children to discuss what they heard and what they read as opposed to learning skills in isolated contexts.

## Vocabulary Development

The size of children's vocabulary knowledge has been shown to have a strong relation to their reading comprehension scores. For the students in this study vocabulary knowledge exerted a strong and direct influence on their reading comprehension and an indirect influence via their oral text comprehension. Tutors/teachers spent time developing students' vocabulary by bringing in realia, visuals, discussion, gestures, and making connections to students' prior knowledge. Students engaged in word study that allowed making new words with familiar patterns. Students would then use these words in their writing. The use of writing helped children move along in their reading development. As they wrote there were coached by their tutor/teacher allowing for the development of phonemic awareness and letter–sound patterns essential to continued progress in reading.

## Language and Literacy

Language-minority children who are successful in school have a strong foundation of reading and writing in their native language (August & Hakuta, 1997; Greene, 1998; Thomas & Collier, 1997). Reading comprehension can be viewed as the product of word decoding, vocabulary knowledge, and oral text comprehension. According to Droop and Verhoeven (2003) during the initial stages of literacy acquisition the combined influence of these factors tends to be much stronger for second-language readers than for first-language readers. Texts that contain language that sounds most like a student's spoken language supports beginning readers. Conducting the tutoring sessions in the child's native language therefore, facilitated their literacy development in all areas of the *Tejas LEE* instrument.

## Additional Contextual Factors Contributing to Students' Success

There are many factors that led to the development of students' literacy. The strategies used based on the critical components of literacy as identified in the literature led to students' success however, there were other contextual factors related to the intervention that warrant discussion.

### Interactions

Besides the strategies used, the interactions that took place between students and tutors were central to student success. Authentic trust and communication between teachers and students frequently can transcend the economic and social disadvantages that afflict communities and schools alike in inner city and rural areas (Cummins, 2000). These interactions are fundamental to the academic success of culturally diverse students. Through the intervention sessions students' sense of self was affirmed. The affirmation of identity established respect and trust between tutors and students that was crucial for the development of students' reading skills. The positive development of students' identities as readers played out in the interactions between instructors and students. Consequently students were more likely to participate actively in instruction and apply themselves to academic effort. The high scores in the area of comprehension may suggest that along with fluency, discussion and interaction play a large role in word recognition and understanding of text.

### High Expectations

Teachers need to have high expectations of their students. High expectations can be defined in two ways. It means cognitively challenging content that is relevant and potentially useful to students and it is significant content that is aimed at developing children's minds, not merely their language knowledge (Jiménez, Moll, Rodríguez-Brown, & Barrera, 1999). The children in this study were thought of as valuable individuals that had many things to offer in their discussions. These expectations translated into actions. Students were motivated and encouraged to try their best without excuses. Slowly children began to believe they too were readers and writers.

### Familial Involvement

Although the tutoring sessions did not allow for the incorporation of thematic-units, tutors attempted to relate their mini lessons to the classroom themes. Because literacy is interrelated, children must be given the opportunity to practice the strands of language arts in connected and purposeful ways. Meaningful and interesting lessons can develop students' language and literacy as well as their critical thinking skills. Classroom teachers were encouraged to use the family's funds of knowledge to develop thematic units or incorporate familial experiences into student writing (Jimenez et al., 1999). In this way, schools can develop an appreciation for personal experiences and connect the world of school to the world of home.

### Classroom Library

In addition, a classroom library with an abundance of books and magazines in both languages was necessary to stimulate children's love of reading. Classroom libraries must offer children a variety of bilingual and Spanish reading materials, some that are easy to read and others that are more challenging and of increasing difficulty and complexity (Alanís, 2004). Likewise, children need access to many books that travel home for reading with family members. Word-less books should be considered as avenues for parents and children to develop vocabulary in any language. Listening to and talking about books on a regular basis provides children with demonstrations of the benefits and pleasures of reading. When considering reading material it is important for educators to use books that respect and celebrate children's home culture, language and experiences so as to help them find a sense of connection and relevance between the home and the school (Barrera & Jiménez, 2000).

Although specific interventions that language-minority children would benefit from have yet to be more fully investigated, it appears that elements known to prevent reading difficulties among monolingual students have much in common with the cognitive development of language-minority children. The results of the present study show many factors intersect to aid in the development of first language reading comprehension and literacy development of struggling Grade 1 language-minority children in a relatively short amount of time. The intervention however, must meet the following criteria (Alanís, Munter, & Tinajero, 2003):

1. Intervention is frequent and of sufficient duration to make a difference.
2. Pupil-to-teacher ratio is kept small (1–4).
3. Texts are carefully selected and sequenced to ensure student success.
4. Word learning activities are used to help children become familiar with print.
5. Vocabulary is taught directly and indirectly in multiple contexts.
6. Writing is used to teach and extend word identification skills.
7. Assessment is meaningful, practical, and ongoing.
8. Pupils build confidence and see themselves as readers.
9. Culturally responsive principles of instruction must be embedded in the model.
10. Use of the native language and familial involvement must be incorporated into the reading intervention in the case of language-minority children.

The general principles of good reading instruction (Weiler, 1998) should be used in intervention programs with a focus on culture and language as assets to enrich language-minority children participation in all levels of literacy learning. Reading intervention projects that employ the use of tutors/teachers with appropriate cultural and linguistic "funds of knowledge" (Grisham, 2000; Gutierrez, 2002) develop an increased sense of responsibility for teaching students in at-risk situations.

## THEORETICAL AND EDUCATIONAL IMPLICATIONS OF THE STUDY

The literacy community must begin to understand the complexities of reading in languages other than English. Although many elements known to prevent reading difficulties among monolingual students have much in common with the cognitive development of language-minority children there are additional issues that must be considered. The results of the present study show many factors interconnect to aid in the development of first language reading comprehension and literacy development of struggling first-grade language-minority children. The use of the native language, the inclusion of family and culture, high teacher expectations and the use of culturally relevant texts all serve to facilitate children's literacy development.

What can I do to help my struggling readers? This question is one that both beginning and experienced bilingual teachers often ask themselves. The answer is not an easy one. Many factors influence the kinds of programs, strategies, and materials teachers develop. With respect to the instruction of language minority children in early elementary school, a strong general focus should be placed on vocabulary acquisition in particular. Children should build a large sight vocabulary in order to access word meanings automatically. Instruction should also be aimed at a deeper level of processing. Rather than focusing primarily on teaching children a large number of letter–sound relationships, numerous encounters with a word in many different contexts should be provided, as students who encounter a word in a variety of activities and different contexts develop more accurate understanding of its meaning and use (Beck & McKeown, 1991). In addition, students with in-depth word knowledge are more likely to use these words in their own speaking or writing (Graves, Juel, & Graves, 1998). Writing of all kinds is also to be encouraged. Writing with invented spelling complements young children's reading development by enhancing perception of phonemes within words, reinforcing knowledge of letter–sound relationships, and helping to make automatic the spellings of high frequency words.

To have an intervention result in true gains structure, training, supervision and planning are needed. School-based preventive efforts should be developed to maintain progress in critical reading skills. Culturally responsive materials in both Spanish and English and instructional strategies should be developed that are well integrated with ongoing classroom instruction. Strategies should center on the critical features of literacy development (e.g., Begorary, 2001; Burns, Griffin, & Snow, 1999; Homan,

King, & Hogarty, 2001) as well as contextual factors, such as the school personnel's use of native language, family involvement, and appreciation of cultural diversity.

Because literacy is so critical for students' academic success, it is important for educators to make informed decisions about their Spanish literacy programs and interventions. The teachers' role is to mediate learning through language and appropriate literacy opportunities that enable children to reach their highest potential. In short, the classroom and the school should represent an environment that minimizes the cultural alienation felt by many language-minority children. Such an environment provides a learning atmosphere that encourages and motivates students to be successful (Alanís, 2004).

## SUGGESTIONS FOR FURTHER RESEARCH

Studies should be conducted to determine which elements of the project plan are most important. This research must also acknowledge and account for the nature of the readers' native language literacy level. In addition to continuing to refine our knowledge about specific instructional techniques and elements, we must examine the intensity and duration of instruction required to eliminate reading failure. And finally, the tutoring model should be tested more carefully to see if similar gains would be obtained in a more controlled situation. It is imperative to keep in mind that although the students who participated in this study have made gains in their reading ability, their classroom peers have also continued to make academic gains. Adequate development of these skills in first grade does not guarantee that children will continue to maintain growth in second grade without additional help.

## LIMITATIONS OF THE STUDY

Some possible limitations on the present study should be mentioned at this point. First, it does not control for all student background variables (i.e., home intellectual climate and motivation) that are likely to have on influence on student achievement. Second, there was no control group to compare between students who did and did not receive the intervention. Third, teacher effect was not taken into account when measuring the intervention effectiveness. Although the results cannot be generalized, the findings obtained from this study will serve as a basis for further investigation.

## REFERENCES

Adams, M. J. (1990). *Beginning to read: Thinking and learning about print*. Cambridge, MA: MIT Press.

Alanís, I. (2004). Effective literacy classrooms: Integrating language and literacy. In C. Salinas, & M. Franquiz (Eds.), *Field of hope: Educating migrant children for the future* (pp. 209–224). ERIC Digest: Charleston, West Virginia.

Alanís, I., Munter, J., & Villamil Tinajero, J. (2003). Preventing reading failure for Language-minority children: Interventions for struggling first grade L2 students. *NABE Journal of Research and Practice, 1*(1), 92–109.

Allington, R. L. (1983). Fluency: The neglected goal. *The Reading Teacher, 36*, 556–561.

Allington, R. L., & Walmsley, S. A. (Eds.). (1995). *No quick fix: Rethinking literacy programs in America's elementary schools.* New York: Teachers College Press.

Anderson, R. C., & Freebody, P. (1981). Vocabulary knowledge. In J. T. Guthrie (Ed.), *Comprehension and teaching: Research reviews* (pp. 77–116). Newark, DE: International Reading Association.

Armbruster B. B., Lehr, F., & Osborn, J. (2001). *Put reading first: The research building blocks for teaching children to read.* Center for the Improvement of Early Reading Achievement (CIERA).

August, A,. & Hakuta, K. (1997). *Improving schooling for language-minority children: A research agenda.* Washington, DC: National Academy Press.

Barrera, R. B., & Jimenez, R. T. (2000). *Literacy practices for Latino students.* Washington, DC: National Clearinghouse for Bilingual Education, The George Washington University, Center for the Study of Language & Education.

Baumann, J. F., & Kameenui, E. J. (1991). Research on vocabulary instruction: Ode to Voltaire. In J. Flood, D. Lapp, & J. R. Squire (Eds.), *Handbook of research on teaching the English language arts* (pp. 604–632). New York: Macmillan.

Beck I., & McKeown, M. (1991). Conditions of vocabulary acquisition. In R. Barr, M. L. Kamil, P. Mosenthal, & P. D. Pearons. (Eds.), *Handbook of reading research 2* (pp. 789–814). New York: Longman.

Begoray, D. (2001). The literacy groups project: investigating the use of Reading Recovery techniques with small groups of Grade 2 students. *Alberta Journal of Educational Research, 47*(2), 141–155.

Blachman, B. (2000). Phonological awareness. In M. Kamil, P. Mosenthal, P. D. Pearson, & R. Barr (Eds.), *Handbook of reading research 3* (pp. 483–502). Mahwah, NJ: Lawrence Erlbaum Associates.

Burns, S., Griffin, P., & Snow, C. (Eds.). (1999). *Starting out right: A guide to promoting children's reading success. Specific recommendations from American's leading researchers on how to help children become successful readers.* Washington, DC: National Academy Press. (ERIC Document Reproduction Service No. ED 439781)

Carrillo, M. (1994). Development of phonological awareness and reading acquisition: A study in Spanish. *Reading and Writing: An Interdisciplinary Journal, 6*, 279–298.

Cunningham, A. E., & Stanovich K. E. (1997). Early reading acquisition and its relation to reading experience and ability 10 years later. *Development Psychology, 33*(6), 943–945.

Cunningham, P. M., & Hall, D. P. (1994). *Making words: Multilevel, hands-on, developmentally appropriate spelling and phonics activities.* Torrance, CA: Good Apple.

Cummins, J. (2000). *Language, power, and pedagogy: Bilingual children in the crossfire.* Buffalo, NY: Multilingual Matters.

Daneman, M. (1991). Individual differences in reading skills. In R. Barr, M., L. Kamil, P., Mosenthal, & P D. Pearson. (Eds.), *Handbooks of reading research. 2* (pp. 512–538). New York: Longman.

Dickinson, D. K., & Tabors, P.O. (2002). Fostering language and literacy in classrooms and homes. *Young Children, 57*(2), 10–19.

Droop M., & Verhoeven, L. (2003). Language proficiency and reading ability in first-and second-language learners. *Reading Research Quarterly, 38*(1), 78–103.

Dowhower, S. L. (1991). Speaking of prosody: Fluency's unattended bedfellow. *Theory into Practice, 30*(3).

Ehri, L. C. (1998). Grapheme-phoneme knowledge is essential for learning to read words in English. In J. Metsala, & L. Ehri (Eds.), *Word recognition in beginning reading* (pp. 3–40). Mahwah, NJ: Lawrence Erlbaum Associates.

Ehri, L. C. (1992). Reconceptualizing the development of sight word reading and its relationship to recoding. In P. Gough, L. Ehri, & R. Treiman (Eds.), *Reading acquisition* (pp. 107–143). Mahwah, NJ: Lawrence Erlbaum Associates.

Escamilla, K., & Andrade, A. (1992). Descubriendo la lectura: An application of Reading Recovery in Spanish. *Education and Urban Society, 24*(2), 212–26.

Freeman, Y. S., & Freeman D. E. (1997). *Teaching reading and writing in Spanish in the bilingual classroom.* Portsmouth, NH: Heinemann Press.

Fornshell, A. C. (2003). *Planning for successful reading and writing instruction in K–2.* Scholastic Professional Books. New York.

Gaskins, I., (1999). A multidimensional reading program. *Reading Teacher, 53*(2), 162–164.

Graves, M. F., Juel, C., & Graves, B. B. (1998). *Teaching reading in the twenty-first century.* Needham Heights, MA: Allyn & Bacon.

Greene, J. (1998). *A meta-analysis of the effectiveness of bilingual education.* Unpublished manuscript, University of Texas at Austin.

Grisham, D. (2000). Connecting theoretical conceptions of reading to practice: A longitudinal study of elementary school teachers. *Reading Psychology, 21*(1), 145–70.

Gullatt, D., & Lofton, B. (1998). Helping at-risk learners succeed: A whole-school approach to success. Window with a view. *Schools in the Middle, 7*(4), 11–14, & 42–43.

Gutierrez, P. (2002). In search of bedrock: Organizing for success with diverse needs children in the classroom. *Journal of Latinos and Education, 1*(1), 49–64.

Hensen, K. T. (1996). Teachers as researchers. In J. Sikula (Ed.), *Handbook of research on teacher education 2* (pp. 53–66). New York: Macmillan.

Homan, S., King, J., & Hogarty, K. (2001). *A small group model for early intervention in literacy: Group size and program effects.* Florida: Reading Recovery Projects. (ERIC Document Reproduction Service No. ED 461095)

Honig, B., Diamond, L., & Gutlohn, L. (2000). *Teaching reading: Sourcebook for kindergarten through eighth grade.* Novato, CA: Arena Press.

McLaughlin, J., Watts, C. & Beard, M. (2000). Just because it's happening doesn't mean it's working: Using action research to improve practice in middle schools. *Phi Delta Kappan, 82*(4), 284–290.

McTaggart, R. (1997). Reading the collection. In R. McTaggart (Ed.), *Participatory action research* (pp. 1–12). Albany, NY: SUNY Press.

Moran, C., & Calfee, R. (1993). Comprehending orthography: Social construction of letter–sound systems in monolingual and bilingual programs. *Reading and Writing. An Interdisciplinary Journal, 5*, 205–225.

National Center for Educational Statistics (1999). *NAEP: Reading subject area.* Accessed at http://nces.ed.gov/nationsreportcard/reading/. March 30, 2004.

National Center for Educational Statistics (2004). *NAEP: Reading subject area.* Accessed at http://nces.ed.gov/nationsreportcard/reading/. March 30, 2004.

National Institute of Child Health and Human Development. (2000). *Report of the National Reading Panel Teaching children to read: An evidence-based assessment of the scientific research literature on reading and its implications for reading instruction* (NIH Publication No. 00–4769). Washington, DC: U.S. Government Printing Office.

National Reading Panel. (2000). *Teaching children to read: Summary report.* Washington, D.C.: National Institute of Child Health and Human Development.

Pearson, P. E., & Gallagher, M. C. (1983). The instruction of reading comprehension. *Contemporary Educational Psychology, 8*, 317–344.

Pinnell, G. S., & Scharer, P. L. (2003). *Teaching for comprehension in reading.* Scholastic Professional Books. New York, NY.

Sensenbaugh, R. (1995). *Reading recovery.* Bloomington, IN: ERIC Clearinghouse on Reading, English, and Communication, Indiana University. (ERIC Document Reproduction Service No. ED 386713)

Snow, C.E., Burns, M. S., & Griffin, P. (Eds.). (1998). *Preventing reading difficulties in young children.* Washington, DC: National Academy Press.

Stahl, S., & Murray, B. (1994). Defining phonological awareness and its relationship to early reading. *Journal of Educational Psychology, 86*, 221–234.

Texas Education Agency (2003). *AEIS Reports*. Austin, Texas: TEA.

Thomas, W., & Collier, V. (1997). *School effectiveness for language-minority children*. Washington, DC: National Clearinghouse for Bilingual Education.

U.S. Census Bureau (2004). Accessed online at http://www.census.gov/ipc/www/usinterimproj. May 18, 2004.

Weiler, J. (1998). *Success for all: A summary of evaluations*. New York: ERIC Clearinghouse on Urban Education, Institute for Urban and Minority Education, Teachers' College. (ERIC Document Reproduction Service No. ED 425250)

Zelasko, N., & Antunez, B. (2000). *If your child learns in two languages: A parent's guide for improving educational opportunities for children acquiring English* as a second language. Washington, DC: National Clearinghouse for Bilingual Education. (ERIC Document Reproduction Service No. ED 337713).

# APPENDIX A

## Lesson Plan Guide Used by University Tutors in School A

| | | |
|---|---|---|
| **Shared Reading** (2 minutes) | Song, listen to a story read by the teacher | Building relationships |
| **Phonological Awareness** (10 minutes) | Review initial sounds Blend, segment, phonemes | Students have opportunities to both blend and segment. All Activities are oral |
| —Syllables | Identifying | Count syllables/use children's names |
| —Onset/rime | Create new patterns | Provide non-examples |
| —Rhymes | Creating/Identifying | Opportunities to practice |
| **Word Study** (3 minutes) Alphabetic Principle | Make a word/ word building | Opportunities to practice |
| **Writing** (3 minutes) | Write letters/words/sentences | Dictation |
| **Closing Activity** (2 minutes) | Talk about something that was learned | Summarize/praise |

Each lesson should follow a predictable sequence that uses what works to help struggling readers develop independent reading strategies. Each component of the lesson has a specific purpose and procedure, which will be described here.

*Shared Reading* (2 minutes): the first two minutes should be used to acquaint your students to the activities and to allow students to share personal experiences related to the text you will be reading.

*Phonemic Awareness Activities* (10 minutes): PA activities include playing with the language, identifying rhymes, counting syllables, and working with onset/rime.

*Word Study/Alphabetic Principle* (3 minutes): Hands-on, manipulative, every-pupil response activity designed to help children learn how letters go together to make words and how small changes make different words (Cunningham).

*Writing* (3 minutes): Writing helps children move along in their reading development. As they write and are coached by the tutor, they develop the PA and letter–sound patterns essential to continued progress in reading. You will also use sound boxes to develop PA.

*Closing Activity* (2 minutes): Review key sounds/words from lesson. Have children summarize their learning. Praise students for their approximations and successes.

## APPENDIX B

### Parts of a Lesson/Timing Guide Used by *Reading Recovery* School B Classroom Teachers

| Minutes | Activity | Examples |
|---------|----------|----------|
| 2 minutes | Fluent writing/Reading | Flash cards, frequency words, dry erase. |
| 10 minutes | Familiar Reading | Re-reading of at least 2 familiar books |
| 10 minutes | Running Record (once each week) | Use results to plan instruction and regroup students |
| 3 minutes | Letter Work/Making and Breaking | Letter names, letter sounds, formation, beginning sounds, embedded |
| 7 minutes | Writing a story | Compose a message that carries meaning |
| 2 minutes | Cut-up story/Sentence | Construct sentences. |
| 3 minutes | Orientation to new book | Use title, illustrations, etc |
| 3 minutes | New book attempted | Encourage children to use reading strategies |
| 2 minutes | Closing | Ask students what they have learned today, praise good behavior, etc. |

# 3

# An Analysis of Second Grade Reading Achievement Related to Pre-Kindergarten Montessori and Transitional Bilingual Education

Linda Rodriguez, Beverly J. Irby, and Genevieve Brown
*Sam Houston State University*

Rafael Lara-Alecio and Martha M. Galloway
*Texas A&M University*

## ABSTRACT

The relationship of participation in a Pre-Kindergarten Montessori bilingual program and a traditional Pre-Kindergarten transitional bilingual program to reading achievement in Spanish and English at second grade was examined. Results indicated that students who participated in the Montessori bilingual program at the Pre-Kindergarten level significantly outperformed students who participated in the traditional transitional bilingual program at Pre-Kindergarten in both English and Spanish reading on the Iowa Test of Basic Skills. The results challenge traditional practices at the Pre-Kindergarten level with English language learners (ELLs) and support the addition of Montessori education in bilingual programs.

## INTRODUCTION

Providing a quality education for English language learners (ELLs) has become critical as nearly 4.5 million children come to school from families where the home language is other than English (U.S. Census, 2000). Yet, Hispanic children continue to score well below their peers in reading throughout the elementary school years and often average about four years behind in their secondary school years as ELLs (Applebee, Langer, & Mullis, 1989; NCES, 2003). Many of these Hispanic students, due to their often impoverished status, are in greatest need to have the support of high quality preschool and primary school environments

(Snow, Burns, & Griffin, 1998); however, it is known that Hispanic children attend preschool at a much smaller rate than their White counterparts (Our Nation, 1996). Access to high quality preschool programs such as the Montessori model, for Hispanic children is even less as a very small percentage of Montessori programs are funded under public education.

As the nation's Hispanic school-age populations dramatically increase, it has become crucial to explore effective practices in prekindergarten programs. Although the pedagogy introduced by Maria Montessori is over a century old, it is remarkably relevant for low socio-economic preschool children of the 21st century. Heinstock (1997) reported that the Montessori approach with primary school children of lower socio-economic status (SES) was more effective than regular public school primary grade programs, regardless of the previous pre-school experience (Heinstock, 1997); however, to date, the literature does not provide sufficient data related to the impact of transitional Montessori bilingual education programs in a prekindergarten (PK) public school. The purpose of our study was to investigate the impact of participation in a PK Montessori bilingual program on low SES, second grade, and Hispanic ELL students' reading achievement scores in Spanish and English.

Following is a discussion Montessori's philosophy and the discrepancies between her original intentions for addressing children's educational needs and modern implementations. Current literature of this topic treats issues of home and school languages, second language acquisition principles, and reading achievement of ELL students. After the general discussion on Montessori, we present the study with the methodology section that includes: (a) the sample population, (b) description of the variable, PK Montessori and traditional bilingual programs, (c) the instrumentation, (d) data collection, and (e) data analyses. We follow that by results and discussion of findings. Lastly we share the significance of the study related to Montessori and second language acquisition theory.

## MONTESSORI: VISION AND REALITY

Maria Montessori was deeply concerned with social injustices for women and children. As she developed her pedagogy and curriculum in 1906, Montessori concentrated her efforts on those women and children of poor socio-economic status (Kramer, 1988). In fact, her first school, *Casa dei Bambini*, served 50 very poor children from a Roman slum (Ruenzel, 1997).

Montessori (1961) stated,

> The poor have not yet had proper consideration, and always there remains one class that was yet more completely ignored, even among the rich. Such was childhood! All social problems are considered from the point of view of the adult and his needs. . . . Far more important are the needs of the child. (p. 120)

Montessori later indicated in the same essay, "Suppose we set up in schools the same social improvement that we are so proud of achieving! Let us feed the children, give them playground, clothing, freedom of speech" (Montessori, 1961, p. 121).

Montessori's intentions of inclusive and accessible educational experiences are contrary to her legacy which is characterized by limited access in terms of: (a) privatization of Montessori's method, (b) high-quality educational programs and materials for non-minority children, and (c) research on Montessori and Hispanic, English language learners.

## Privatization

Despite the fact that Montessori focused her initial work toward poor children, society has promoted Montessori primarily for an exclusive private education. For example, according to Ruenzel (1997), only four percent (200) of the approximately 5000 Montessori schools in the United States are funded under public education. Thus, the social justice for which Montessori worked is diminished as the schools bearing her name and promoting her methodology and philosophy are limited primarily to those children whose parents have the resources to afford private school education.

## Programs and Materials

Kagan (1989) stated, "There are vast inequities regarding children's eligibility and access to programs. Children are segregated by income, with limited choices and resources for low-income families" (Kagan, 1989, p. 234), and, this situation ". . . does not reflect the law or spirit of our nation" (Kagan, 1989, p. 235). According to the National Center for Educational Statistics, only 50% of children living in households with incomes of $10,000 or less receive care and education from persons other than their parents, in comparison to 77% of children in households with incomes in excess of $75,000 (National Center for Education Statistics [NCES], 1999). From 1973 to 1993, Hispanic three- and four-year old enrollment in preschool remained flat (about 15%), while White preschool enrollment steadily grew from 18 to 35% (Our Nation, 1996). Often, low-income Hispanic families believe their home environments are better for their children than programs like Head Start, because many early childhood services are not prepared to deal with the linguistic and cultural diversity of their children (ibid). To emphasize the need for high-quality preschool programs, consider that at age four, Hispanic children tend to have less-developed, school-related skills than do White children (ibid). In 1993, for example, Hispanic four-year old children were less able than their White counterparts to identify basic colors (61% compared to 91%), recognize all letters of the alphabet (12% to 31%), count up to 50 or more (11% to 22%), and write their first name (59% to 74%) (ibid). This inadequate introduction to schooling may have long-term negative consequences for Hispanic students. The concerns related to high quality early childhood programs, particularly for Hispanic students, is deserving of attention because it has been projected that by the year 2030, Hispanic students will be at almost 16 million—25 % of the total school population (ibid).

Because minority children are three times more likely to be poor than majority children (Children's Defense Fund, 2000), their access to Montessori programs and materials is drastically reduced. Additionally, materials for teaching in Montessori programs are currently developed primarily in English, and they are not specific to the Hispanic culture; thus, the access to Montessori for children who are in the low socio-economic status (SES), ELLs, and Hispanic is further limited.

## RESEARCH

Even in the professional literature, there is a paucity of references to Montessori and SES and/or to Montessori and Hispanic ELL children and corresponding bilingual educational programs. In an exhaustive review of literature, only two studies were found which related to low SES; i.e., Jackson (1980) and Wheeler (1998). Further, those were the only two studies found related to ELL children.

### Montessori Bilingual Education

Renton (1998) indicated that Montessori (1949) spoke of young children as natural linguists. In Montessori's view, children unconsciously learn about the language itself and how it operates. It was the exposure that children had to one or more languages that determined whether their linguistic potential was developed. In the cases of some children, a natural linguist was "awakened" by their family context, where the child might grow up with two or more languages being spoken at home. In the case of other children, their potential was developed at school, where their native language was used to introduce a second, dominant language. Yet other children in many Montessori programs are exposed to two or more languages with the purpose of developing true bilingual skills (Renton, 1998).

The complex multicultural and multilingual reality of American education today is affecting Montessori programs, especially in the public schools (Renton, 1998). Issues in early childhood education are of concern in an increasingly changing society. This was why, as Renton indicated, Montessorians worldwide are developing creative responses to this challenge. These responses include Montessori schools' support for home language maintenance, second language, bilingual and multicultural education, and immersion programs whose aim is to utilize the sensitive period for language development more fully, from PK through elementary.

According to Renton (1998), the home and the language of culturally and linguistically diverse learners should not only be respected, but also maintained and developed as fully as possible. For these children, the mastery of the dominant language was also of vital importance. Culturally and linguistically diverse children should consider themselves functional in two cultures and in two languages.

With the belief that primary language skills in a first language was the base for developing skills in a second language, Renton (1998) presented five basic principles of current second language acquisition approaches that she suggested can be successfully implemented in a Montessori environment.

First, Renton (1998) stated that second language acquisition happens most naturally when the process closely resembles first-language acquisition. Second, the environment that should promote second language acquisition must provide comprehensible input and a supportive affective climate. This principle means that language should be understandable and meaningful. Undoubtedly, the concept of context plays a critical role in making language understandable and meaningful. According to Renton (1998), the concrete materials used in the Montessori method have proved attractive to children while at the same time they "embody specific concepts, and invite exploration through movement and the senses" (p. 31).

Third, second language acquisition should foster a basic communicative proficiency and a cognitive academic proficiency. In a Montessori learning environment, both levels of language are continually being constructed and practiced (Renton, 1998). Social conversations among the learners and the teacher and lessons that target concept development are combined in the instruction of children. The environment that promotes second language acquisition must provide comprehensible input (Krashen, 1988) and a supportive affective climate.

Fourth, second language acquisition requires time. The three-year cycle proposed by Montessori programs provides time for children to move through various levels of second language development.

Finally, the fifth principle presented by Renton (1998) stated that languages are inseparable from culture, and the former are always learned most effectively in a cultural context. Indeed, as Renton (1998) indicated, "culture shapes the child's first experiences, from which language arises" (p. 31).

One study (Jackson, 1980) purported to describe and to evaluate the first year of a Montessori bilingual early childhood program. The evaluation of the program included language testing for comprehension and production of Spanish and English as ELLs as observational data from the Spring and Fall semesters of 1980. The obtained results suggested that regarding English and Spanish comprehension and production, the gains made in each case (English/Spanish) were highly significant, using the correlated $t$-tests. However, given the lack of a comparison group, these changes could not necessarily be attributed to the Montessori bilingual treatment.

Other researchers (Farmer, 1998; Thomas & Collier, 2002) noted that children who have been pushed to English usually attain a fragmented education and are more likely to drop out before they complete high school. Conversely, Farmer (1998) determined that in Montessori bilingual preschool programs, teachers who are native Spanish speakers guide children who are from Spanish-speaking homes. These children master the content in Spanish and then transition to English.

According to the Montessori philosophy, children construct their identity from what is offered in the environment (Standing, 1957). Hence, it is important that children's first school experience be a smooth transition from home, where teachers speak the children's native language and understand children's native culture. Farmer (1998) stated that if the school program was in a language and a culture dissimilar to the children's, the vital cognitive and socializing experiences at school do not connect with the home experiences.

Rosanova (1998) found that young children's growth to bilingualism was both resilient and robust under the right circumstances. He further indicated the bilingual Montessori classroom was an exceptionally good environment for the development of what, in second language acquisition theory, was termed as basic interpersonal skills and cognitive academic language.

Supportive of the Montessori philosophy, the maturational/linguistic worldview of the young child with special foci on bilingualism was advocated by Saville-Troike (1973), McLaughlin (1978, 1987), and Chaudron (1988). In this view, the child's primary language is used as a mode of instruction with additive English occurring when the child had mastered concepts in his primary language. Cummins (1986) indicated that content areas of instruction provide a rich source of comprehensible input for ELL children who often experience anxiety and hostility toward learning in general and toward English in particular. Such attitudes reduce the amount of input that can be acquired and slow down the development of English as a second language (Chomsky, 1988; Cummins, 1986; Krashen, 1985).

## Reading Achievement and ELL Students

Few significant research studies exist related to reading instruction and second language acquisition. Garcia (1987) determined that ELLs may misinterpret English words or reading passages based on erroneous lexical or semantic associations with their own language or on different cultural schemata or personal experiences. Strengthening ELL students' Spanish literacy also enables them to use their native language, enhancing their bilingual capacity (August, Calderon, & Carlo, 2001). Those students who had the greatest opportunity to develop their Spanish between kindergarten and sixth grade increased their standardized English language and reading test performance at a significantly higher rate than students in the other programs and in the normed sample from the standardized test (Garcia, 1999).

According to The National Research Council and the Committee on the Prevention of Reading Difficulties in Young Children, among the most important factors for successful reading were the child's: (a) intellectual and sensory capacities, (b) positive expectations about and experience with literacy from an early age, (c) support for reading-related activities and attitudes so that he or she is prepared to benefit from early literacy experiences and subsequent formal instruction in school, and (d) instructional environments conducive to learning (Snow, Burns, & Griffin, 1998). Academic language develops gradually over time. Ovando, Collier, and Combs (2003) maintained that the development of academic language is a continuous process throughout a student's schooling.

## METHODOLOGY

Our study was established with a correlation research design. Since the empirical research was found to be scant in our area of investigation, we determined that an initial correlation design to examine the extent to which ELLs achievement in English and Spanish was related to an early experience in specific classroom environment or method would be appropriate to add to the knowledge base. Our study was guided by the following research question: Is there a significant difference in second grade reading achievement scores in both English and Spanish between two groups of ELLs students (a) those who participated in a PK Montessori bilingual program and (b) those who participated in a PK traditional bilingual program?

### Sample and Context of Study

The population included in this study was 450 Second Grade ELL students enrolled in a large urban school district in southeast Texas in 2000–2001 who had participated in either (a) a PK Montessori bilingual program in 1998–1999 or (b) a PK traditional bilingual program in 1998–1999. Students who had been enrolled in the PK Montessori bilingual program were considered the experimental group, while students who had been enrolled in the PK traditional bilingual program were considered the control group. All participants were of Hispanic origin, had Spanish as their primary language, and were of low socio-economic status.

### Sample

According to Gall, Borg, and Gall (1996), if a large effect size is anticipated, a more rigorous statistical power level of .70 at .05 level of significance should be considered. Following that recommendation, calculations recommended a minimum number of participants to be at least 40. Considering the maximum factors that affect the internal validity of the study, specifically mortality, ten more participants in each intervention were added. There were two samples, each one included 50 (experimental and control) with total of 100 participants per sample.

To answer the research question as related to Spanish reading achievement, a stratified random sample was conducted with a population of 450 second grade

ELL students from eight elementary campuses that served the majority of ELL students within the same school district. Students in the population were then reduced to a sample characterized by (a) their participation in either program type (a PK Montessori bilingual program or a traditional bilingual PK program), (b) those who had taken the Aprenda achievement test in second grade, and (c) those who were enrolled during the 2000–2001 school year. As a result 200 students met the prescribed characteristics—100 from each program type. To increase the internal validity of the study, 10 more students than the minimum 40 needed for power sampling were added for random selection. From 100 students per program type, a random selection was conducted, consisting of 50 students who had participated in a PK Montessori bilingual program and a random selection of 50 participants who had participated in a traditional bilingual PK program.

To answer the research question as related to English reading achievement, a stratified random sample was conducted with a population of 450 second grade ELL students from eight elementary campuses that served the majority of ELL students within the same school district. Students in the population were then reduced to a sample characterized by (a) their participation in either program type (a PK Montessori bilingual program or a traditional bilingual PK program), (b) those who had taken the Iowa Test of Basic Skills achievement test in second grade, and (c) those who were enrolled during the 2000–2001 school year. As a result 200 students met the prescribed characteristics—100 from each program type. To increase the internal validity of the study, 10 more students than the minimum 40 needed for power sampling were added for random selection. From 100 students per program type, a random selection of 50 students who had participated in a PK Montessori bilingual program and a random selection of 50 participants who had participated in a traditional bilingual PK program was conducted.

## Context: PK Montessori Bilingual Program

The PK Montessori Center is a public school supported through federal funds. Eighty-nine percent of the children were identified at the poverty level. Of the 690 children on the campus, 80% were Hispanic, 14% African-American, and 6% other. Sixty-two percent of the children were categorized as ELLs and were served in bilingual classrooms (Texas Education Agency [TEA], 2001). The PK Montessori Center, opened in the fall of 1998, was a result of school district's successful passage of a 20 million dollar bond election to support the building of four early childhood centers. A 40,000 square foot urban campus, the Center housed 18 classrooms, a multi-purpose room, library, teacher workroom, lounge, nurse's' station, parent workroom, diagnostician office, counseling room, speech therapy room, and an office area. Each classroom was equipped with its own lavatory, drinking fountain, and sink. Twelve classrooms were in open areas, while six were self-contained. Nine of the classrooms were designated as bilingual classrooms (five self-contained; four open). The campus sits on the corner of a busy

Houston intersection and is surrounded by a grass-covered playground. On one side of the campus is a wooded area, on another side is a large church, and on the other side is a large Hispanic flea market. The eight elementary campuses from which the sample of second grade ELL students was drawn were located within a five-mile radius of the Center. None of the elementary campuses continued the Montessori program in kindergarten, first, or second grade.

At the Montessori Center, each classroom is equipped fully with quality Montessori materials, more than is observed in many private school Montessori classrooms. Each classroom has new materials that are ELLs cared for by the teacher and the students, because in the Montessori environment everything has its proper place and must be kept in order. Each classroom cost is at least $10,000. Materials, many three dimensional and multi-sensory, are arranged in centers. Each center is correlated to the curriculum that is sequential, integrated, and aligned to the state standards for PK, the district benchmarks, and the Montessori methodology and philosophy.

Each teacher in the Montessori Center is certified by the state. In addition, each teacher receives five weeks of mandatory Montessori training from the National Center for Montessori Education at a cost of $5000 per teacher. Training continues throughout the following school year with a certified trainer with ongoing curriculum and instructional support. In Montessori, the teacher is trained to prepare an environment responsive to the needs of the learner and to prepare the learners to meet their own needs and encourage conversation with the children. These conversations among the children and the teacher encourage the unfolding, or development, of the language. A Montessori teacher is also trained to teach the children how to have poise, order, and equilibrium while working in centers or individually. Lessons in the Montessori method are individualized, concise, simple, objective, and allow for teacher observation. Teachers are trained to observe and take records. The teacher is trained to develop a classroom focused on creating a love of order, love of work, profound spontaneous concentration, attachment to reality, the love of silence and of working alone, sublimation of the possessive instinct, power to act from real choice and not from curiosity, obedience, independence and initiative, spontaneous self-discipline, and joy. The teaching staff and administrators share a common educational philosophy and have collaboratively developed expected levels of students' achievement with daily observations and formal assessments conducted every three weeks.

Montessori training is intensive and imparts an attitude as ELLs as information. The training includes Montessori child psychology, educational theory, material demonstrations, supervised practice with Montessori materials, observation of Montessori classrooms, supervised practiced teaching, and extensive written and oral exams. Multi-aged clusters enhance the Montessori dynamic by reducing competition, maximizing curriculum options available to any one child, providing a family atmosphere that plays a vital role in socialization, and permitting older children to model advanced work for younger children.

The Montessori Center takes a holistic approach to educating the child. Parents are trained in the Montessori philosophy and are required to volunteer time at the school. The school is welcoming, and over 20,000 volunteer hours are logged annually.

The principal at the PK Montessori bilingual program makes every effort to (a) recruit highly qualified bilingual early childhood teachers, (b) provide additional training and other support to ensure student achievement success, (c) offer time for teachers to plan together, and (d) create a collective awareness among teachers about their reading program in Spanish.

## PK Traditional Bilingual Centers

The three PK traditional bilingual centers, Centers A, B, and C, were funded with federal funds that support low-income children. In Center A, 87% of the student population was economically disadvantaged. Although, 35% of the children were categorized as ELLs, only 40% of the 35% were served in bilingual classrooms. Of the 582 children on the campus, 51% were Hispanic, 41% African-American, and 8% other. In Center B, 89% of the student population was economically disadvantaged. Of the 592 children on the campus, 88% were Hispanic, 5% African-American, and 7% other. While 56% of the children were categorized as ELLs, only 30% of the 56% were served in bilingual classrooms. In Center C, 90.2% of the student population was economically disadvantaged. Of the 510 children on the campus, 62.5% were Hispanic, 26% African-American, and 14.4% other. Forty-three percent of the children were categorized as ELLs; however, only 20% of the 43% were served in bilingual classrooms (TEA, 2001).

## Instrumentation

Participants were administered the reading section of the Aprenda (Spanish) and the Iowa Test of Basic Skills (ITBS; English). The ITBS and the Aprenda tests used in the study are administered to ELL students on an annual basis by the school district to measure student progress. The ITBS English test is administered to ELL students who have some English skills. If students do not have English skills, they are exempt from taking the ITBS test.

### Aprenda

The purpose of the Aprenda test is to measure the academic achievement of Spanish-speaking students. The Aprenda Spanish test is a written test that contains the following sections: Word Reading, Reading Comprehension, Language, and Listening (Harcourt Brace, 1998).

*Reliability and validity of Aprenda Spanish Test.*    Aprenda was normed in the spring and fall of 1996 on approximately 56,000 students in a nationwide sample of Spanish speaking students. Test–retest reliability in pre-reading and reading portions of this assessment battery were in the 0.85 range for children in Grades K–2. Criterion validity was assessed by comparing performance on this version of Aprenda with the previous version of Aprenda. Kuder–Richardson Formula #20 Reliability Coefficient of .94 for second grade students for Total Reading was determined (Harcourt Brace, 1998).

### Iowa Tests of Basic Skills (ITBS)

The purpose of the ITBS test is to measure the academic achievement of Spanish-speaking students in English. The ITBS is used by the district for second grade ELL students as a pretest and as a posttest to measure reading achievement gains in English.

*Reliability and validity of ITBS.* The ITBS was normed using a national sample at the beginning and end of the school year in 1995 utilizing Kuder–Richardson Formula 20 (KR–20) procedures, the reliability coefficient of .943 for Total Reading for second grade students in the spring (Riverside, 1995). This formula provided a reliability estimate equaling the average of all split-half coefficients available on all possible divisions of the test into halves (Gall, Borg, & Gall, 1996).

Although the ITBS had a high coefficient, the technical manuals did not discuss the appropriateness or inappropriateness of the tests for ELL students. Small percentages of ELL students were included in the ITBS standardization sample, ranging from a high of 1.5% in Grade 6 to a low of 0.3% in Grade 12. Students enrolled in bilingual or ESL programs ranged from 1.7% of the ITBS national standardization sample in Grade 3 to 0.5% in Grades 9, 10, and 12 (Zehler, Hopstock, Fleischma, & Greniuk, 1994). The ITBS was selected by the district and administered annually to all students; therefore, it was used in our study despite the fact that the appropriateness for this particular form of the ITBS for second grade ELL students had not been established.

## Data Collection and Analysis

The Aprenda Spanish reading achievement scores and the ITBS reading achievement scores for Grade 2 students in the Fall of 2001 (Aprenda—October, 2001; ITBS—September, 2001) were collected from district records. Computer coding identified two groups of students, one being enrolled in a PK Montessori bilingual program and one in a PK traditional bilingual program. Data were analyzed using SPSS 10.

## Statistical Design

An independent t-test was conducted to determine if there were statistically significant differences between the two groups of students on the Aprenda reading subtest. Because Normal Curve Equivalents (NCEs) are the most useful in manipulating test data for comparison of scores across tests across subjects, NCEs scores were used in the calculation of the *t*-test. An effect size using Cohen's *d* also was calculated.

An independent *t*-test was conducted to determine if there were statistically significant differences between the two groups of students on the ITBS reading subtest. Standard scores were used in the calculation of the *t*-test because NCEs were not reported to the district. An effect size using Cohen's *d* also was calculated.

## RESULTS

### Spanish Reading Results

The results of the independent *t*-test, depicted in Table 3.1, indicated statistical significance ($p \le .05$), with ELL students who had participated in a PK Montessori bilingual program significantly outscoring the ELL students who had participated in a PK raditional bilingual program on the Spanish reading subtest of the Aprenda. The confidence interval as reported on the difference was at 95% confidence interval [CI] = .0024538 – 9.9906. Less variance was found in the Montessori group's Spanish reading scores (SD = 11.3468) as opposed to the traditional group's scores (SD = 13.6086). Cohen's *d* was calculated resulting in a .4005 which is considered a low medium effect size.

### English Reading Results

Table 3.2 depicts the results of the independent *t*-test for the ITBS English reading subtest for two groups of Grade 2 ELL students: (a) students who participated in a PK Montessori bilingual program, and (b) students who participated in a PK traditional bilingual program. The results of the independent *t*-test indicated a significant difference ($p \le .05$) between the children who had participated in a PK Montessori bilingual program and the children who had participated in a PK traditional bilingual program on the English reading subtest of the ITBS, with the PK Mon-

TABLE 3.1
Independent *t*-Test for the Aprenda Spanish Reading Subtest

| PK Program | *n* | *M* | *SD* | *SE* | 95% Confidence Interval | | *t* | *df* | *p* |
| --- | --- | --- | --- | --- | --- | --- | --- | --- | --- |
| | | | | | *Lower* | *Upper* | | | |
| Montessori Bilingual | 50 | 67.8640 | 11.3468 | 1.6047 | 4.538E-.02 | 9.9906 | 2.003 | 98 | .048 |
| Traditional Bilingual | 50 | 62.8460 | 13.6086 | 1.9245 | | | | | |

$p \le .05$.

TABLE 3.2
Independent *t*-Test for the ITBS English Reading Subtest

| PK Program | n | M | SD | SE | 95% Confidence Interval | | t | df | p |
|---|---|---|---|---|---|---|---|---|---|
| | | | | | Lower | Upper | | | |
| Montessori Bilingual | 50 | 146.6000 | 10.4080 | 1.4719 | 5.6623 | 12.6877 | 5.179 | 98 | .000 |
| Traditional Bilingual | 50 | 137.4200 | 6.9842 | .9877 | | | | | |

*p* ≤ .05.

tessori group outscoring the tradition PK group. The confidence interval as reported on the difference was at 95% confidence interval [CI] = 5.6623 – 12.6977. There was more variance among the Montessori group's English reading scores (SD = 10.4080) as opposed to the traditional group's scores (SD = 6.9842). Cohen's *d* was calculated with a 1.035, which is considered a large effect size.

## DISCUSSION

The results of the analysis of the Spanish Reading Aprenda and the English Reading ITBS indicated that second grade ELL students who participated in a PK Montessori bilingual program scored significantly higher than second grade ELL students who participated in a PK traditional bilingual program.

These findings could be interpreted in light of Montessori philosophy, characteristics, and practices unique to the PK Montessori bilingual program and exposed to the children at an early age: (a) high expectations, (b) strong instructional leadership, (c) focused and sustained professional development, (d) comprehensive oracy and literacy development, (e) rich physical environment, (f) aligned curriculum, (g) parent support, and (h) Montessori philosophy shared by the trained faculty. The above characteristics are supported by educational research and practice at the Montessori PK campus and are discussed briefly as follows.

### High Expectations

The PK Montessori bilingual program sets expectations ELLs above the district benchmarks. It is the expectation of the school district that schools implement vertically aligned benchmark targets developed by the school district. For example, one of the benchmark targets states that students in PK will master 10 initial letter sounds by the end of the school year. The PK Montessori bilingual program sets the benchmark expectations at 26 initial letter sounds, clearly above the district's expectations.

Additionally, expected levels of achievement are collaboratively developed by the administrators, teachers, and support staff, are implemented school wide, and are frequently assessed. Ladson-Billings (1994) maintained that teachers of successful learners of color believe that students are capable of excellence, and they assume responsibility for ensuring that their students achieve that excellence. Scheurich (1998) stated that just succeeding with the children in one's classroom is not sufficient; each teacher must work together with administrators and other teachers to ensure success for all children.

## Strong Instructional Leadership

Goldenberg and Sullivan (1994) emphasized the principal's role as crucial and fundamental to providing support and exerting pressure toward improvement and accountability. At the PK Montessori bilingual Center, strong instructional leadership was evident as the principal placed high priority on (a) recruiting highly qualified bilingual early childhood teachers, (b) providing sustained and relevant training to ensure student achievement success, (c) providing time for teachers to plan together, (d) creating a collective awareness among teachers and parents about the importance of reading, and (e) instilling a sense of accountability for the success of all children.

## Sustained and Focused Professional Development

Focused and sustained staff development was determined to be an integral component to the program at the PK Montessori campus. Teachers are provided staff development during a five-week period during the summer on Montessori education, as ELLs as release time to attend follow-up or enrichment Montessori training during school hours. A Montessori trainer provides these follow-up sessions on-site. Additionally, during the school year and the summer, teachers are provided professional development in bilingual literacy issues, phonemic awareness, emergent reading and writing, curriculum development, parent/family involvement, and self-assessment and improvement.

Sufficient time, before, during, and/or after the school day, is allocated for teacher learning, implementation, and reflection. Weekly grade level meetings and Montessori teacher training promote collegial sharing and honest discussion to respond to the challenge of meeting the PK student needs based on an examination of patterns of student strengths and weaknesses. The principal ensures that the program builds "internal capacity" among the campus teachers so that they can provide the leadership to new teachers on the campus and share the high expectations related to the district and state benchmarks. The PK Montessori program makes ongoing, sustained, and focused professional development a priority and has done so since the opening of the school.

## Comprehensive Oracy and Literacy Development

In the Montessori learning environment, both languages, primary and target, should be continually constructed and practiced (Renton, 1998). Social conversations among the learners and the teacher and lessons that target concept development were observed to be combined in the instruction of children in the PK Montessori bilingual classrooms. Students exposed early to this particular Montessori environment are afforded rich access to their native Spanish language, which apparently broadened their oral language development, a critical factor in learning to read.

In the observed PK Montessori bilingual program, children first are expected to develop social and cognitive strategies that enable them to understand and eventually to develop a receptive vocabulary. Rosanova (1998) identified four developmental stages of communication in a Montessori community, namely, the preproduction, the early production, the speech emergence, and the intermediate fluency stages. In the early production stage in this Montessori environment, many children begin to produce a variety of simple words and short phrases in the target language, and they also respond with one-word answers to questions in the target language. Communication was observed to get stronger in the Montessori program as children helped their peers interpret and understand spoken language. In the speech emergence stage, coherent dialogues begin to emerge, as some children begin to speak the target language in longer phrases and more fluently. We determined that teachers in the PK Montessori program established survival vocabulary goals and exposed children to a richer vocabulary than did teachers in the PK traditional programs. Additionally, the PK Montessori program teachers used rhyme and movement to enhance oracy.

The PK Montessori bilingual curriculum and standard Montessori practices appear to supply the rudiments of what most children need for a foundation for reading in the native as ELLs, as the target language. The PK Montessori bilingual program focused specifically on (a) teaching letter sounds through hands-on approach by using objects and sandpaper letters, (b) a curriculum aligned with the district benchmark targets and state standards for PK and second language acquisition, (c) oral language development, and (d) phonemic awareness. Snow, Burns, and Griffin (1998) in *Preventing Reading Difficulties in Young Children*, recommended that early childhood reading instruction encompass both the mechanics of reading (e.g., practice with the sound structure of words, recognition of letters, and purposes for reading) and the development of text comprehension (e.g., talk about books, reading strategies, and the development of conceptual knowledge), all of which were found to exist in the observed PK Montessori bilingual program.

Although the target language is approached and integrated within the curriculum, literacy in a child's native language is the foundation of the PK Montessori bilingual program. Such a foundation establishes a knowledge, concept, and skills base that transfers from native language reading to reading in a second language (Collier & Thomas, 1992; Cummins, 1989; Escamilla, 1987; Modiano, 1968; Rodriguez, 1988). Moreover, it has been established that, for Spanish-speaking children, there is a high and positive correlation between learning to read in Spanish and subsequent reading achievement in English (Collier & Thomas, 1992; Greene, 1998; Krashen & Biber, 1987; Lesher-Madrid & García, 1985; Ramírez, Yuen, & Ramey, 1991). Escamilla (1998) stated that there is strong theoretical and empirical evidence to suggest that teaching Spanish-speaking children in the U.S. to read and write first in Spanish constitutes both sound policy and "best practice."

## Physical Environment

In the PK Montessori bilingual classroom the environment is carefully prepared. The physical environment is orderly, precise, and attractive. It invites learning without being over-stimulating. It is controlled, allowing the children to experience success, but also allowing for creative extensions of the exercises so they become truly meaningful to each child. The psychological environment set by the teacher is encouraging and supportive of purposeful activity. Children have a freedom within limits to pursue their own needs while learning to respect the needs of others and while developing independence.

If a young child is placed in an environment rich in materials that meet his/her developmental needs and he/she is given the freedom to choose activities according to these needs, he/she learns spontaneously, effortlessly and joyously (Montessori, 1964). The multisensory and print-rich environment (in the native language primarily, but enhanced with the target language) was a hallmark of the PK Montessori bilingual program and likely influenced the higher reading scores of the students identified in our study.

## Aligned Curriculum

Curriculum alignment is the process of organizing three key elements in a classroom so that they are closely matched (aligned). The three elements are (a) instruction and materials, (b) outcomes or standards, and (c) tests. The supposition is that the most efficient and effective student learning will result when classroom instruction and materials align with outcomes and standards and these align with tests (Gorin & Blanchard, 2004). We found the PK Montessori bilingual curriculum to be completely aligned with the philosophy of Montessori, Montessori instructional strategies, the PK curriculum, which is the DLM Early Childhood Express (Schiller, Clements, Lara-Alecio, Samora, & Irby, 2003), and the state and district standards or benchmarks which are aligned to the benchmark tests that relate to the third grade Texas Assessment of Knowledge and Skills (TAKS). There is consistent monitoring of the alignment.

## Parent Support

Our findings indicated that the PK Montessori campus engaged parents in a contract by which they had to commit to 20 hours of service over the year. Parent and volunteer time was logged at over 20,000 hours. Parents were provided the tools to understand the philosophy of Montessori, strategies to improve their children's reading and math skills, and helpful instruction on how to be a better parent in relation to (a) encouraging their children in schoolwork, (b) providing enriching opportunities, (c) offering a print-rich home environment, and (d) disciplining children with appropriate strategies.

## Shared Montessori Philosophy

The Montessori philosophy offers a broad vision of education as an aid to life. Every teacher hired at the PK Montessori campus was expected to embrace and develop that philosophy. A philosophy of respect for each child's differences must be visibly demonstrated with kindness and soft teaching and corrective reasoning voices. Observations of the teachers at the Montessori campus revealed their belief in the Montessori philosophy which advocates that the children's task is an inner construction as they grow from childhood to maturity through natural development. Each individual child's inner directives freely guide the child toward wholesome growth. The principal helped to establish this shared vision. According to Betances (1992), students likely will be more successful when a collaborative vision that is clear and compelling and that is connected to teaching and learning is evident. This vision focuses attention on students.

## CONCLUSIONS AND RECOMMENDATIONS
## FOR EDUCATIONAL PRACTICE

The purpose of our study was to investigate the impact of a PK Montessori bilingual program on low-socioeconomic, second grade, Hispanic ELL students' reading achievement scores in Spanish and English. The results indicated that ELL students who participated in a PK Montessori bilingual program scored higher in Spanish and English reading on standardized tests during the first semester of second grade than did those ELL students who participated in a traditional bilingual PK program during the same time period. Based on the results of our study, participation in a PK Montessori bilingual program appears to positively impact reading achievement in both English and Spanish. We hypothesize that this positive impact was related to the comprehensive and systemic approach to PK Montessori bilingual education described in this paper.

For those considering a PK Montessori bilingual program, the following elements are important to incorporate as the program is planned and implemented. First, the PK Montessori bilingual curriculum is a total curriculum approach that is integrated and sequential. Teachers' common understanding of their lesson planning and curriculum scope and sequence is essential to the success of the program. Second, full benefits can be achieved only if a well-trained Montessori teaching staff that shares a common educational philosophy that is supported by the campus principal understands the dynamic of the total program. Third, teachers need to be certified in bilingual/ESL education and in Montessori education so that the two fields can be integrated well in the classroom. Fourth, the Montessori material is costly; therefore, additional funding might be necessary. Fifth, expected levels of student achievement should be developed school-wide. All staff working at a Montessori PK Bilingual Center should embrace high expectations for the students. Sixth, parents/families should be fully integrated into the school and must be educated about the Montessori philosophy. Related to this is the reporting of skill achievement to parents. It is recommended that the district report card be altered to exemplify the skills taught within the PK Montessori bilingual program.

## SIGNIFICANCE AND RELATIONSHIP TO THEORY

The significance of our study is the strong support it provides for the implementation of a *public school* PK Montessori bilingual program. The PK Montessori bilingual education program appears to be a superior beginning program to offer at the preschool level to that of just a regular, transitional bilingual program. The theory of Montessori education offers the basis of respect for the ELL child and his/her language, and the theory of language acquisition is embedded in the public school PK Montessori environment observed in our study.

In the PK Montessori bilingual program there was an aligned focus on oral language development with comprehensible input surrounded by a supportive affective climate. Teachers developed the language of the child in situations of respect—teacher-to-teacher and child-to-child. The Montessori environment naturally supported and promoted such situations in which the teacher structured that environment to make social and academic language understandable and meaningful with hands-on activities, concrete materials, and much discussion and exploration by the children.

The hope that Maria Montessori had for children of lower socioeconomic status is realized in such a public school program and provides encouragement that PK Montessori bilingual programs lay a strong foundation for later academic achievement.

## REFERENCES

Applebee, A., Langer, J., & Mullis, I. (1989). *Crossroads in American education*. Princeton, NJ: Educational Testing Service.

August, D., Calderon, M., & Carlo, M. (2001). *The transfer of skills from Spanish to English: A study of young learners*. Retrieved June 3, 2002, from http://www.cal.org/pubs/articles/skillstransfer-nabe.html

Betances, S. (1992, July). *Presentation at the Summer Institute of North Central Regional Educational Laboratory Academy for Urban School Leaders.* Retrieved May 31, 2002, from http://www.ncrel. org/sdrs/areas/issues/educatrs/leadrshp/betantrns1.htm

Chaudron, C. (1988). *Second language classrooms.* Cambridge, England: Press Syndicate of the University of Cambridge.

Children's Defense Fund. (2000). *The state of American's children yearbook 2000.* Retrieved March 3, 2001, from www.ecs.org

Chomsky, N. (1988). *Language and problems of knowledge.* Cambridge, MA: MIT Press.

Collier, V., & Thomas, W. (1992). A synthesis of studies examining long-term language minority student data on academic achievement. *Bilingual Research Journal, 16*(1–2), 187–212.

Cummins, J. (1986). Empowering minority students: A framework for intervention. *Harvard Educational Review, 56,* 18–36.

Cummins, J. (1989). *Empowering minority students.* Ontario, CA: California Association for Bilingual Education.

Escamilla, K. (1987). *The relationship of native language reading achievement and oral English proficiency to future achievement in reading English as a second language.* Unpublished doctoral dissertation, University of California, Los Angeles.

Escamilla, K. (1998). *Bilingual means two: Assessment issues, early literacy and Spanish-speaking children.* Retrieved May 31, 2002, from http://www.ncbe.gwu.edu/ncbepubs/symposia/reading/bilingual5

Farmer, M. (1998). Creating Montessori bilingual programs. *Montessori Life, 10*(2), 22–25.

Gall, M., Borg, W., & Gall, J. (1996). *Educational research: An introduction.* White Plains, NY: Longman.

García, G. (1987). *Factors influencing the English reading test performance of Spanish–English bilingual children.* Unpublished doctoral dissertation, University of Illinois at Urbana–Champaign.

García, G. E. (1999). *Bilingual children's reading: An overview of recent research.* Retrieved on May 31, 2002, from http://www.cal.org/ericcll/News/199909/main.html

Goldenberg, C., & Sullivan, J. (1994). *Making change happen in a language minority school: A search for coherence.* Santa Cruz, CA: National Center for Research on Cultural Diversity and Second Language Learning.

Gorin, J. S., & Blanchard, J. (2004, April 12). *Strategies for improving mathematics and reading: Interventions and impact.* Paper presented at the annual meeting of the American Education Research Association, San Diego, CA. Retrieved May 31, 2004, from http://convention.allacademic. com/aera2004/view_paper_info.html?pub_id=1352&part_id1=31420

Greene, J. P. (1998). *A meta-analysis of the effectiveness of bilingual education.* University of Texas at Austin. Retrieved May 31, 2002, from http://ourworld.compuserve.com/homepages/JWCRAWFORD/greene.htm

Harcourt Brace. (1998). *Aprenda: La prueba de logros en español.* San Antonio, TX: Harcourt Brace Educational Measurement.

Heinstock, E. G. (1997). *The essential Montessori.* New York: Plume.

Jackson, S. (1980). *Formative evaluation of a Montessori bilingual preschool program.* Unpublished doctoral dissertation, University of Texas at Austin.

Kagan, S. L. (1989). Normalizing preschool education: The illusive imperative. In E. Flaxman & A. H. Passow (Eds.), *Changing populations/changing schools: Ninety-fourth yearbook of the National Society for the Study of Education* (pp. 840–101). Chicago, IL: National Society for the Study of Education.

Kramer, R. (1988). *Maria Montessori. A biography.* Chicago: University of Chicago.

Krashen, S. (1985). *The input hypothesis: Issues and implications.* New York: Longman.

Krashen, S. (1988). *Second language acquisition and second language learning.* Oxford: Pergamon Press.

Krashen, S., & Biber, D. (1987). *On course: Bilingual education's success in California.* Sacramento: California Association for Bilingual Education.

Ladson-Billings, G. (1994). *The dreamkeepers: Successful teachers of African American children.* San Francisco: Jossey Bass Publishers.

Lesher-Madrid, D., & García, E. (1985). The effect of language transfer on bilingual proficiency. In E. García & R. Padilla (Eds.), *Advances in bilingual education research* (pp. 53–70). Tucson: The University of Arizona Press.

McLaughlin, B. (1978). *Second-language acquisition in childhood.* Hillside, NJ: Lawrence Erlbaum Associates, Inc.

McLaughlin, B. (1987). *Theories of second-language learning.* London: Edward Arnold Publishers, Ltd.

Modiano, N. (1968). National or mother tongue in beginning reading: A comparative study. *Research in the Teaching of English, II*(1), 32–43.

Montessori, M. (1949). *The absorbent mind.* Adyar, India: Vasanta Press.

Montessori, M. (1961). *To educate the human potential.* India: Kalakshetra Publications.

Montessori, M. (1964). *The Montessori method.* New York: Schocken Books.

National Center for Education Statistics (NCES). (2003). *Average reading scales scores, by race/ethnicity. 1992–2003.* Retrieved June 20, 2004, from http://nces.ed.gov/nationsreportcard/reading/results2003.

National Center for Educational Statistics (2002). *Public school student, staff and graduate counts by state, school year 2000–2001.* U.S. Dept. of Education.

Our Nation on the Fault Line. (1996). *Our nation on the fault line: Hispanic American education.* Retrieved October 2000, from http://www.ed.gov/pubs/FaultLine/call.html

Ovando, C. J., Collier, V. P., & Combs, M. C. (2003). *Bilingual & ESL classrooms: Teaching multicultural contexts* (3rd ed.). Boston: McGraw-Hill.

Renton, A. (1998). Cultivating the natural linguist. *Montessori Life, 10*(2), 31–33.

Riverside. (1995). *Iowa tests of basic skills: Norms and score conversions with technical information.* Itasca, IL: Riverside Publishing.

Rodríguez, A. (1988). Research in reading and writing in bilingual education and English as a second language. In A. Ambert (Ed.), *Bilingual education and English as a second language.* New York: Garland Pub.

Rosanova, M. (1998). Early childhood bilingualism in the Montessori children's house. *Montessori Life, 10*(2), 37–48.

Ruenzel, D. (1997). *The Montessori method.* Retrieved October 8, 2001, from http://www.edweek.org/tm/1997/07mont.h08

Saville-Troike, M. (1973). *Bilingual children: A resource document, 2.* Washington, DC: Center for Applied Linguistics.

Scheurich, J. (1998). Highly successful and loving, public, Pre-K–5 schools populated mainly by low SES children of color: Core beliefs and cultural characteristics. *Urban Education, 33*(4), 451–491.

Schiller, P., Clements, D. H., Lara-Alecio, R., Samora, J., & Irby, B. (2003). *DLM early childhood express. Teacher's Edition.* Columbus, OH: SRA/McGraw-Hill.

Snow, C., Burns, M., & Griffin, P. (Eds.). (1998). *Preventing reading difficulties in young children.* Washington, DC: National Academy Press.

Statistical Package for the Social Sciences (SPSS). (2001). Retrieved May 31, 2002, from http://www.utexas.edu/cc/stat/software/spss/#Intro

Standing, E. M. (1957). *Maria Montessori. Her life and work.* New York: Plume.

Texas Education Agency (TEA). (2001). *AEIS Report.* Retrieved November 25, 2001, from http://www.tpri.org/

Thomas, W., & Collier, V. (2002). *A national study of school effectiveness for language minority students' long-term academic achievement final report: Project 1.1.* Retrieved May 31, 2002, from www.crede.ucsc.edu

U.S. Government Census Bureau. (2000). *U.S. Census Report 2000.* Available from http://www.census.gov/population/cen2000/phc-t1/tab04.pdf

Wheeler, K. (1998). *Bilingualism and bilinguality: An exploration of parental values and expectations in an American sponsored overseas school.* Unpublished doctoral dissertation, University of Minnesota, Minnesota.

Ramirez, J. D., Yuen, S. D., & Ramey, D. R. (1991). *Longitudinal study of structured English immersion strategy, early-exit and late-exit transitional bilingual education programs for language-minority children.* San Mateo, CA: Aguirre International.

Zehler, A., Hopstock, P., Fleischma, H., & Greniuk, C. (1994). *An examination of assessment of limited English proficient students.* Arlington: U.S. Department of Education.

# 4

# Cultural, Linguistic, and Socioeconomic Factors Influencing Monolingual and Bilingual Children's Cognitive Development

Virginia Gonzalez
*University of Cincinnati*

## ABSTRACT

This study illustrates the effect of cultural, linguistic, socioeconomic status (SES), and developmental factors on young minority and majority children's cognitive development. The objective is to study developmental, SES, and linguistic factors affecting the performance of three groups of young children (i.e., monolingual mainstream, monolingual Hispanic, and bilingual Hispanic) in an alternative assessment of cognition and language (i.e., the Qualitative Use of English as Spanish Tasks, QUEST; Gonzalez, 1994, 1995). The methodology includes a quasi-experimental design using five independent variables as predictors: language of administration and response for QUEST (English and/or Spanish), low and middle-high SES, age (4 to 9 years of age), and gender. The dependent variable, the children's performance on QUEST, was analyzed using one-way ANOVA and multiple regression models.

Results showed the presence of a major pattern indicating that SES, developmental (age), linguistic (i.e., language of administration and response—including code switching and code mixing, and linguistic characteristics of Spanish and English), and cultural factors (content knowledge represented by stimuli) significantly influence monolingual and bilingual children's verbal and non-verbal concept formation processes. Thus, allowing children to use their strongest language and cultural style of communication (including code switching and code mixing) is an important variable in cognitive assessment. Thus, the fact that most language-minority children come from disadvantaged SES backgrounds, rather than they speak Spanish or are limited-English proficient, is the most important variable influencing their performance in cognitive developmental tasks.

The most important theoretical contribution was the empirical validation of a complex revised model showing: (1) support for the complex interaction of cognitive, linguistic, and cultural factors influencing verbal and non-verbal concept construction processes measured by alternative assessments; and (2) similarities and differences between monolingual and bilingual children, in comparison to previous findings (Gonzalez, 1991, 1994, 1995; Gonzalez, Bauerle, & Felix-Holt, 1996). Practical contributions of the study for the assessment of young children indicate that the performance of bilingual low SES students, as well as of monolingual children, is affected by the language of administration and response, and cultural attributes of alternative measures of cognitive and language development. The alternative assessment used, QUEST, provided an opportunity for bilingual children to demonstrate how their understanding of different languages and cultures had enhanced their cognitive development. QUEST provided a window to observe the presence of different content cultural knowledge domains learned, and cognitive processes that are nurtured by bilingual and bicultural settings.

## OBJECTIVES AND PURPOSES

Since the 1960s until the present, methodological problems of measuring validly and reliably cognitive development, first-and-second-language (L1 and L2) proficiency, and SES has become a traditional source of flaws present in research on the relation between children's cognitive development and bilingualism. This study has the objective of comparing the performance of monolingual and bilingual, low and middle-high SES children in an alternative measure of cognitive and language development.

The purpose is to attempt to control for sources of developmental, linguistic, and cultural methodological flaws in the measurement of cognitive and language development in bilingual children through the use of an alternative measure (i.e., QUEST, Gonzalez, 1994, 1995). Through a series of studies conducted (e.g., Gonzalez, 1991; Gonzalez, Bauerle, & Felix-Holt, 1996) QUEST has demonstrated to be a valid and reliable measure for bilingual and monolingual young children. This alternative measure uses verbal and non-verbal classification tasks that are developmentally appropriate for young children. In addition, QUEST represents the culture and the language of Hispanic children in its stimuli, instructions, administration and scoring procedures, and diagnostic categories. I consider that SES factors are mediating variables confounding the effect of L2 learning and bilingualism on cognitive development. Thus, I also attempt to understand the effect of SES factors, by comparing young monolingual and bilingual children from low and middle-high SES backgrounds.

## A STATE-OF-THE-ART CONCEPTUAL
## FRAMEWORK FOR STUDYING THE EFFECT
## OF MONOLINGUALISM AND BILINGUALISM
## ON CHILDREN'S COGNITIVE DEVELOPMENT

As a context for understanding methodological problems, I will briefly discuss in sections presented below, the most important studies on the effect of monolingualism and bilingualism on children's cognitive development. The first studies controlling for confounding factors affecting the positive influence of bilingualism on cognitive development in children were conducted during the early 1960s. A landmark study was conducted in Canada by Peal and Lambert (1962). This study had a between subjects design, which compared monolingual and bilingual children, and controlled for the first time for SES factors. It was not until the middle 1980s that researchers started to conduct and endorse studies with between bilingual subject designs, which compared low versus high L1 proficiency in bilingual children from low SES backgrounds. This methodological design was abandoned in the late 1980s for within bilingual subject designs and regression models, which could control statistically for individual differences in L1 and L2 proficiency levels, language dominance, and SES factors in language-minority low SES children.

Even though there have been improvements in the methodological designs of research studies conducted since the 1960s until the present, there are still methodological problems in the actual instruments used to measure the level of L1 and L2 proficiency, language dominance, and cognitive development in language-minority children. At present, most studies conducted on bilingualism and cognition control for confounding factors, and aim to demonstrate the advantages of early bilingualism on cognition. However, few of the studies conducted since the 1960s until the present have used valid alternative assessments of cognition and language for minority low SES children. Most studies conducted until the late 1990s have been reduplicative and descriptive, and have followed a very traditional theoretical and methodological framework.

As the extensive and meticulous literature search conducted revealed, since the early 1960s until the present most research studies on bilingualism and cognitive development still continue to use discrete-point standardized tests that assess:

1. Limited language skills (e.g., only vocabulary at the receptive level), instead of the multidimensionality of interactive expressive and receptive language skills (i.e., writing, reading, speaking, and listening) in different linguistic areas (pronunciation, vocabulary, syntax, grammar, and semantics—understanding symbolic and sociocultural meaning, and pragmatics—social use of language for communicating within a culture).

2. Unidimensional aspects of cognitive development, focusing primarily on logico-mathematical skills, and not representing other cultural dimensions of contemporary models of intelligence that could open a new line of inquiry.

These standardized tests were originally developed during the early and middle decades of this century under the influence of the medical traditional assessment model. These traditional tests have been demonstrated to be invalid and unreliable for bilingual children from minority and low SES backgrounds by numerous research studies conducted during the 1970s and 1980s (for an extended discussion see Gonzalez & Yawkey, 1993; Gonzalez, Brusca-Vega, & Yawkey, 1997). However, these standardized tests continue to plague with methodological flaws most contemporary research studies on bilingualism and cognition, resulting in the invalid measurement of these variables in low SES language-minority children. Even contemporary studies conducted in the 1990s, which recognize the need for the change of theoretical and methodological paradigms for the study of bilingualism and cognition, still use standardized tests for the measurement of these variables. Thus, even though the weight of research evidence is overwhelming for the methodological flaws of standardized tests when used with language-minority children, there is still need to develop experimentally an alternative way of measuring cognition and language in bilinguals.

The QUEST, developed by Gonzalez (1991, 1994, 1995), provides an alternative way of measuring experimentally cognition and language in low SES bilingual children. With this valid and reliable alternative measure, developed based on a strong theoretical model (Gonzalez, 1991, 1994, 1995), researchers can control successfully for linguistic and cultural confounding variables when measuring cognitive development in bilinguals. In addition to accurate measures there is need to use robust qualitative and statistical designs, such as developmental categories and regression models. As results of previous validation studies conducted have shown (e.g., Gonzalez, et al., 1996), QUEST has also demonstrated to provide an experimental way of controlling for individual differences and developmental factors affecting the measurement of cognition and language in bilinguals.

In addition, most contemporary studies on cognitive development in bilinguals recognize the overwhelming effect of:

1. SES factors (e.g., maternal and paternal occupations and educational levels, whether or not the mother works outside the home, number of siblings).
2. Sociocultural environmental factors present in the home and school settings (e.g., language use at home by parents and siblings, L1 and L2 proficiency levels of parents).

Thus, the objective of this study was to contribute to the understanding of how SES, developmental, linguistic, and cultural factors affect cognitive and linguistic development in bilinguals by implementing experimentally sound methodological changes in the measurement of these variables with QUEST.

In the three sections presented below, I will discuss critically methodological problems present in three clusters of studies conducted with minority children:

1. Between subjects design studies comparing cognitive development in bilingual and monolingual children.
2. Within subjects design studies comparing low versus high L2 proficiency effects on bilingual children' s cognitive development, divided into studies using standardized tests and experimental tasks in order to discuss their effect on research findings.
3. Studies focused on the effect of SES factors on minority children's development.

## METHODOLOGICAL PROBLEMS PRESENT IN MEASURING COGNITIVE DEVELOPMENT, L1 AND L2 PROFICIENCY, AND SES FACTORS IN BILINGUALS

### Between Subjects Designs: Bilinguals Versus Monolinguals

The comparison of bilingual and monolingual children's cognitive development is a complex and difficult task still to be solved by researchers, due to the lack of valid measures appropriate for both groups. Actually, I propose that measures should represent the developmental characteristics of young children from both majority and minority backgrounds (e.g., short attention spans, unfamiliarity with testing situations and schooling, language and social development in progress, etc.). Compounding to the challenge posed by developmental factors, young bilingual children's language and cognition is influenced by two cultural and linguistic systems.

Then, I propose that the valid measure of cognitive and language development in between-subjects design studies, needs to be done by alternative assessments that accommodate for developmental, cultural, and linguistic factors present in majority monolingual children; and more importantly in minority, bilingual, and bicultural children. Another methodological problem present in between-subjects design studies is the difficulty of controlling for individual differences of bilingual children's cognitive and language development.

In spite of these methodological problems, between-subjects designs studies conducted during the past 35 years have consistently shown that bilingual children's cognitive processes develop at higher levels in comparison to monolingual counterparts. More importantly, this consistent evidence has been found in studies using qualitative as well as standardized measures of cognitive and language development. Research evidence has demonstrated that bilingualism influences positively young children's performance in qualitative cognitive tasks involving concept formation processes such as classification, metalinguistic awareness, creativity, analogical reasoning, and problem-solving abilities (e.g., Bialystock,

1991; Diaz, 1985; Hakuta & Diaz, 1985). In addition, since the landmark study conducted by Peal and Lambert's (1962), most studies using standardized measures of cognitive development have demonstrated that bilingual children outperformed monolingual counterparts, when controlling for mediating variables (e.g., SES, proficiency levels in first-and-L2).

However, the methodological problems of operationally defining and measuring cognitive and language development in young majority and minority children, have been present in most studies using standardized tests such as the pioneer Peal and Lambert's (1962) study. Interestingly, even though Peal and Lambert used the Raven Progressive Matrices as a measure of cognitive development, they still found that bilinguals performed at higher levels than monolinguals. Another problem that I find in Peal and Lambert's hypothesis is that they compared monolingual with balanced bilingual children, raising a methodological problem of the operational definition and measurement of L1 and L2 proficiency and language dominance. Furthermore, I also wonder whether individual differences present in monolingual and bilingual children's cognitive abilities introduced confounding effects and subsequently methodological flaws to Peal and Lambert's (1962) study. That is, were the balanced bilinguals selected for the study potentially more intelligent than other non-balanced bilingual children, or than monolingual children; even before they became bilingual? That is, balanced bilingualism may not be the result of learning two languages (as was explained by Peal & Lambert, 1962), but the result of individual differences present in children prior to their bilingualism (for a more detailed discussion of this issue see Clark & Gonzalez, 1998).

One of the most common arguments to explain the evidence supporting the positive effect of bilingualism on cognition has been the code-switching hypothesis proposed originally by Peal and Lambert (1962). This hypothesis states that the advantage of cognitive flexibility was the result of bilingual children's ability to think in two languages. More recently, Diaz and Klingler (1991) questioned Peal and Lambert's code-switching hypothesis due to the absence of empirical evidence that bilinguals actually use both languages when performing cognitive tasks. Instead, they explained the early advantages of bilingualism as the result of the function of language as a self-regulatory executive control process, which can lead to metacognitive abilities and metalinguistic awareness. That is, private speech available to bilinguals in two different symbolic systems allows them to separate form and meaning, and to access implicit knowledge resulting in metacognitive (thinking about thinking) and metalinguistic (thinking about language) processes.

Later, Lambert and Tucker (1972) developed another explanation for the advantages of bilingualism shown in the St. Lambert experimental bilingual program offered to French speaking and English speaking children: The transfer of skills and content learned across languages. They raised an important issue of knowledge representation in bilinguals, in which verbal concepts in first and L2 could have a common underlying non-verbal dimension. With this explanation they recognized that bilingual research could open a new window to the traditional problem of the relationship between language and thought (for a more detailed discussion of this issue see Gonzalez & Schallert, 1999).

Thus, the cause and the effect direction of the relationship between bilingualism and cognition has not been demonstrated yet by an explanatory model. This study opens the question of whether the direction of this relationship could be demonstrated by more sophisticated contemporary research designs, such as regression models. As proposed by Bialystock and Cummins (1991) and by Diaz (1985), by now researchers are aware that the use of longitudinal designs would be the ideal research strategy for the control of individual differences present in between-subjects comparisons of cross-sectional designs. However, there are still other methodological flaws that need to be resolved even when using within-subjects designs: the valid and reliable measure of other important confounding variables, besides individual differences, such as SES factors and the influence of bilingualism and biculturalism on cognition. I attempt to start accomplishing this challenging task in this study by controlling for linguistic, cultural, and developmental factors by using an alternative qualitative method for the accurate measure of cognition and language in bilinguals called QUEST.

## Within Bilingual Subjects Designs: Low Versus High L2 Proficiency Studies Using Standardized Tests

The within subjects design started to be used during the 1980s, and was proposed and endorsed by researchers such as Kenji Hakuta and Rafael Diaz (1985), who categorized degrees of bilingualism in three groups: proficient, partial, and limited bilinguals. However, I can identify a methodological flaw present in some of the within subjects design studies, that is the use of standardized measures assessing discrete cognitive and language abilities. Even though a positive influence of bilingualism on cognition is shown by these studies, the use of standardized discrete measures narrows the scope of cognitive and linguistic abilities assessed. I argue that when other alternative, experimentally based, measures are used by researchers, different and broader dimensions of bilingual children's cognitive and linguistic abilities may be assessed.

Moreover, I find serious methodological flaws in studies conducted during the 1980s using the within subjects designs, due to the invalid psychometric characteristics of standardized tests of language proficiency and cognitive development. I propose that studies using the Raven Progressive Matrices as a measure of nonverbal cognitive abilities in bilinguals, and the Picture Vocabulary Test (PPVT) as a measure of language proficiency (e.g., Diaz, 1985; Hakuta, 1988; Hakuta & Diaz, 1985) have major validity problems, especially for Spanish dominant children with low English proficiency levels. It seems to me that when studies use the Raven Progressive Matrices as a measure of cognitive abilities in bilingual children, results do not show an attenuation of cognitive advantages due to bilingualism (as it is argued by Diaz, 1985; Hakuta & Diaz, 1985). Actually, I explain differently the findings obtained by these studies: For older children with higher degrees of English-as-a-L2 proficiency; the Raven test may be a more valid measure of their non-verbal, and spatio-temporal cognitive abilities. Therefore, the children's higher degree of bilingualism explains a lower percentage of the variance of the Raven's scores within a regression model; and vice versa, for younger children with lower degrees of English-as-a-L2 proficiency. However, I consider that for all bilingual children, regardless of their levels of L1 and L2 proficiency, discrete point standardized tests (e.g., the Raven Progressive Matrices and the PPVT) are unidimensional measures of the multidimensionality of cognition and language.

Thus, I consider that there are two major methodological problems in studies obtaining different findings for older and younger children's degree of bilingualism on cognition:

1. The narrow or discrete domain of cognitive abilities measured by standardized tests (Gonzalez, et al., 1997; Oller, 1991; Oller & Damico, 1991), such as the Raven test which only assesses spatio-temporal relationships representing perceptual and non-verbal concept formation processes.
2. The lack of validity and reliability of the Raven test for minority children due to the influence of schooling, learning, standardization, cultural, and linguistic factors on their test performance (Rogoff & Chavajay, 1995).

Therefore studies are influenced by interfering variables such as:

1. Schooling and learning effects.
2. Lack of validity due to bilingual children's linguistic and cultural unfamiliarity with test items, and to standardization problems.
3. Lack of construct validity of theoretical frameworks underlying standardized tests when used with low SES, language-minority children.

## Within Bilingual Subjects Designs:
## Low Versus High L2 Proficiency
## Studies Using Experimental Tasks

Findings of studies using experimental tasks of verbal and non-verbal abilities have also shown a positive relationship between bilingualism and cognitive development (e.g., Diaz & Padilla, 1985; Gonzalez, et al., 1996). Diaz and Klingler (1991) recognized that "a major problem in understanding and explaining the relationship between bilingualism and cognitive development is that research has focused mostly on outcome rather than process variables" (p. 180). Bialystock (1991) asserted that it is only recently that the study of the relationship between bilingualism and cognition has shifted "from product description to process models" (p. 5).

I consider that the current research focus on outcome is due to the widespread use of standardized tests of cognition and language, which have a discrete and narrow scope, reducing the multidimensional complexity of these variables to unidimensional views. I propose that the use of experimental, higher-level, cognitive tasks (such as the verbal and non-verbal classification tasks included in QUEST) can offer a window to cognitive and semantic processes in bilinguals (such as thinking styles and strategies, and metacognitive and metalinguistic processes). In addition, I consider that it is also important to analyze these experimental tasks measuring higher-level cognitive processes not only statistically, but also qualitatively such as the scoring system used with QUEST in this study. The qualitative analysis allows researchers to understand and explain why bilingual children's thinking processes are different than their monolingual counterparts.

Actually, the verbal and non-verbal classification tasks included in QUEST measure conceptual formation from perceptual to metalinguistic levels. Bilingual children are asked probing questions and provided with counterexamples that contrast form and meaning, and stimulate children to think about language. In the several validation studies conducted with QUEST (e.g., Clark & Gonzalez, 1998; Felix-Holt & Gonzalez, 1999; Gonzalez, et al., 1994, 1996, 1999; Gonzalez & Clark, 1999; Oviedo & Gonzalez, 1999), it has been found that a high proportion of bilingual children tend to think at metalinguistic levels in both non-verbal and verbal tasks, showing a positive influence of bilingualism on cognition.

Even when children showed low levels of L1 and L2 proficiency, Gonzalez and collaborators have found non-balanced bilinguals to perform at high developmental levels, such as metalinguistic, in non-verbal classification tasks of QUEST. Young non-balanced bilingual children from low SES backgrounds were able to use metaphors, to think about the meaning of words, to understand that labels are independent from the attributes of the real-world object, to understand that labels are the result of cultural and linguistic conventions, and to think creatively and humorously with language. Relatedly, Diaz and Klingler (1991) stated that "bilingual children show consistent advantages in tasks of both verbal and non-verbal abilities" (p. 183), because "the cognitive effects of bilingualism appear relatively early in the process of becoming bilingual and do not require high levels of bilingual proficiency nor the achievement of balanced bilingualism" (p. 184).

Thus, it is not that non-balanced bilingual children do not have the potential to show the advantages of bilingualism in their testing performance. Rather, I consider that very few developmentally, culturally, and linguistically sensitive instruments exist that can provide higher-level tasks for non-balanced bilinguals to show their high cognitive potential. In this study, QUEST provides language-minority, low SES children an opportunity to demonstrate their learning and cognitive potential; which has not yet been actualized in the form of knowledge, skills, or abilities.

In addition, Gonzalez and collaborators have found that it is also important to compare non-balanced bilingual children's performance on QUEST when administered in their first-and-L2. This form of comparison was described by Bialystock and Cummins (1991) as "... an evaluation of the way in which bilingual children approach a particular task in their first and L2" (p. 228). That is the reason why the qualitative analysis of higher-level conceptual tasks, such as QUEST, is so important for understanding the qualitative differences of how bilingual children think in their first-and-L2, and the cultural and linguistic differences in their cognitive processes when compared with monolingual children. That is, there is consistent research evidence that bilingual children think qualitatively different than monolingual children.

Thus, it is important to use valid alternative measures of cognitive processes that are sensitive to the cultural and linguistic differences of language-minority children. On the other hand, it is also important to compare bilingual with monolingual children in order to understand "... those aspects that are unique to speakers of two languages and those that appear not to be influenced by linguistic competence (Bialystock & Cummins, 1991, p. 228). It is in this spirit that I have designed this between and within subjects design study that compares bilingual and monolingual, low and middle-high SES, children's cognitive processes, when measured by a developmentally, culturally, and linguistically sensitive alternative assessment.

In doing these comparisons, it is also important not to loose sight of individual differences, which prevail over the issue of how bilingualism or monolingualism influences similarly or differently children's cognitive development. For instance, Gonzalez (1991) found that cultural and linguistic factors influenced whether bilingual children would form one or two semantic representations; and that the same bilingual child would present both forms of representations, unique and common for both languages. Actually, these within subject differences were related to the cultural and linguistic characteristics of stimuli and classification tasks used.

In conclusion, the contribution of this study is to provide empirical evidence of the cognitive advantages of bilingualism, even of non-balanced bilingual children from low SES backgrounds, by evaluating validly their higher-level cognitive processes through the use of QUEST. As discussed by Hakuta (1982), historically research has focused on "good" and "bad" bilingualism and intelligence. However, as discussed in this paper, contemporary researchers have realized that cognitive development in bilingual children is a multifaceted, complex variable influenced by numerous factors such as SES. The cognitive development of monolingual and bilingual children can not solely be researched as an issue of language acquisition; but must be researched thoroughly taking into account external social, economic, and cultural factors as discussed in the section below.

## Methodological Problems Present in Measuring
## SES Factors in Minority Children

Current studies of bilingualism and cognitive development have found that the SES of a child can be a powerful predictor of cognitive development (e.g., Diaz, 1985; Hakuta, 1991). However, researcher studies have been plagued by methodological problems, due to the difficulties of accurately measuring the SES variable. Controversy has arisen over the methods of measuring SES factors because they do not reliably provide complete information about the everyday living conditions of the child. Then, compounding to the problem discussed in the section above, of how to measure L1 and L2 proficiency levels in bilinguals, there are also variations in SES levels within groups of bilingual children.

Some of the studies on SES effects in minority children's development focus on some language-minority groups, such as Hispanics and African-Americans (e.g., Bradley, Whiteside, & Mundfrom, 1994; Duncan, Brooks-Gunn, & Kato, 1994; Walker, Greenwood, Hart, & Carta, 1994). However, these studies do not recognize the compounding effect of the possible presence of two languages or two cultures on other developmental variables. Moreover, most researchers do not differentiate between ethnicity, culture, and race; resulting in confounding factors and methodological flaws. For instance, even though Mexican-Americans and Puerto Ricans share the same overall Hispanic cultural background, there are very specific dialectal and ethnic idiosyncratic characteristics that differentiate these subgroups. Moreover, individuals who have inherited similar or different genetic make-ups, labeled commonly racial characteristics, can also be nurtured under similar or different sociocultural settings.

This lack of differentiation between race, ethnicity, and culture studies is compounded in these studies with the use of invalid standardized tests for measuring developmental variables (e.g., intelligence, language, and emotional development). In the descriptions of their samples these studies just recognize the presence of different ethnic groups as a factor within the complex SES variable; but do not explore the presence of a minority language effect on other developmental areas, such as cognition. The lack of control for the degree of L1 and L2 proficiency in language-minority children is not even recognized as a limitation in these SES effects on developmental outcome studies. For instance, the fact that some of the children in these developmental outcome studies of at-risk conditions could have been bilingual is never explored (e.g., studies of resiliency in minority children, Bradley et al., 1994). Moreover, the lack of sensitive measures to represent the qualitative different nature of cultural and linguistic thinking styles, creates in the results of these developmental studies a confounding effect between nature and nurture aspects of cognition in minority children.

Thus, compounding the scarcity of studies with bilingual children, there is the presence of major methodological flaws in controlling for the effect of SES factors when selecting subject samples and measuring developmental complex variables (e.g., cognitive and L1 and L2 proficiency levels). As stated by Diaz (1985), there is still a major methodological flaw present in most contemporary studies conducted with bilingual children, and I would add with minority children in general, that is ". . . in certain bilingual populations in the United States, degree of bilingualism is somewhat confounded with socioeconomic variables" (p. 1384). Diaz (1985) found that when using LISREL models that take into account the simultaneous effect of variables, bilingualism seems to be the cause of cognitive advantages present in young children, even when SES factors were controlled for. That is, he found that ". . . significant initial group differences [based on extreme high and low L2 proficiency] in cognitive variables disappeared when SES and parental employment were used as covariates" (Diaz, 1985, p. 1385). In this study, I will follow Diaz's suggestion (1985), to use as independent variables or predictors language of administration and language of response, as well as SES factors.

In sum, this study attempted to merge three areas of research:

1. Studies showing the positive effects of bilingualism when alternative measures of cognition (such as QUEST) represent diverse cultures and languages, and allow for accommodating the language of administration and language of response to the linguistic needs of the children (using both Spanish and English, and allowing the use of code mixing and code switching).
2. The powerful impact of external factors, such as SES background, on the cognitive development of language-minority (bilingual and monolingual) low SES children.
3. The importance of using alternative measures that methodologically control for linguistic, cultural, and developmental factors affecting cognitive development in both bilingual and monolingual, minority and mainstream young children.

## Research Questions

Five research questions were addressed in this study:

1. What is the influence of linguistic (i.e., language of administration and language of response matching the children's monolingual or bilingual background; and particular language characteristics of the Spanish and English languages in relation to general and linguistic-gender classification criteria or scoring systems) and cultural (content knowledge represented by animate and inanimate object referents) factors on the bilingual and monolingual, minority and mainstream, young

children's performance in language and conceptual development, and verbal and non-verbal classification tasks?

2. What is the effect of language of administration and language of response for QUEST on bilingual and monolingual, minority and mainstream, young children's performance in language and conceptual development, and verbal and non-verbal classification tasks?

3. What is the effect of developmental factors on bilingual and monolingual, minority and mainstream, young children's performance in language and conceptual development, and verbal and non-verbal classification tasks?

4. What is the effect of gender factors on bilingual and monolingual, minority and mainstream, young children's performance in language and conceptual development, and verbal and non-verbal classification tasks?

5. Of the variables used in this study (i.e., language of administration of QUEST, and children's SES and age), which is the best predictor of the word knowledge, and non-verbal and verbal concept formation process of bilingual and monolingual, minority and mainstream, young children?

## METHOD

### Design

The methodology includes a quasi-experimental design using four independent variables as predictors:

1. Language of administration for QUEST (English and/or Spanish).
2. Language of response for QUEST (English and/or Spanish).
3. Low and middle-high SES.
4. Age (in 6 months ranges from 4 to 9 years of age).

The dependent variable, the children's performance on QUEST, was analyzed by sub-task within a one-way ANOVA model, and by clusters of sub-tasks (using a Principal Components Analysis resulting in 6 independent factors of verbal and non-verbal concept formation) within a multiple regression model.

QUEST controlled for methodological confounding variables stemming from developmental, linguistic, and cultural factors. QUEST represents cultural, linguistic, and cognitive variables corresponding to the sociocultural experience of both Hispanic and mainstream children.

### Subjects

The total number of subjects was 120, comprised of three subgroups:

1. Ninety low SES Hispanic children from the Southwest region of the US, who presented different degrees of bilingualism and differed also in their language dominance (Spanish or English). These children were attending public schools located in low SES Hispanic "barrios." All the monolingual Spanish and bilingual Hispanic children were attending bilingual classrooms, and were first-second-third generation Mexican-Americans. The monolingual English children were attending regular classrooms.

2. Fifteen monolingual Spanish, Hispanic, middle-high SES children attending a regular classroom in a preschool in Lima-Perú.

3. Fifteen monolingual English, middle-high SES children living in the Southwest region of the US. These children were attending regular classrooms in a private preschool associated with a Christian church.

All the subjects were referred for evaluation by their teachers and/or parents as potentially gifted. The ages of the children ranged between 4 to 9 years of age. The majority of children were in the age bracket of 5 years to 6 years and 6 months of age (comprising 89 subjects, 74%). The remaining children were either older, in the age bracket of 7 years to 9 years of age (comprising 24 subjects, 20%); or younger, in the age bracket of 4 years to 4 years and 6 months (comprising 8 subjects, 6%). The number of boys and girls was about equal, with 67 male and 63 female subjects.

## Instruments

### Qualitative Use of English and Spanish Tasks (QUEST)

The QUEST was used as an alternative measure of cognitive and language development in bilingual and monolingual children. Gonzalez's (1991, 1994, 1995) developed a model that explained the concept formation process in bilingual children and identified two knowledge representational systems dependent on the particular cognitive, linguistic, and cultural characteristics of the content learned. The first conceptual representational system is abstract, universal, and non-verbal; and the second one is semantic, verbal, and culturally-linguistically bound. Cognitive factors were considered abstract knowledge representations instantiated in cultural symbolic conventions and in linguistic structures and markers. Cultural and linguistic factors were selected because Spanish assigns linguistic gender for both animate and inanimate abstract conceptual categories, corresponding to culturally important symbolic distinctions, which are expressed through linguistic rules and markers. In contrast, English only assigns linguistic gender to some animate conceptual abstract categories. The model from which the classification tasks were derived was based partially on Piagetian theory (Piaget, 1967) and on the constraint model (Markman, 1984; Waxman, 1990), and it was found to have construct validity as shown by parametric and non-parametric tests (Gonzalez, 1991).

The derived verbal and non-verbal classification tasks were designed to assess bilingual children's general and linguistic gender conceptual processes for two different abstract, symbolic and linguistic semantic categories represented by animals (animate) and food (inanimate) objects. Stimuli used for the five classification tasks were plastic full-color objects representing 14 groupings reflecting the interaction of cognitive, cultural, and linguistic factors. Stimuli groupings were validated using judges for assuring construct validity and three pilot tests for assuring content validity (Gonzalez, 1991, 1994, 1995).

Three of these five classification tasks are verbal including labeling, defining, and verbal justification of sorting; and two tasks are non-verbal including sorting and category clue. Tasks will be described following the pre-established order of administration (for a more complete description of tasks see Gonzalez, 1995). For the labeling task, the child is presented plastic objects and asked to name them (What *do you call this?*), while giving her one item at a time, followed by the defining task at the production level in which the child is asked four different probes to elicit a description of the object(s) (*What is a __?*, *What is a __ like?*, *Tell me something about a ___*, and *What does a ___ look like?*). After, for tapping the comprehension level of the defining task, the child is given a definition that points to verbal and non-verbal clues for class inclusion categories of objects (taxonomic categories: superordinate, intermediate, and subcategories). This definition is repeated three times, and after the child is asked to define three different kinds of items. For the sorting task, the child is asked to group the objects by linguistic gender; followed by the verbal justification of sorting task in which the child is asked to explain the order imposed on the objects, and she is presented with metalinguistic counterexamples that change groupings and labels. Finally, for the category clue task, the child is provided with a model of how to group objects by linguistic gender using two pictures of identical dolls; and then she is asked to sort the objects following the model provided, to explain her groupings, and to answer metalinguistic counterexamples that change groupings and labels.

## Procedure

Once the classroom teachers filled out the surveys, the parents of the selected potentially gifted children were asked to give consent for their children's participation in the study. Children were assessed in one or two language administration sessions of QUEST, depending on whether they were monolingual or bilingual. Each administration session lasted for approximately one hour. Two parallel sets of QUEST were used to avoid transfer of learning effect between the Spanish and the English administrations in bilingual children. Always, the first administration of QUEST was conducted in the dominant language of bilingual children. Individual assessments were conducted, and there were at least two weeks between the two language administrations for bilingual children. Assessments were conducted in different rooms available at the schools that offered a quiet environment, free of distractions (e.g., the principal's office, an empty classroom, etc.).

The author of this study assessed and scored the performance of about half of the participants in this study, with the help of two graduate students of Educational Psychology acting as research assistants. The other half of the sample was assessed and their performance scored by graduate students taking a course on testing of minorities (taught by the author of this paper). These graduate students received 10 hours of training in administering QUEST, including watching 3 administration videos, and hands-on practice sessions where pairs of students administered the assessment to each other and scored protocols. Monolingual English and bilingual Spanish/English evaluators were paired, one served as an administrator of QUEST and the other one as a recorder. Each pair of evaluators, recorded responses in protocols, made a diagnosis on the children's verbal and non-verbal conceptual developmental levels, and wrote a summary report.

## Description of Data Analysis

Qualitative analysis of data included the complex scoring system for QUEST, according to which children's responses were assigned nominal categories that described their verbal and non-verbal conceptual development achieved across classification tasks. The scoring system is divided into five point assignment areas including language development, verbal and non-verbal general, and verbal and non-verbal gender areas; based on which children are diagnosed on conceptual development (for an extended description of the scoring system see Gonzalez, 1995). General areas include any valid criteria that the child uses for classification (e.g., color, functions, subcategories, etc.). Gender areas include classification criteria based on physical gender for animate object referents, linguistic gender assignment for inanimate object referents, or functional use (related to gender assignment, e.g., this food is for mom, and this food is for dad) for both animate object referents and inanimate object referents.

The language development area includes only the labeling task. The verbal general and gender-based areas include defining and verbal justification of sorting tasks, and the non-verbal general and gender-based areas include sorting and category clue tasks. Thus, children's responses to the five tasks administered in both languages were scored twice, assigning points for both general and gender areas. The language development area was categorized into three levels: (a) low (0–2 points), (b) moderate (3–5 points), and (c) high (6–8 points); according to the number of labels produced by the child. For the other four areas children's responses were categorized into five stages based partially on Piaget's theory (1965): (1) no classification (affective responses, juxtaposed groupings and graphic collections), (2) pre-conceptual: perceptual (extralinguistic features—

color, size, shape, parts of objects), (3) pre-conceptual: functional (thematic relations), (4) concrete (taxonomic categories showing class-inclusion), and (5) metalinguistic (taxonomic semantic categories). In order to be diagnosed in any of these five developmental stages for any of the five verbal and non-verbal tasks, children's responses needed to be at that level at least for three out of the eight items that were included in the tasks.

## RESULTS AND DISCUSSION

### Data Analysis Design

Thus, since the number of children in each of the three subject groups was unequal and also because degree of bilingualism is a difficult variable to measure validly and reliably, the variable of monolingualism or bilingualism was confounded. I decided to group together the monolingual and bilingual children regardless of their degree of first-and-L2 proficiency levels. However, language dominance remained as an independent variable since children were administered QUEST in their dominant language, and they were allowed to respond in either Spanish or English or using simultaneously both Spanish and English (allowing code switching and code mixing). That is, language of administration and language of response for QUEST were used both in the one-way ANOVA and regression tests as independent variables. Administrators of QUEST provided instructions to the children in their preferred language for communication. Children were given full credit for responses provided in any of their two languages, and also when they used code switching and/or code mixing.

Two major reasons motivated the researcher to make this decision:

1. The absence of valid and reliable criteria and tests for assessing first-and-L2 proficiency levels.

2. Previous research results obtained in validation studies of QUEST (see e.g., Gonzalez, et al., 1995; Oviedo & Gonzalez, 1999; Felix-Holt & Gonzalez, 1999) pointing to the need to use both languages simultaneously as a tool for administration and response. By using dual language administration and response, Hispanic children could express verbally their thinking and a more accurate measure of bilingual children's genuine verbal and non-verbal cognitive developmental potential could be done.

As discussed above, a major methodological problem is the difficulty of forming bilingual Spanish–English subject groupings, and thus using an experimental design, due to lack of valid and reliable language proficiency tests. Then, only the variables of language of administration and language of response for QUEST, SES, and age remained as viable independent variables for conducting one-way

ANOVA tests and multiple regression analyses. Thus, in this study data analysis was conceptualized as a General Lineal Model (GLM) multivariate procedure for repeated measures, which provides analysis of variance and regression tests for multiple dependent variables by one factor variable or covariate.

Two sets of one-way ANOVA tests were conducted with language of administration, language of response, age, and gender (each entered in separate tests) as the independent variable for all subjects and their QUEST performance by the 20 sub-task as the dependent variables. Results were also analyzed using multiple regression tests entering the three predictors (language of administration of QUEST, SES, and age) simultaneously and one factor in QUEST performance at a time as the dependent variable. When a predictor was found to be significant, a second regression test was run, procedure that resulted in significant predictors for four factors of QUEST performance.

The factors in QUEST performance were obtained by conducting a Principal Components Analysis procedure in order to reduce the number of sub-tasks into clusters that would:

1. Result in a revised model for furthering our understanding of the influence of cognitive, linguistic, and cultural factors on the conceptual formation and developmental process in young children (stated in Research Question 1).
2. Provide more statistical power for conducting regression tests.

The 20 sub-tasks were checked in a Principal Component Analysis by the two linguistic (i.e., language of administration and language of response matching the children's monolingual or bilingual background; and particular language characteristics of the Spanish and English languages in relation to general and linguistic-gender classification criteria or scoring systems) and cultural (content knowledge represented by animate and inanimate object referents) factors that had proven to be significant in previous model construction and validation studies (see e.g., Gonzalez, 1991, 1994, 1995; Gonzalez, et al., 1996). Thus, this Principal Components Analyses procedure also served to analyze the influence of cognitive, linguistic, and cultural factors on low and mid-high SES, bilingual and monolingual children's conceptual development. The resulting principal components or rotated factors were uncorrelated, or orthogonal, among themselves. This characteristic is a very important one, because when predictors are uncorrelated in the stepwise multiple linear regression analyses, they can explain a higher amount of variance on the dependent variables and it is possible to talk about the unique contribution of each predictor. As a result, the problem of multicollinearity which causes unstable regression equations is reduced or eliminated.

Below the major findings will be reported and interpreted in relation to the major purpose and objective of this study: To provide an empirical evidence for the effect of SES, linguistic (language of administration and language of response for QUEST), cultural (general and linguistic-gender scoring systems, and content knowledge—animate object referents and inanimate object referents), and developmental factors (age) on the verbal and non-verbal concept formation in monolingual and bilingual low and middle-high SES children. First, the Principal Components Analysis results will be reported in relation to Research Question 1, followed by the three sets of one-way ANOVA tests conducted in relation to Research Questions 2, 3, and 4. Finally, the results of the regression analyses conducted for the four predictors used, in relation to Research Question 5, will be presented. Only the tests with a probability level over .05 are reported here.

## What Is the Influence of Linguistic and Cultural Factors on Children's Conceptual Development?: Research Question 1

When conducting the Principal Components Analysis procedure, the critical value of the correlation coefficient taken as part of a factor was .50 or higher. Most of the tasks were at a very high range of correlations, for the rotated factor patterns and also for the final communality estimates, between .85 and .95. The Kaiser criterion was used for deciding which factors to retain. This criterion retains only those factors with an eigenvalue (i.e., the percent of the variance each factor accounts for) that are greater than 1 on the scree plot.

In addition, the principal components or rotated factors were uncorrelated, or orthogonal, among themselves. The pattern of rotated variables had a high loading only on one of the factors with an eigenvalue greater than 1. That is, the pattern underlying the principal components was a clear and simple one. This is considered to be a good characteristic of constructs underlying a model, as it is related to the principle of scientific parsimony. The factors were rotated using the varimax procedure, which gives an orthogonal transformation matrix. The interpretation of the factors was focused on the varimax rotated loadings, as they are easier to interpret.

Some similar and different results were found when comparing: (1) the empirical clustering of the variables in this study conducted with both monolingual and bilingual children, including a wider age range (comprising 4 to 9 year-olds); with (2) previous findings of studies (Gonzalez, 1991, 1994, 1995; Gonzalez, et al., 1996) conducted with bilingual Hispanic children only, with a narrower age range (comprising 5 to 7 year-olds). The first similarity between this study and previous studies is the presence of a Language Development Factor (called Factor 1) that included only the labeling task for both general and linguistic-gender scoring systems, and for both animate (animals) and inanimate (food) object referents. That is, the performance of bilingual children in the labeling task was correlated when word knowledge referred to the use of linguistic-gender assignments for animals and food object referents. This first factor was present only in the Spanish language, and therefore was shown only in the bilingual children's performance.

The second similarity is the presence of a verbal representational system common to animate and inanimate object referents (called Factor 2), with a culturally-linguistically bound classification system (linguistic-gender scoring system) for the Spanish language only. That is, bilingual children did show some uniqueness in their representational systems of verbal concepts, associated with the particular characteristics of the Spanish language only. Then, bilingual children would construct symbolic meanings of sociocultural conventions and linguistic structures and markers that were common for both animate and inanimate objects in the Spanish language. Thus, the addition of a L2 did make a difference in how bilingual children constructed verbal concepts.

The third similarity is the presence of a verbal representational system for abstract (universal) concepts (called Factor 3), which was represented by the general scoring system, and was common to the English and Spanish languages. Thus, both monolingual and bilingual children constructed common classifications for both animate and inanimate objects based on general criteria (e.g., color, size, parts of the objects, classes, and/or metalinguistic criteria—e.g., number of syllables in the object names).

There were also differences between this study and previous studies. These differences showed specific interrelations among the levels of the linguistic, cultural, and cognitive variables; which were more complex than had been originally found in the model constructed with bilingual children only (Gonzalez, 1991, 1994, 1995; Gonzalez, et al., 1996). The first difference found is the presence of a relationship between verbal and non-verbal, abstract and linguistic and culturally-bound representational systems for *animate object referents* (animals) object referents (called Factor 4); which corresponded to a *general* and *linguistic-gender* classification criteria (or scoring system). These verbal and non-verbal concepts formed were common to monolingual and bilingual children, due to similarities between semantic categories present in the Spanish and English languages for representing linguistically animate objects. That is, both Spanish and English showed a correspondence between feminine and masculine physical gender categories, and symbolic meanings of sociocultural conventions represented by linguistic structures and markers. For instance, in English and Spanish two different words mark the assignment of linguistic gender, which corresponds to the external world reality of the existence of a feminine (e.g., hen, cow, woman, girl; corresponding to *gallina, vaca, mujer,* and *niña* in Spanish) and a masculine (e.g., rooster, bull, man, boy; corresponding to *gallo, toro, hombre,* and *niño* in Spanish) referent for each kind of animate object.

The second difference found is the existence of a relationship between verbal and non-verbal representational systems for *inanimate* object referents (called Factor 5); which corresponded only for the *general* classification criteria (or scoring system). Both monolingual and bilingual children constructed abstract categories in relation to universal or general classification criteria (e.g., color, form, parts of the objects, classes, or metalinguistic classifications—e.g., based on the first letter of object names). However, the English and Spanish languages differ in their semantic representation, and in their corresponding symbolic meanings of sociocultural conventions and linguistic structures and markers. Only the Spanish language, among other Latin languages, represents linguistic gender for inanimate objects, such as food. For instance, the food object "apple" in English will be represented with a linguistic-gender marker in Spanish "*la manzana*," with the "*a*" ending marking a feminine noun requiring a feminine marker also in the corresponding article "*la*." Then, only some bilingual children (especially the English dominant bilinguals), and none of the monolingual English children could form verbal and non-verbal concepts for inanimate objects (food) based on linguistic-gender classification criteria.

Thus, Factor 5 corresponding to inanimate object referents, was found to be a separate cluster from Factor 4, corresponding to animate object referents. Then, monolingual and bilingual children showed a different verbal and non-verbal concept construction performance in relation to linguistic and cultural content knowledge, represented in this study as linguistic representations in Spanish and English of inanimate and animate object referents. These separate factors indicate the presence of separate representational systems for how monolingual and bilingual children represent animate and inanimate verbal and non-verbal concepts when Spanish and English share similar cultural and linguistic characteristics.

Comparing the findings of this study with previous results (Gonzalez, 1991, 1994, 1995; Gonzalez, et al., 1996), it can be observed that the presence of similarities and differences indicate that cultural (i.e., content cultural knowledge, animate or inanimate object referents) and linguistic factors have an interactional effect on how monolingual and bilingual children construct verbal and non-verbal concepts. Thus, this study provides empirical support for a revised model of the complex interaction of cognitive, cultural, and linguistic factors previously found for bilingual children only (Gonzalez, 1991, 1994, 1995; Gonzalez, et al., 1996), now with a modified model for commonalties found between monolingual and bilingual children (see Fig. 4.1).

In sum, overall common findings with previous studies show that:

1. Bilingual children construct a separate language representation, corresponding to word knowledge for the linguistic-gender scoring system, and for the Spanish language only (Factor 1).

2. Bilingual children construct a verbal representational system based on a culturally-linguistically bound classification system, corresponding to the linguistic-gender scoring system, common to animate and inanimate objects, present only in the Spanish language (Factor 2).

3. Monolingual and bilingual children share representational systems for verbal concepts based on an abstract (universal) classification system, corresponding to a general scoring system, common to animate and inanimate objects, and present in Spanish and English (Factor 3).

By comparing Factors 2 and 3, it can observed that bilingual children had constructed two different verbal concepts, common to animate and inanimate object

| Content Cultural Knowledge | General Classifications (Scoring System) | Linguistic-Gender Classifications (Scoring System) |
|---|---|---|
| **COMMON TO ANIMATES & INANIMATES** Similar to Original Model derived from bilingual children samples (Gonzalez, 1991, 1994, 1995; Gonzalez, Bauerle, & Felix-Holt, 1996) | | **FACTOR 1** • Language Development: Word Knowledge • *General & Linguistic-Gender Scoring Systems* • **Spanish Only** • **Bilingual children only** |
| | **FACTOR 2** • **Verbal Concepts** • Culturally-Linguistically Bound Classification System • *Linguistic-Gender Scoring System* • **Spanish Only** • **Bilingual children only** **FACTOR 3** • **Verbal Concepts** • Abstract (Universal) Classification System • *General Scoring System* • **Common to Spanish & English** • **Common to Bilingual & Monolingual children** | |
| **ANIMATES** Different from Original Model derived from bilingual children samples (Gonzalez, 1991, 1994, 1995; Gonzalez, Bauerle, & Felix-Holt, 1996) | **FACTOR 4** • **Verbal & Non-Verbal Concepts** • Abstract (Universal) & Culturally-Linguistically Bound Classification Systems • *General and Linguistic-Gender Scoring Systems* • **Common to Spanish & English** • **Common to Bilingual & Monolingual children** | |
| **INANIMATES** | **FACTOR 5** • **Verbal & Non-Verbal Concepts** • Abstract (Universal) Classification System • *General Scoring System* • **Common to Spanish & English** • **Common to Bilingual & Monolingual children** | |

FIG. 4.1.  Revised Model of the Influence of Cognitive, Cultural, and Linguistic Factors on the Construction of Abstract and Semantic Categories on Monolingual and Bilingual Children.

referents, resulting into two different linguistic instantiations (one for Spanish only, Factor 2; and another one common to Spanish and English, Factor 3) and two different re-representations of semantic categories (one for a culturally and linguistically bound classification system, Factor 2); and another one for an abstract classification system, Factor 3). Then, it can be concluded that a separate semantic representational system will be constructed, when verbal concepts are represented differently by Spanish and English languages. Thus, bilingual children do receive a positive influence from their dual language stimulation, resulting in the construction of an additional verbal classification system for representing the unique symbolic cultural and linguistic categories present only in one of their languages (called Factor 2 in this study).

In addition, specific findings that make a difference between bilingual and monolingual children present only in this study show a relationship between verbal and non-verbal representational systems, common to the Spanish and English languages, that will be present in both monolingual and bilingual children for:

1. Animate object referents (animals) in relation to abstract (universal) and culturally-linguistically bound classification systems, corresponding to both the general and linguistic-gender scoring systems (Factor 4).
2. Inanimate object referents (food) in relation to abstract (universal) classification systems, corresponding to a general scoring system (Factor 5).

It can be observed that content cultural knowledge, whether language represents animate or inanimate referents, makes a difference in how monolingual and bilingual children construct verbal and non-verbal concepts. An interaction between abstract and semantic representations was constructed by all children in order to link the real-world characteristics of animate objects (existence of physical gender) with their symbolic and semantic representations (linguistic gender assignment), which was present in both Spanish and English (Factor 4). In contrast, when dealing with inanimate objects, monolingual and bilingual children only shared the construction of a common interactional verbal and non-verbal concept, that corresponded to a general or abstract classification system (Factor 5). As discussed above, bilingual children added a separate verbal representational system (Factor 2) that was culturally and linguistically bound, and corresponded only to the Spanish language for representing animate and inanimate object referents Then, as interpreted based on the similar findings listed above, bilingualism brings to children the opportunity to add another semantic representational system, which serves as a cognitive tool to form new verbal concepts. Thus, bilingualism also brings new cultural or symbolic and linguistic or semantic mental concepts as tools for thinking. That is, bilingualism also means biculturalism and bicognitivism; changing qualitatively development as it adds new dimensions to bilingual children's mental representations.

It seems that QUEST provided an opportunity for bilingual children to demonstrate how their understanding of different languages and cultures had enhanced their cognitive development. QUEST provided a window to observe the presence of different content cultural knowledge domains learned, and of cognitive processes that are nurtured by bilingual and bicultural milieus.

## What Is the Effect of Language of Administration and Language of Response on Children's Conceptual Development?: Research Question 2

Results of the ANOVA tests (see Table 4.1) indicated that *language of administration* (either Spanish or English, or Spanish and English—bilingual administration) and *language of response* (either Spanish or English, or Spanish and English—*code switching* and *code mixing* were allowed) had an *independent effect* on children's QUEST performance for:

1. The labeling task (measuring language development in relation to word knowledge) for animate object referents at the general and linguistic-gender level, and inanimate object referents at the linguistic-gender level.
2. The category clue task (measuring non-verbal concept formation) for animate object referents at the general level.

As discussed above in relation to the results of the Principal Components Analysis and Research Question 1, the two specific ANOVA results above also show the presence of a pattern for bilingual children to form a separate semantic representational system for linguistic-gender of inanimate object referents, present only in the Spanish language. At the same time, these results also show a pattern for monolingual and bilingual children to form a common abstract, and sometimes even a common semantic representation, when forming verbal and non-verbal concepts for animate object referents in Spanish and English. This latter pattern was present when there were commonalties between the Spanish and English semantic or linguistic representations for the physical gender of animate objects.

However, when analyzing the second result of an effect of language of administration and response for QUEST on the monolingual and bilingual children's performance in the category clue task, it can be observed that these two independent factors had an effect on their non-verbal concept formation for animate object referents. Then, it seems that the specific language(s) used for administering and responding influenced the children's developmental level attained, corresponding to their ability level to understand the underlying linguistic-gender classification system used for animate object referents (following a model of separating animals by physical gender using the "feminine" and "masculine" linguistic categories); which in turn seems to have influenced the children's ability to classify animate object referents using a general criteria.

In addition, *language of administration* had an effect on the verbal justification task (measuring verbal concept formation) for inanimate object referents at the

TABLE 4.1
Analysis of Variance for Language of Administration and Language
of Response for QUEST, and Age as Independent Variables (IVs)
and Monolingual and Bilingual Children's Performance
on QUEST Sub-Tasks as Dependent Variables (DVs)

| Source | df | Sum of Squares | Mean Square | F Ratio | Probability |
|---|---|---|---|---|---|
| *For Language of Administration of QUEST as the IV* | | | | | |
| Labeling Task for Animals, General Level | | | | | |
| • Between Groups | 1 | 1.301 | 1.301 | 4.134 | .045 |
| • Within Groups | 104 | 32.737 | .315 | | |
| • Total | 105 | 34.038 | | | |
| Labeling Task for Food, Linguistic-Gender Level | | | | | |
| • Between Groups | 1 | 1.592 | 1.592 | 4.595 | .034 |
| • Within Groups | 104 | 36.031 | .346 | | |
| • Total | 105 | 37.623 | | | |
| Verbal Justification Task for Animals, General Level | | | | | |
| • Between Groups | 1 | 6.611 | 6.611 | 4.044 | .047 |
| • Within Groups | 104 | 170.031 | 1.635 | | |
| • Total | 105 | 176.642 | | | |
| Category Clue Task for Animals, General Level | | | | | |
| • Between Groups | 1 | 6.715 | 6.715 | 4.120 | .045 |
| • Within Groups | 104 | 169.521 | 1.630 | | |
| • Total | 105 | 176.236 | | | |
| *For Language of Response for QUEST as the IV* | | | | | |
| Labeling Task for Animals, General Level | | | | | |
| • Between Groups | 1 | 1.902 | 1.902 | 6.156 | .015 |
| • Within Groups | 104 | 32.136 | .309 | | |
| • Total | 105 | 34.038 | | | |
| Labeling Task for Food, Linguistic-Gender Level | | | | | |
| • Between Groups | 1 | 1.733 | 1.733 | 5.021 | .027 |
| • Within Groups | 104 | 35.890 | .345 | | |
| • Total | 105 | 37.623 | | | |
| Verbal Justification Task for Animals, General Level | | | | | |
| • Between Groups | 1 | 9.578 | 9.578 | 5.963 | .016 |
| • Within Groups | 104 | 167.063 | 1.606 | | |
| • Total | 105 | 176.642 | | | |
| Verbal Justification Task for Animals, Linguistic-Gender Level | | | | | |
| • Between Groups | 1 | 7.650 | 7.650 | 3.741 | .056 |
| • Within Groups | 104 | 212.690 | 2.045 | | |
| • Total | 105 | 220.340 | | | |

*(Continued)*

TABLE 4.1
(Continued)

| Source | df | Sum of Squares | Mean Square | F Ratio | Probability |
|---|---|---|---|---|---|
| *For Language of Response for QUEST as the IV* | | | | | |
| Category Clue Task for Animals, General Level | | | | | |
| • Between Groups | 1 | 7.426 | 7.426 | 4.575 | .035 |
| • Within Groups | 104 | 168.809 | 1.623 | | |
| • Total | 105 | 176.236 | | | |
| *For Age as the IV* | | | | | |
| Labeling Task for Animals, Linguistic-Gender Level | | | | | |
| • Between Groups | 11 | 7.370 | .670 | 1.956 | .043 |
| • Within Groups | 87 | 29.802 | .343 | | |
| • Total | 98 | 37.172 | | | |
| Labeling Task for Food, Linguistic-Gender Level | | | | | |
| • Between Groups | 1 | 7.427 | .675 | 2.043 | .033 |
| • Within Groups | 87 | 28.755 | .331 | | |
| • Total | 98 | 36.182 | | | |
| Defining Task for Animals, General Level | | | | | |
| • Between Groups | 1 | 14.256 | 1.301 | 2.209 | .021 |
| • Within Groups | 87 | 52.019 | .598 | | |
| • Total | 98 | 66.545 | | | |
| Sorting Task for Animals, General Level | | | | | |
| • Between Groups | 1 | 22.337 | 2.031 | 2.093 | .029 |
| • Within Groups | 87 | 84.410 | .970 | | |
| • Total | 98 | 106.747 | | | |
| Sorting Task for Food, Linguistic-Gender Level | | | | | |
| • Between Groups | 1 | 38.357 | 3.487 | 1.901 | .050 |
| • Within Groups | 87 | 159.603 | 1.835 | | |
| • Total | 98 | 197.960 | | | |
| Verbal Justification Task for Animals, General Level | | | | | |
| • Between Groups | 11 | 37.607 | 3.419 | 2.335 | .014 |
| • Within Groups | 87 | 127.382 | 1.464 | | |
| • Total | 98 | 164.990 | | | |
| Verbal Justification Task for Animals, Linguistic-Gender Level | | | | | |
| • Between Groups | 11 | 52.542 | 4.777 | 2.658 | .006 |
| • Within Groups | 87 | 156.367 | 1.797 | | |
| • Total | 98 | 208.909 | | | |

*(Continued)*

TABLE 4.1
(Continued)

| Source | df | Sum of Squares | Mean Square | F Ratio | Probability |
|---|---|---|---|---|---|
| *For Age as the IV* | | | | | |
| Verbal Justification Task for Food, General Level | | | | | |
| • Between Groups | 11 | 43.769 | 3.979 | 2.503 | .009 |
| • Within Groups | 87 | 138.312 | 1.590 | | |
| • Total | 98 | 182.081 | | | |
| Verbal Justification Task for Food, Linguistic-Gender Level | | | | | |
| • Between Groups | 11 | 37.181 | 3.380 | 2.124 | .027 |
| • Within Groups | 87 | 138.455 | 1.591 | | |
| • Total | 98 | 175.636 | | | |
| Category Clue Task for Animals, Linguistic-Gender Level | | | | | |
| • Between Groups | 11 | 33.352 | 3.032 | 1.664 | .095 |
| • Within Groups | 87 | 158.486 | 1.822 | | |
| • Total | 98 | 191.838 | | | |
| Category Clue Task for Food, Linguistic-Gender Level | | | | | |
| • Between Groups | 11 | 39.318 | 3.574 | 2.266 | .018 |
| • Within Groups | 87 | 137.228 | 1.577 | | |
| • Total | 98 | 176.545 | | | |

general level, and *language of response* had an effect on the verbal justification task for animate object referents at the general and linguistic-gender levels. Again, complementing findings of the Principal Components analysis conducted in relation to Research Question 1, ANOVA results also indicated that language of administration influenced the specific verbal conceptual developmental level, based on general classification criteria, attained by monolingual and bilingual children, in relation to inanimate objects. This particular result is similar to Factor 3, in which commonalties between the Spanish and English languages result in a common semantic or verbal representational system for the abstract (or universal) properties of inanimate object referents (e.g., color, shape, number of parts, class, or metalinguistic criteria).

Finally, language of response influenced the monolingual and bilingual children's ability to form verbal concepts for animate object referents, at both an abstract and a semantic representational system level. This particular result is similar to results obtained in previous studies conducted with bilingual children only (see Gonzalez et al., 1996). That is, the particular language(s) chosen by children to respond (either Spanish or English, or both Spanish and English—using code switching or code mixing) had an effect on their ability level attained to explain their non-verbal sorting, both at a general level (using general criteria, e.g., color, size, parts of the item, functions, classes, or metalinguistic criteria) and also at a linguistic-gender level (using linguistic structures and markers that refer to "feminine" or "masculine" classifications—e.g., "this is the mommy kangaroo and this is the daddy kangaroo," "this is a she seal, and this is a he seal," or "this is the lion, and this is the lioness").

These results also coincide with similar findings in previous studies conducted with bilingual children only (Gonzalez et al., 1996), in which language of administration made a difference in cognitive developmental levels achieved by bilingual children (as analyzed using chi-square tests). More specifically, Gonzalez and collaborators (1996) found that bilingual children attained higher cognitive developmental levels when QUEST was administered in Spanish. These latter results were also present even in balanced bilinguals, due to the new cultural and linguistic conceptual dimensions open by the Spanish language administration (presence of linguistic-gender for all animate and inanimate object referents), which are not present in the English language. In addition, Gonzalez and collaborators (1996) also noticed the importance of allowing non-balanced bilingual children to use code switching for responding when assessed with QUEST. This individualization of assessment to the linguistic needs and ability levels of the child resulted in the enhancement of their cognitive and linguistic developmental levels attained across verbal tasks.

Moreover, these results also coincide with another pattern found by Gonzalez and collaborators (1996), showing a pattern for verbal and non-verbal procedures to provide new and valuable complementary information. That is, this pattern indicated that verbal and non-verbal classification tasks made a significant difference in bilingual children's performance. In general, previous findings show that bilingual children could sort objects (in the sorting task) using general criteria in English, and linguistic-gender criteria in Spanish; but they could not verbally explain their groupings (in the verbal justification of sorting task) with the same easiness in both languages. In addition, the presence or absence of linguistic-gender assignments for animate and inanimate object referents influenced the conceptual developmental level attained by bilingual children. More specifically, the Spanish administration for non-verbal tasks for inanimate referents create for bilingual children the opportunity to think at a higher metalinguistic level (Gonzalez et al., 1996). Previous studies also demonstrate that content cultural knowledge also made a significant difference in bilingual children's performance, showing that when they were familiar with the assessment stimuli, such as inanimate referents (food), they tended to perform at higher non-verbal conceptual levels (Gonzalez, 1991, 1994, 1995; Gonzalez et al., 1996).

Therefore, results indicate that adapting administration and response procedures to suit children's individual needs (in this case their bilingual idiosyncratic linguistic and cultural styles of communication) and abilities, allows them to demonstrate their verbal conceptual understanding of different languages and cultures. Thus, there is need to individualize assessment for measuring the unique individual effect of cognitive, cultural, and linguistic factors influencing bilingual children's verbal concept formation process. Moreover, QUEST provides bilingual children with the opportunity to perform differently when being assessed using two languages and cultural contents. The multidimensionality of QUEST allows evaluators to individualize assessment by providing a window for observing the interaction of cognition, language, and culture. In this manner, qualitative alternative assessments, such as QUEST, provide a holistic perspective that helps to understand and improve traditional methodological problems still present when assessing bilingual children.

## What Is the Effect of Developmental Factors on Children's Conceptual Development?: Research Question 3

In addition, ANOVA tests (see Table 4.1) indicated that age had a significant effect on children's QUEST performance for most sub-tasks:

1. The labeling task (measuring language development at the level of word knowledge) for animate object referents and inanimate object referents at the linguistic-gender level.
2. The defining task (measuring verbal concepts) for animate object referents at the general level.
3. The sorting task (measuring non-verbal concepts) for animate object referents at the general level, and for inanimate object referents at the linguistic-gender level.
4. The verbal justification of sorting task (measuring verbal concepts) for animate object referents and inanimate object referents at both general and linguistic-gender levels.
5. The category clue task (measuring non-verbal concepts) for animate object referents and inanimate object referents at the linguistic-gender level.

These results show that age had a significant effect on children's concept formation developmental levels attained, in relation to content cultural knowledge (with different patterns emerging for animate and inanimate object referents), and also in relation to verbal and non-verbal tasks. In most instances, children had a harder time forming both verbal and non-verbal concepts for inanimate objects at a linguistic-gender level. That is, because concept formation for inanimate object referents requires a metacognitive level of understanding of the abstract symbolic criteria underlying cultural and linguistic conventions, represented by linguistic structures and markers. However, the formation of verbal and non-verbal concepts for inanimate object referents using a general classification criteria (e.g., color, shape, function, classes, and metalinguistic criteria) seemed to be less influenced by the age of the children.

Actually, these emerging patterns are similar to previous findings (Gonzalez, 1991, 1994, 1995; Gonzalez, et al., 1996) showing that bilingual kindergartners and first graders performed at higher conceptual developmental levels with inanimate rather than with animate object referents. This similar pattern may be the result of the effect of cultural content knowledge and level of familiarity with sociocultural experiences in relation to object referents. That is, children are much more familiar with food than with animals, as the food items represented in QUEST are encountered by the children on their real-life experiences on a daily bases (which is not the case for animals).

In addition, the age of children also had a significant effect on their performance on verbal and non-verbal tasks. Results show that children's age non-verbal concepts mostly at the linguistic-gender level, but not at the general level (especially for inanimate object referents, except for animate object referents in the sorting task). Then, it seems that concept formation for inanimate object referents, as explained above the most familiar content cultural knowledge, seemed not to be affected by developmental factors. However, the harder and higher conceptual processes of forming non-verbal and verbal concepts for inanimate object referents at the linguistic-gender level was significantly affected by age, due to requiring metacognitive and metalinguistic abilities to problem-solve the proposed tasks. These findings coincide with previous studies conducted (Gonzalez et al., 1996) in which bilingual kindergartners and first graders performed at above-normal developmental levels in non-verbal classification tasks of QUEST, and at normal developmental levels in verbal tasks; both patterns related to the specific cognitive, cultural, and linguistic characteristics of the content represented in QUEST.

It is also important to note that this age effect on the children's performance in classification tasks of QUEST may have also been confounded with language of administration and language of response effects, which also proved to be significant when tested independently (as explained above). Thus, it should be considered that this significant age effect as additive on the previous significant findings of language of administration and response for QUEST. Then, Spanish (and not English) is the language that shows linguistic-gender for inanimate object referents; which has proven to have an effect on children's performance on verbal and non-verbal tasks (Gonzalez, 1991, 1994, 1995; Gonzalez, et al., 1996). Thus, using a qualitative assessment method that reflects content that may be similar or different across languages allows evaluators to gain a more holistic view of the interaction of cognition, culture, and language.

## What Is the Effect of Gender Factors on Children's Conceptual Development?: Research Question 4

ANOVA tests (see Table 4.1) indicated that the gender variable did not have an effect on any sub-task of QUEST. Even though an equal number of boys and girls were present in the sample, and therefore the gender of the subjects was controlled as a variable in the quasi-experimental design of the study, children performance in QUEST tasks was not affected by their gender. No previous studies conducted with QUEST had tested the effect of gender on children's performance.

## Which Is the Best Predictor of Children's Conceptual Development?: Research Question 5

Step-wise multiple regression analyses results (see Table 4.2) indicated that three independent variables (SES, language of administration, and age) were significant predictors of children's performance on four factors of QUEST:

1. Step 1, First Model: SES and language of administration of QUEST were significant predictors of Factor 1 (language development in relation to word

TABLE 4.2
Summary of Multiple Linear Regression Analyses Using SES, Language of Administration for QUEST, Language of Response for QUEST, and Age as Predictors; and QUEST Factors as Dependent Variables

| DV(s) IV(s) | Source | SS | df | MS | F | R squared | p |
|---|---|---|---|---|---|---|---|
| **Step 1/First Model: SES and Language of Administration** as Predictors for **Factor 1**: Language Development in Relation to Word Knowledge, Common to Animates and Inanimates, Abstract (Universal) & Culturally-Linguistically Bound Classification Systems, Spanish and Bilinguals Only | | | | | | | |
| Factor 1 | Multiple reg. | 16.147 | 2 | 8.074 | 9.359 | .154 | 0.024 |
| SES & Language of Administration on X variable | | | | | | | |
| Residual | | 88.853 | 103 | .863 | | | |
| Total | | 105.000 | 105 | | | | |
| **Step 2/Second Model**: SES as Predictor for **Factor 2**: Verbal Concepts, Common to Animates and Inanimates, Culturally-Linguistically Bound Classification System, Present only in Spanish and in Bilingual Children | | | | | | | |
| Factor 2 | Multiple reg. | 7.820 | 1 | 7.820 | 8.369 | 0.074 | 0.005 |
| SES on X variable | | | | | | | |
| Residual | | 97.180 | 104 | .934 | | | |
| Total | | 105.000 | 105 | | | | |
| **Step 3/Third Model**: SES as Predictor for **Factor 4**: Verbal and Non-Verbal Concepts, for Animates Only, Abstract (Universal) & Culturally-Linguistically Bound Classification Systems, Common to Spanish & English, Common to Monolinguals and Bilinguals | | | | | | | |
| Factor 4 | Multiple reg. | 16.191 | 1 | 16.191 | 18.960 | .154 | 0.012 |
| SES on X variable | | | | | | | |
| Residual | | 88.809 | 104 | .854 | | | |
| Total | | 105.0001 | 105 | | | | |
| **Step 4/Fourth Model**: Age as Predictor for **Factor 5**: Verbal and Non-Verbal Concepts, for Inanimates Only, Abstract (Universal) Classification System, Common to Spanish and English, Common to Monolinguals and Bilinguals | | | | | | | |
| Factor 5 | Multiple reg. | 5.946 | 1 | 5.946 | 6.009 | .058 | 0.016 |
| Age on X variable | | | | | | | |
| Residual | | 95.986 | 97 | .990 | | | |
| Total | | 101.932 | 98 | | | | |

knowledge for animate object referents and inanimate object referents at the general and linguistic-gender levels).

2. Step 2, Second Model: SES was a significant predictor of Factor 2 (verbal concepts for animate object referents and inanimate object referents at the linguistic-gender level).

3. Step 3, Third Model: SES was a significant predictor of Factor 4 (verbal and non-verbal concept formation for animate object referents, both at the general and linguistic-gender levels).

4. Step 4, Fourth Model: Age was a significant predictor of Factor 5 (non-verbal and verbal concepts for inanimate object referents at the general level).

All these 4 significant models are reported in Table 4.2, presenting a summary of the step-wise multiple linear regression analysis conducted. In the first model, the language of administration had an effect on a QUEST factor component: Labeling at the linguistic-gender level for animate object referents (present both in Spanish and English) and inanimate object referents (present only in Spanish). Then, findings in the ANOVA tests were coincident with the regression results in terms of showing a language of administration influence on the children's word knowledge levels for inanimate object referents at the linguistic-gender level. Thus, again the particular content cultural knowledge and the linguistic characteristics represented symbolically and semantically in inanimate object referents seem to have an effect on children's performance. In this case, only Spanish showed linguistic-gender for inanimate object referents, and therefore language of administration did influenced the children's performance, making a difference between monolingual and bilingual children. It is only bilingual children the ones who can use their cultural and linguistic specific knowledge in Spanish (i.e., in terms of linguistic-gender assignments for inanimate object referents) in the labeling task.

Second, regression tests results (see Table 4.2) also indicated that the most significant predictor was the children's SES, which had an effect on their developmental level on two main QUEST factor components:

1. Second model: Verbal conceptual development at the linguistic-gender level for animate (present in both Spanish and English) and for inanimate object referents (present only in Spanish), called Factor 2.

2. Third model: Non-verbal and verbal conceptual development at the general and linguistic-gender levels for animate object referents (present in both Spanish and English), called Factor 4.

These results point to a pattern indicating that: Whether children came from a low or middle-high SES background predicted their verbal and non-verbal conceptual development, in relation to specific cultural (content knowledge—animate and inanimate object referents) and linguistic factors (structures and markers characteristics of Spanish and English in relation to general or linguistic-gender classification criteria and scoring systems). This pattern supports findings of the Principal Components Analysis and the ANOVA tests discussed above; which all support the significant effect of cultural and linguistic factors on the verbal and non-verbal concept formation processes of both monolingual and bilingual children. Indeed commonalties were found in how monolingual and bilingual children form verbal and non-verbal concepts (indicated by Factors 3, 4, and 5). However, also special differences have also been discovered in this study for how conceptual, cultural, and linguistic differences found between the Spanish and the English languages do affect how bilingual children form new representational systems (Factors 1 and 2), unique only to the Spanish language. Therefore, bilingualism does have a significant effect on how children develop bicognitive and bicultural conceptual processes and representational systems.

Moreover, the fourth model indicates that age was also a significant predictor of the children's developmental level in QUEST, specifically for verbal and non-verbal concept formation for inanimate objects at the general level. It seems that monolingual and bilingual children shared the ability to represent verbal and non-verbal concepts using general classification criteria only. Therefore, the age variable predicted the commonalties (general classification criteria) in monolingual and bilingual children's performance in verbal and non-verbal concept formation for inanimate objects. As discussed above, the content cultural knowledge *does* influence the children's performance, especially in relation to linguistic instantiations (structures and markers) that are present only in the Spanish language.

In sum, considering together results of the Principal Components Analysis, ANOVA tests, and regression tests, the presence of three patterns emerge:

1. SES, developmental, linguistic (i.e., language of administration and language of response matching the children's monolingual or bilingual background; and particular language characteristics of the Spanish and English languages in relation to general and linguistic-gender classification criteria or scoring systems), and cultural (content knowledge represented by animate and inanimate object referents) factors are significantly influencing monolingual and bilingual children's verbal and non-verbal concept formation levels (as measured by alternative instruments).

2. Language of administration and language of response for QUEST have a significant influence on monolingual and bilingual children's verbal and non-verbal concept formation processes. These results indicate that allowing children to use their strongest language and cultural style of communication (including code switching and code mixing) is an important variable in cognitive assessment.

3. Thus, the fact that most language-minority children come from disadvantaged SES backgrounds, rather than they speak Spanish or are limited-English

proficient, is the most important variable influencing their performance in cognitive developmental tasks.


## CONCLUSIONS: THEORETICAL AND PRACTICAL CONTRIBUTIONS OF THE STUDY

The most important finding was the empirical validation of a more complex revised model showing similarities and differences between monolingual and bilingual children's verbal and non-verbal concept construction processes. Then, this study provides empirical support for a revised model (comparing similarities and differences in monolingual and bilingual children) of the complex interaction of cognitive, linguistic, and cultural factors previously found by Gonzalez (1991, 1994, 1995; Gonzalez et al., 1996) only in bilingual children.

In addition, this study adds a new set of independent variables, with coincident findings from ANOVA and regression tests, showing the significant effect of SES, developmental (age, comparing ages ranging from 4 to 9 years), linguistic (i.e., language of administration and language of response matching the children's monolingual or bilingual background; and particular language characteristics of the Spanish and English languages in relation to general and linguistic-gender classification criteria or scoring systems), and cultural (content knowledge represented by animate and inanimate object referents) factors on monolingual and bilingual, low and middle-high SES children's performance on an alternative cognitive and language development measure (QUEST). Thus, results of this study show that the process of concept construction is related to the cultural and/or linguistic nature of the representations, which may show similarities and differences when comparing Spanish and English monolingual children with English/Spanish or Spanish/English bilinguals (with different degrees of fluency in both languages). Therefore, concept construction was shown to be a cultural and linguistic content driven process.

Thus, both the new revised model and the new independent variables contribute to the literature in bilingual education as well as in cognitive and developmental psychology areas. As discussed in the critical theoretical framework proposed in this study, there is scarcity of multidimensional studies that empirically test the effect of SES, developmental, linguistic, and cultural variables on the development of cognitive processes in bilingual children. The major contribution of this study is the validation of a data-driven model explaining why and how bilingualism affects cognition, taking into account age, and cultural and linguistic factors affecting cognition.

This theoretical contribution also results in practical contributions, by deriving specific similarities and differences in how monolingual and bilingual children construct verbal and non-verbal processes. The significance of the SES variable for predicting the monolingual and bilingual children's performance in verbal and non-verbal concept formation tasks, becomes the most important practical implication of the study. That is, it is the fact that most bilingual children in the public US schools come from a low SES background, and not their English language proficiency or the presence of a minority L1, what affects their cognitive and language development.

This study also demonstrated that the performance of bilingual low SES students, as well as of monolingual children, is affected by the language of administration and response, and the cultural attributes of the specific cognitive and language development measure used. Thus, when alternative assessments represent appropriate developmental, cultural, linguistic factors; bilingual children are provided an equal opportunity to show how bilingualism enhances their bicognitive and bicultural development. In fact, two new ways of representing verbal concepts and word knowledge were found in bilinguals, when compared with monolingual counterparts of similar or different low or mid-high SES backgrounds.

An important practical implication points to the validation of QUEST, also supported by a series of previous studies (Clark & Gonzalez, 1998; Felix-Holt & Gonzalez, 1999; Gonzalez & Clark, 1999; Gonzalez et al., 1994, 1996, 1998, 1999), demonstrating that this alternative qualitative assessment, using verbal and non-verbal classification problem-solving tasks, has proven to be useful for validly assessing cognitive and language development in young bilingual children. Then, when a model that represents the cultural and linguistic advantages of bilingualism is empirically tested in an alternative, problem-solving measure of the process of concept construction, bilingual children can show the advantages of bilingualism on their cognitive and language development. This study also proves that QUEST can methodologically control for the significant effect of linguistic and cultural factors on how monolingual and bilingual children construct verbal and non-verbal concepts. This series of studies have proven that regardless of degree of language proficiency in first and L2, bilingual children (even the so considered limited English proficient) show advantages in how they construct verbal and non-verbal concepts. More specifically, as this study shows, bilingualism opens for children new ways of representing culturally and linguistically real-life animate and inanimate object referents; opportunities for stimulating the potential of symbolic development not enjoyed by monolingual children (regardless of their SES background and level of proficiency in their L1).

By relating the five factors emerging from the revised model, and the complex pattern of interaction among variables found in the ANOVA and regression tests, findings can be summarized in the following statement: Verbal and non-verbal conceptual development is influenced by idiosyncratic linguistic structures and markers of each language, their sociocultural meanings for linguistic conventions, and their related underlying abstract and semantic conceptualizations, that may be similar or different across cultures and languages. Even though specific differences were found in this study when comparing monolingual and bilingual children, in general findings of this study are complementary to the interaction between cognitive, linguistic, and cultural factors found in previous validation studies conducted only with bilingual children (Gonzalez, 1991, 1994, 1995; Gonzalez et al., 1996).

## LIMITATIONS OF THE STUDY AND NEED FOR FUTURE STUDIES

Even though this study had a rather large sample, an unequal number of low and middle-class children were compared. Then, there is need to administer QUEST to a larger number of children who are monolingual Spanish or English and come from a middle-high SES background. However, the particular low SES and bilingual characteristics of the major portion of the sample in this study represent the larger portion of language-minority Hispanic children attending US public schools presently, who are at-risk of developing learning problems (see e.g., Gonzalez et al., 1997 for some demographic data on this at-risk children).

As presented in the critical discussion of the framework and methodology sections, the language proficiency level of the bilingual children could not be controlled due to methodological problems in currently available standardized tests. However, the language of administration and language of response for QUEST were used as independent variables in the ANOVA tests, or as predictors in the multiple regression tests; leading to coincident significant results.

This study was also limited by the higher percentage of subjects (74% of the sample) represented by the age bracket of 5 years to 6 years, 6 months of age. The older (in the age bracket of 7 years to 9 years of age, 20%) or younger children (in the age bracket of 4 years to 4 years and 6 months, 6%) were not equally represented. A future study should increase the number of children in the older and younger brackets, in order to further test (with a higher level of power) the developmental effect on verbal and non-verbal concept formation processes.

Although some important limitations can be found in this study, the major core research questions of how linguistic, cultural, developmental, and SES factors affect verbal and non-verbal concept construction in monolingual and bilingual children could be answered, with a number of coincident significant findings across parametric tests, as well as in comparison with a series of previous studies. In addition, the most important confounding methodological cultural, linguistic factors could be controlled by the alternative measure used (QUEST), as well as could be represented as independent variables or predictors of the cognitive and language developmental performance of monolingual and bilingual children. Thus, it can be argued that the weight of the empirical evidence, provided by this and other quasi-experimental studies, seems to support the advantages of bilingualism on bicognitivism and biculturalism in young children.

## ACKNOWLEDGMENTS

The author wants to recognize the contributions of Dynah M. Oviedo and Kathleen O'Brien de Ramirez for the data collection and analysis phase of this study. Their bilingual and bicultural backgrounds became valuable assets for the study.

## REFERENCES

Bialystock, E. (1991). Introduction. In E. Bialystock (Ed.), *Language processing in bilingual children* (pp. 1–9). Cambridge University Press: Cambridge, Great Britain.

Bialystock, E., & Cummins, J. (1991). Language, cognition, and education of bilingual children. In E. Bialystock (Ed.), *Language processing in bilingual children* (pp. 222–232). Cambridge University Press: Cambridge, Great Britain.

Bradley, R. H., Whiteside, L. Y., & Mundfrom, D. J. (1994). Early indications of resilience and their relation to experiences in the home environments of low birth-weight, premature children living in poverty. *Child Development, 65*, 346–360.

Clark, E. R., & Gonzalez, V. (1998). *Voces* and voices: Cultural and linguistic giftedness. *Educational Horizons, 77*(1), 41–47.

Diaz, R. M. (1985). Bilingual cognitive development: Addressing three gaps in current research. *Child Development, 56*, 1376–1388.

Diaz, R. M., & Klingler, (1991). Towards an exploratory model of the interaction between bilingualism and cognitive development. In E. Bialystock (Ed.), *Language processing in bilingual children* (pp. 167–192). Cambridge University Press: Cambridge, Great Britain.

Diaz, R. M., & Padilla, K. A. (1985). *The self-regulatory speech of bilingual preschoolers*. Paper presented at the April Meeting of the Society for Research in Child Development. Toronto, Canada.

Duncan, G. J., Brooks-Gunn, J., & Kato, P. K. (1994). Economic deprivation and early childhood development. *Child Development, 65*, 296–318.

Felix-Holt, M, & Gonzalez, V. (1999). Alternative assessment models of language-minority children: Is there a match with teachers' attitudes and instruction? In V. Gonzalez (Vol. Ed.), *Language and cognitive development in L2 learning: Educational implications for children and adults* (pp. 190–226). Needham Heights, MA: Allyn & Bacon.

Gonzalez, V. (1995). *Cognition, culture, and language in bilingual children: Conceptual and semantic development*. Bethesda, MD: Austin & Winfield.

Gonzalez, V. (1994). A model of cognitive, cultural, and linguistic variables affecting bilingual Hispanic children's development of concepts and language. *Hispanic Journal of Behavioral Sciences, 16*(4), 396–421.

Gonzalez, V. (1991). *A model of cognitive, cultural, and linguistic variables affecting bilingual Spanish/English children's development of concepts and language*. Doctoral Dissertation. Austin, Texas: The University of Texas at Austin. (ERIC Document Reproduction Service No. ED 345 562).

Gonzalez, V., Bauerle, P., Black, W., & Felix-Holt, M. (1999). Influence of evaluators' beliefs and cultural-linguistic backgrounds on their diagnostic and placement decisions for language-minority children. In V. Gonzalez (Vol. Ed.), *Language and cognitive development in L2 learning: Educational implications for children and adults* (pp. 269–297). Needham Heights, MA: Allyn & Bacon.

Gonzalez, V., Bauerle, P, & Felix-Holt, M. (1996). Theoretical and practical implications of assessing cognitive and language development in bilingual children with qualitative methods. *Bilingual Research Journal, 20*(1), 93–131.

Gonzalez, V., Bauerle, P., & Felix-Holt, M. (1994). A qualitative assessment method for accurately diagnosing bilingual gifted children. *NABE Annual Conference Journal 1992–1993*, 37–52. Washington, DC: NABE.

Gonzalez, V., Brusca-Vega, R., & Yawkey, T. D. (1997). *Assessment and instruction of culturally and linguistically diverse students with or at-risk of learning problems: From research to practice.* Needham Heights, MA: Allyn & Bacon.

Gonzalez, V., Clark, E. R., Bauerle, P; & Black, W. (1998). *Cultural and linguistic giftedness in Hispanic bilingual kindergartners: Analyzing the validity of alternative and standardized assessments.* Poster presented at the AERA Annual Meeting, San Diego, CA.

Gonzalez, V., & Clark, E. R. (1999). *Folkloric* and *historic* views of giftedness in language-minority children. In V. Gonzalez (Vol. Ed.), *Language and cognitive development in L2 learning: Educational implications for children and adults* (pp. 1–18). Needham Heights, MA: Allyn & Bacon.

Gonzalez, V., & Schallert, D. L. (1999). An integrative analysis of the cognitive development of bilingual and bicultural children and adults. In V. Gonzalez (Vol. Ed.), *Language and cognitive development in L2 learning: Educational implications for children and adults* (pp. 19–55). Needham Heights, MA: Allyn & Bacon.

Gonzalez, V., & Yawkey, T. (1993). The assessment of culturally and linguistically diverse students: Celebrating change. *Educational Horizons, 72*(1), 41–49.

Hakuta, K. (1991). *Mirror of language: The debate on bilingualism.* New York: Basic Books.

Hakuta, K. (1988). Why bilinguals. In F. S. Kessel (Ed.), *The development of language and language researchers: Essays in honor of Roger Brown* (pp. 229–318). Hillsdale, NJ: Lawrence Erlbaum Associates.

Hakuta, K. (1982). *The L2 learner in the context of the study of language acquisition.* Paper presented at the Society for Research in Child Development Conference on Bilingualism and Child Development, New York University, June.

Hakuta, K., & Diaz, R. M. (1985). The relationship between degree of bilingualism and cognitive ability: A critical discussion and some new longitudinal data. In K. E. Nelson (Ed.), *Children's language,* Vol. V. Hillsdale, NJ: Lawrence Erlbaum Associates.

Lambert, W. E., & Tucker, G. R. (1972). *Bilingual education of children: The St. Lambert experiment.* Newbury House: Rowley, MA.

Markman, E. M. (1984). The acquisition of hierarchical organization of categories by children. In C. Sophian (Ed.), *Origin in cognitive skills.* The 18th Annual Carnegie Symposium on Cognition (pp. 376–406). Hillsdale, NJ: Lawrence Erlbaum Associates.

Oller, J. W., Jr. (1991). Language testing research: Lessons applied to LEP students and programs. Paper conducted at the *First Research Symposium on Limited English Proficient (LEP) Students' Issues: Focus on Evaluation and Measurement.* Washington DC: Office of Bilingual Education and Minority Languages Affairs, US Department of Education.

Oller, J. W., Jr. & Damico, J. S. (1991). Theoretical considerations in the assessment of LEP students. In E. V. Hamayan & J. S. Damico (Eds.). *Limiting bias in the assessment of bilingual students* (pp. 77–110). Austin, Texas: Pro-Ed.

Oviedo, M. D., & Gonzalez, V. (1999). Case study comparisons of standardized and alternative assessments: Diagnoses accuracy in minority children. In V. Gonzalez (Vol. Ed.), *Language and cognitive development in L2 learning: Educational implications for children and adults* (227–268)**.** Needham Heights, MA: Allyn & Bacon.

Piaget, J. (1967). Piaget's theory. In P. H. Mussen (Ed.), *Carmichael's manual of child psychology,* Vol. I (pp. 703–732). New York: John Wiley.

Peal, E., & Lambert, W. E. (1962). The relation of bilingualism to intelligence. *Psychological Monographs, 76,* 1–23.

Rogoff, B., & Chavajay, P. (1995). What's become of research on the cultural basis of cognitive development? *American Psychologist, 50*(10), 859–877.

Walker, D., Greenwood, C., Hart, B., & Carta, J. (1994). Prediction of school outcomes based on early language production and socioeconomic factors. *Child Development, 65,* 606–621.

Waxman, S. R. (1990). Linking language and conceptual development: Linguistic cues and the construction of conceptual hierarchies. *The Genetic Epistemologist, 17,* 13–20.

# II

# APPLIED EDUCATION/
# ACTION RESEARCH

# 5

# A Rationale for Connecting Dual Language Programs with Gifted Education

Jaime A. Castellano and Margarita Pinkos
*School District of Palm Beach County, Florida*

## ABSTRACT

Gifted education and dual language programs have a propensity to attract our country's best and brightest students. Both programs challenge them academically and linguistically, and the outcomes of each prepare these students to successfully participate in a global society that is culturally, ethnically, and linguistically diverse. The hope is that they will be able to compete with the world's best by orienting their opportunities to develop and extend convergent and divergent thinking skills, investigative processes, effective communication skills, and the development of a healthy affect, among other cognitive, academic, and linguistic skills.

The purpose of this article is to offer a rationale for connecting dual language programs with gifted education. Because both programs share common characteristics and the caliber of students also exhibit parallel levels of intelligence and verbal/linguistic strengths the collaboration between the two categorical entities seems to make sense. It is a logical evolution in this age of bridge building coalitions, particularly in light of cost-cutting measures that are currently impacting schools across the country. Furthermore, bilingual dual language programs specific to the School District of Palm Beach County, Florida will be examined; gifted education program models will be reviewed; and the connection between the two will be presented.

## SHIFTING THE PARADIGM

Few educators would disagree with the benefits that dual language and gifted education programs have to offer their students, especially with the mandates required by the No Child Left Behind (NCLB) legislation, which, some would argue, reflects a deficit model of education. Both programs allow schools to successfully account for all their students, as opposed to those that are the least able. Advocacy from parents, teachers, and administrators can result in the successful development of these programs in order to meet the needs of our nation's outstanding public school students.

While educators in gifted education may disagree about identification procedures and the meaning of giftedness, they usually agree that the primary purpose of gifted education is to meet the unique educational needs of either exceptionally bright or talented students or to maximize the talents they already possess (Castellano, 2002). They contend that the regular curriculum does not allow these students sufficient avenues to expand their talents and abilities, and that students whose abilities are not tapped sufficiently will not meet their potential. Proponents of gifted education also maintain that without adequate educational experiences that challenge high ability students, a vast resource will be lost to American society (Office of Educational Research and Improvement, 1993, 1998; Diaz, 2002). While they do not take issue with the contention that education needs to improve for all students, they have particular concern with those bearing special talents. That is, those they see as most likely to benefit society in a variety of leadership, academic, creative, and artistic capacities (Office of Educational Research and Improvement, 1998). Meeting the needs of gifted students can be done through any number of program options, including inter-collaborative relationships with other categorical programs like bilingual education, particularly dual language programs.

Cloud, Genesee, and Hamayan (2000) suggested that there are educational, cognitive, socio-cultural, and economic benefits to individuals as well as society at large as the result from intensive study of second and even third languages in enriched educational programs, i.e., dual language programs. If our nation is to compete on a global scale our schools need to produce students who are proficient and efficient in their communication skills in various languages. Dual language programs can serve this roll. They go on to say that the development of advanced levels of language competence, in a primary or second language, is most successful when it occurs in conjunction with meaningful, important, and authentic communication. In school settings, this can be communication about academic subjects. Thus, including second languages not only as subjects of study, but also as vehicles for teaching and learning other academic subjects is a logical and effective way of extending students' language competence. These programs tend to attract students who already have a solid foundation in their first language and who are linguistically and scholastically capable of doing well learning content in another language (Cenoz & Genesee, 1998; Thomas & Collier, 1998).

## Benefits of Bilingualism

Just as the merits of gifted education continue to be debated, so do the benefits of bilingualism. For example, the relationship between bilingualism and cognitive development is frequently misunderstood. As Hakuta (1990); Lindholm (1992), and

Lessow-Hurley (2000) pointed out, there is a lingering belief in some quarters that bilingualism is something negative, rather than something positive. This conviction, he argues, stems from long-held attitudes about immigrants as somehow inferior to mainstream Americans even though the United States is predominately a nation of immigrants. Despite this view, there is a significant body of research that shows bilingualism is associated positively with greater cognitive flexibility. In comparisons of bilingual and monolingual children, there is evidence that bilingualism leads to what Hakuta terms "superior performance on a variety of intellectual skills" (p. 5). The eagerness with which some schools have greeted this expanded view of intelligence suggests that many educators find these theories and research findings validated in their experience and congruent with the democratic ideals of schooling (Lockwood, 1997b). Our goal as educators should be to develop programs that match the cognitive and linguistic needs that students have, not to force them into programs that do not challenge them to fly to their greatest heights.

## DUAL LANGUAGE PROGRAMS IN THE SCHOOL DISTRICT OF PALM BEACH COUNTY, FLORIDA

The School District of Palm Beach County began implementation of dual language programs in 1998, in one geographically isolated, low-performing rural school. Throughout the years, and amid success beyond expectations, the program has blossomed and evolved into a significant district initiative (School District of Palm Beach County District Plan, 2004). The district has clearly delineated a spectrum of services for second language learners where the dual language program anchors the limits that separate foreign language instruction and English for Speakers of Other Languages (ESOL) services. The different components of this spectrum of services are clearly defined for the purposes of monitoring optimal implementation and program evaluation.

At the elementary level, the program has been implemented school-wide in one school, and partial or as a strand within a school in nine other district school centers. The target language of these programs is Spanish, with one exception, where the target language is French with a strong component of Haitian culture and additional exposure to Haitian Creole. The most popular model of dual language is the two-way immersion model presented in Table 5.1. The instructional day is usually allotted equally to both English and the target language in a 50–50 model. Most participating schools follow a daily schedule whereas a few follow an alternating day schedule.

Participating schools have a large percentage of language minority students and family income levels that earn the schools Title I qualification. Students are assigned to the program on a voluntary basis and those schools that implement the program school wide allow students and their families to opt out of the program and the school entirely upon request. Funding for the programs comes from a

TABLE 5.1
Two-Way Immersion Model

| School | Language of Instruction | Years in Place | Instructional Model |
|--------|------------------------|----------------|---------------------|
| Gove Elementary | English/Spanish | 8 | K–2 (50/50)<br>3–5 (1 class: 50/50)<br>3–5 (25–75) |
| North Grade Elementary | English/Spanish | 6 | K–3 (50/50)<br>4th (25–75) |
| Indian Pines Elementary | English/Spanish | 6 | K–3 (50/50)<br>4th (25/75) |
| Hagan Road Elementary | English/Spanish | 3 | K–2 (50/50) |

combination of sources. The schools receive an ESOL allocation based on the number of students in the program who have been identified as limited English proficient (LEP) using the Florida State Department of Education's identification criteria.

Upon initial entry a public school in the School District of Palm Beach County, Florida the Home Language Survey on the registration form must be completed, signed, and dated for all students by the parent/guardian registering the student. For those students requiring additional screening, a state approved age appropriate Language Assessment Scale (LAS, Duncan & DeAvila, 1986) test is used to assess students' aural/oral ability. The results of the assessment indicate that a student scores in one of the following levels and language categories: (1) level 1: Category A -non-speaker, (2) level 2: Category B -limited speaker, (3) level 3: Category C -limited speaker, (4) level 4: Category D -fluent speaker, and (5) level 5: Category E -fluent speaker.

Students in K through 12th Grade scoring as non-speakers or limited English speakers (levels 1–3) on the LAS-O qualify for English for speakers of other languages (ESOL) services. Students in K though Grade 3 scoring as fluent English speakers (levels 4 or 5) on the LAS-O do not qualify for ESOL program services, unless recommended by the school's LEP Committee. Students in Grades 4–12 scoring as fluent English speakers (levels 4 or 5), based on the LAS-O assessment results, are assessed by the additional administration of the LAS Reading/Writing assessment (Duncan & DeAvila, 1986). In addition, schools use their basic regular operating budget to fund teachers as necessary. In several schools Title I funds and/or special magnet school funding is used to supplement the program.

At the secondary level, three middle schools are currently completing their first year of implementation. In these schools the models show more variety as each school has found its own niche based on the identified needs of their specific

TABLE 5.2
School Models

| School | Language of Instruction | Years in Place | Instructional Model |
|---|---|---|---|
| Jefferson Davis Middle School | Spanish/English | 2 | Two-Way Immersion<br>Students take 2 of the 2 courses offered in Spanish<br>• Language Arts<br>• Math |
| Okeeheelee Middle | Spanish/English | 1<br>International Spanish Academy | Two-Way Immersion<br>Students take 2 or 3 of the 4 courses offered in Spanish<br>• Language Arts<br>• Math<br>• Physical Education<br>• Theatre |
| Conniston Middle | Spanish/English | 1 | Two-Way Immersion<br>Students take 2 of the 3 courses offered in Spanish<br>• Language Arts<br>• Social Studies<br>• Physical Education |

populations (see Table 5.2). One of the middle schools serves an overwhelmingly large Hispanic population. Most of their students come to this school with middle to advanced levels of native language literacy. As a response to the characteristics of the school population, the school has adopted a school wide model where every student takes a minimum of two out of six academic classes in Spanish. The second middle school has focused on the area of the arts. The school has implemented an arts choice program. In their quest for integrating their Spanish-speaking population into the arts program and hoping to enhance the language skills that the students have brought with them in their native language, this school has enhanced their existing ESOL program with an emphasis on native language content instruction. Finally, the third middle school has implemented a program strand within the school where native Spanish speakers choose to take at least two academic subjects in Spanish and monolingual English speakers who have not been exposed previously to a dual-language program take one content area of their choice in Spanish, as well as an intensive Spanish language instruction class. During their content area class, the students are grouped heterogeneously with native Spanish speakers learning Spanish side-by-side with their non-native peers. In the Spanish language instruction classes, however, only those students who are beginning learners of Spanish are in attendance. In addition to the concept of a partial school model, this third secondary school has engaged in a partnership with the Ministry of Spain and has been recognized as the district's first International Spanish Academy.

All district programs, regardless of level, enjoy a great deal of support from the community. School Advisory Councils (SAC) are required to vote in the majority before the implementation of a dual language program in a school. The faculty of each school is required to follow a similar approval process. Although daunting at times, each school makes every effort to recruit quality teachers who have been educated in the target language and are thus fully bilingual and bi-literate as well as certified in the area of instruction (Bernal, 2002). These efforts have taken school officials to recruit as far away as Spain, Venezuela, Puerto Rico, Mexico, and Haiti.

Finally, when describing the school models, it is important to point out that each program has a very strong staff development component supported and facilitated both at the school site and at the district level. The focus for staff development includes strong emphasis in the areas of balanced literacy, second language acquisition, teacher collaboration, assessment for learning, analysis of student data, and others as identified by the school staff. Each year, the school conducts a self-assessment, program evaluation, and refinement of the program based on concrete evidence of program strengths and weaknesses directly related to student achievement.

One of the most rewarding outcomes of the dual language programs in the School District of Palm Beach County has been the dramatic impact on the students' academic performance measured in both formative and summative assessments. A large majority of schools at the elementary level began the program categorized in the lowest ranks of the Florida Department of Education's accountability system. Slowly and steadily, all dual language programs in the district have demonstrated significant increases in student achievement. As a result, these schools presently form part of the top ranked schools in the district. Most of their grade "A" labels in the State's accountability plan contrast poignantly with schools that share similar demographics but sport a much lower grade in the same grading system (see Table 5.3).

TABLE 5.3
Grades of Palm Beach County Schools
with Two-Way Dual Language Programs

| School | Year | | | | |
|--------|------|------|------|------|------|
|        | 2004 | 2003 | 2002 | 2001 | 2000 |
| Gove Elementary | A | A | A | C | D |
| North Grade | A | B | A | A | C |
| Indian Pines | A | A | A | B | C |
| Hagan Road | A | A | A | C | A |
| Jefferson Davis | B | B | B | C | C |

## Instructional Strategies

A great variety of instructional strategies are used at each district dual language school. There is no attempt at the district level to standardize the delivery models, but flexibility is encouraged and valued as to ensure that the programs are responsive to the specific needs of the students served in each school. Nevertheless, there are some aspects of the instructional program that are common to all district dual language schools, either by design or as a consequence of the programs themselves. For example, to promote increased academic achievement of all students, graphic organizers are used, critical thinking and problem solving skills are weaved through all content areas, and there is an emphasis on high expectations.

## Celebration of Multilingualism

One of the most common characteristics of dual language programs in the district is that they all advocate an organizational culture that celebrates multilingualism. English language learners are not identified as students in need of "overcoming a deficiency," but as members of a student body that is actively engaged in the business of learning a second language (Slavin & Cheung, 2003). Thus, the power structure is different than in many other schools where there is a clear status attached to the majority language. In dual language programs, proficiency in either language is equally valued. Students regard each other as powerful resources in their shared quest for bilingualism. In most cases, this phenomena extends to the community and it is not uncommon for parents to actively schedule after school visits and play dates with linguistically diverse peers in an effort to increase the opportunities of their children to practice the language.

Visible signs of both languages are common throughout the schools: announcements are made in at least two languages, casual conversations in many languages are overheard in hallway and lounges, multicultural fairs are organized and highly attended, teachers and parents conduct after-hour language classes for each other, and in many instances, schools have added additional foreign language instruction in a third language as part of the school day. Without exception, the culture of language celebration extends to a general feeling of openness and tolerance for all diversity, and the schools are characterized by a positive school climate where all students thrive in the common culture (Christian & Genesee, 2001; Thomas & Collier, 1998).

## Commitment to Additive Pedagogy

Another common thread identified in all the schools is a commitment to additive instruction. And although these are not only descriptive of gifted and dual language programs only, they are viewed as one of enrichment that values the skills all students bring with them. These schools have high expectations for all language groups and closely monitor the progress of each individual student towards the established goals in both languages. For this purpose, the district has placed a premium on the development of native language assessments that parallel the English assessments used in the district. Teachers use data from assessments in both languages to diagnose strengths and weaknesses of the students and to adjust the educational plans as necessary. Discussions and educational planning are geared to the non-negotiable goal for students to become literate in a second language as they gain and maintain a high level of literacy in their native language.

District dual language programs also demonstrate a commitment to additive instruction in their decision to include appropriate areas of content in the instructional day. This decision obligates teachers to plan collaboratively in great detail to avoid repetition or overlap in a limited instructional day. One of the traditional difficulties in 50:50 models is the reduction of instructional time due to class switching. This situation is aggravated by the pressure from state and federal accountability systems to perform at high levels in state achievement tests. In many instances, schools in the district have sacrificed areas of content such as science, social studies, and fine arts to increase the literacy instruction period. Dual language programs in the School District of Palm Beach County have generally resisted the impulse to subtract content instruction even as their instructional time has the additional challenge of having to be divided in two district language settings. Schools have been recompensed by their efforts with steady gains in the state assessment results for participating students.

## Focused Professional Development

The importance of professional development cannot be overemphasized. It is recognized that teaching content in two languages and keeping the level of instruction simultaneously focused on student achievement and language acquisition is an extremely difficult task. The district's dual language schools share the strength of highly structured, student-centered staff development plans. Training components are not exclusively delivered to the staff currently teaching in a dual language class, but it is rather extended to all staff members in each school. It is the philosophy of the district that in a dual language school all faculty members are indeed dual language teachers even if the school has only implemented a strand. The purpose of this philosophy is manifold. First, it is important that when the program is implemented in a school, the climate and culture of the school are permeated with the value and understanding of the principles of second language acquisition and enriched education (Bernal, 2002; Crawford, 1997). It is not uncommon for a dual language program to suffer and even fail due to the lack of understanding of the school staff and the impact of the comments to the outside community!

The second purpose in addressing the entire staff of a school when planning professional development is to foster an atmosphere of collaboration and reflection among all staff members. It is critical to the success of the program that this atmosphere exists. Teachers are trained to participate in professional dialogue to analyze a wide range of topics, from school improvement to analysis of individual student achievement; from review of current educational literature to assessment of school needs; and from discussion of successful instructional practices to the development and evaluation of instructional material.

Finally, the focus of the staff development plan in the district dual language schools should not be placed on second language acquisition in isolation. Rather, the focus should rely more on the areas of balanced literacy and student centered instructional practices that embrace second language acquisition principles. Just as students are not taught language as an isolated content, but are rather taught content in two languages, second language acquisition practice is not taught in isolation but as it relates to effective educational practices.

## Gifted Education Program Models

In the School District of Palm Beach County, Florida students identified as gifted are given the option of either participating in a part-time or full-time gifted education program. Part-time, pullout programs are a popular model of choice for those schools that do not have enough students to offer a full-time program. The emphasis in this model is on interactive learning following the content area standards in the core curriculum areas mandated by the state department of education. The resource room model, which is implemented as a send-out program from the regular classroom for a portion of the school day is for students who are gifted and excelling at a level the regular classroom teacher cannot easily challenge.

Furthermore, certain advantages are offered through this send-out resource model. Gifted students, for example, are grouped with their intellectual peers, an integral component of high-quality programming for this population of students. The model is flexible enough to tailor curriculum and instruction to the abilities and interests of individual students. It also offers the opportunity for cooperation between regular classroom teachers and gifted education teachers (Castellano, 2002). Of particular importance is the fact that this model allows students with uneven academic development to participate in regular education classrooms for grade appropriate skills and in the resource room for skill-area strengths. The resource room delivery model provides enrichment activities that both enhance the grade-appropriate curriculum and reflect students' interests. Accelerated learning opportunities also challenge students' strengths. The learning environment further requires the application of higher-level thinking skills and develops divergent and creative thinking essential to problem-solving life experiences. In addition, stimulating activities allow for students to extend learning well beyond the regular classroom and that are commensurate with their abilities. Flexible grouping patterns (performance, interest, multiage) is also used in the part-time, pullout program to optimize learning (Castellano, Faivus, & White, 2003).

The gifted center model, which groups gifted students together in classes for the entire school day is offered to those who need the challenge of a comprehensive curriculum above the level of need for their age peers. These self-contained classrooms at the elementary level extend and enrich the curriculum by promoting higher order and critical thinking skills and are staffed by teachers endorsed in gifted education. In addition to covering prescribed grade-level objectives—and usually extending beyond them—a variety of enrichment, personal-development, and skill-development experiences are planned (Castellano, 2002). Typically found at the middle/junior high school and senior high school levels, cluster grouping calls for students to be grouped for the purpose of instruction in a specified content area. Providing opportunities to accelerate or enrich their academic experiences in the different subject areas allows their high-level needs to be met. Another program option implemented in the continuum of services offered to gifted students in Palm Beach County is the inclusive education model. This model is implemented in the regular classroom with the teacher providing a number of curricular options including curriculum compacting, alternative assignments, independent study, and grouping for instruction. This model is appropriate for students who are identified as gifted but only have one or two areas of strengths (Castellano, et al., 2003).

If the needs of gifted learners are to be met, we must have a planned, coordinated, continuous program. This program must be open and responsive to the changing individual, while providing a continuous challenge and an adequate diversity of content and process. While we may draw from more traditional gifted education models, our own communities, our parents, our students, and our staffs must make decisions regarding structure and intent (Clark, 1992). Traditional gifted education models can also work for those English language learners identified as gifted. Like adapting and modifying curriculum-differentiation to meet the needs of diverse student levels- gifted education program delivery models can be adapted and modified with little or no emphasis on cost.

## BUILDING BRIDGES BETWEEN DUAL LANGUAGE PROGRAMS AND GIFTED EDUCATION

More and more school districts across the United States are just beginning to discover the importance of matching the needs of the students to the most appropriate delivery model while maintaining the integrity and respect of their cultural, ethnic, and linguistic diversity (Castellano, 2002). The program options available to schools and school districts for educating their most able students are numerous. Clark (1992) maintained that among other considerations, the planning necessary to develop a gifted program should provide the best match for the needs of the students. Therefore, special considerations must be given to those students whose primary language is other than English. For students identified as gifted, as well as limited English speaking, dual language programs should be on the short list for consideration. This same option is also viable for gifted students who are monolingual English speakers and who possess advanced levels of verbal ability. Expanding services by connecting dual language programs and gifted education seems to be a logical evolution of both programs because they are very similar. Both programs challenge students academically, in addition to advancing their overall language development. Both programs prepare students to successfully participate in a global society, and both programs advocate a healthy nurturing learning environment, among others.

Over the past few years the popularity of dual language bilingual programs has dramatically increased. In this instructional delivery model speakers of two languages are placed together in a bilingual classroom to learn each other's language and work academically in both languages. Most common in the United States are programs that simultaneously teach Spanish to English background children and English to Hispanics, while cultivating the native language skills of each. This type of enrichment program assumes a pluralistic model in that the goal is to make students bilingual and bi-literate (Kogan, 2001). Gifted education programs across the country are also being proactive in their identification of students who are culturally and linguistically diverse. Some are under orders from the Office for Civil Rights, while others have been awarded federal dollars to make access to gifted education a priority. Both dual language programs and gifted education offer the academic framework that embraces students who are academically talented and excel in language development. In some schools students have access to both. Program similarity allows this to happen.

The outcome for students enrolled in a dual language program is congruent to that of students receiving a gifted education. Specifically, in dual language the outcome is to develop students who can speak, read, and write in two languages at age and grade appropriate levels or beyond, while in gifted education the outcome is to provide an appropriately challenging education for students based on their individual academic and cognitive development. In the field of bilingual education, dual language programs are perceived as effective in promoting advanced academic achievement and language development. The similarities in outcomes and characteristics of effective dual language and gifted education programs is presented in Table 5.4, and the similarities in student characteristics in dual language and gifted education programs is presented in Table 5.5.

Cloud, Genesee, and Hamayan (2000), Gallagher (2002), and Henderson and Berla (1995) asserted that in dual language programming parent involvement is integral to program success. Informing parents and getting them involved from the on-set is important so that they are fully aware of the structure and goals of the program and so they are prepared to make the long-term commitment of time and involvement that successful participation requires. In the world of gifted educa-

TABLE 5.4

Similarities of Outcomes and Characteristics
of Effective Dual Language and Gifted Education Programs

| Dual Language | Gifted Education |
|---|---|
| **Outcome:** To develop students who can speak, read, and write in two languages at age and grade appropriate levels. | **Outcome:** To provide an appropriate education for students based on their individual academic and cognitive development. |

| Characteristics of Effective Programs | |
|---|---|
| *Dual Language* Cloud, Genesee, and Hamayan (2000) | *Gifted Education* Castellano (2004) |
| 1. High level of parental involvement | 1. Community awareness and parental involvement |
| 2. High standards | 2. National standards |
| 3. Strong leadership | 3. Administrative support |
| 4. Program is developmental | 4. Readiness levels |
| 5. Instruction is student-centered | 5. Interest inventories |
| 6. Challenging academic instruction | 6. Pace, complexity, depth |
| 7. Reflective teachers | 7. Teachers ask, "What if?" |
| 8. Integration of programs | 8. Program options |
| 9. Additive environment | 9. Enrichment and acceleration |

TABLE 5.5

Similarities of Outcomes and Characteristics of Students
in Dual Language and Gifted Education Programs

| Dual Language | Gifted Education |
|---|---|
| **Outcome:** To develop students who can speak, read, and write in two languages at age and grade appropriate levels. | **Outcome:** To provide an appropriate education for students based on their individual academic and cognitive development. |

| Characteristics of Students | |
|---|---|
| *Dual Language* Cloud, Genesee and Hamayan (2000) | *Gifted Education* |
| 1. Attitudes towards language | 1. Emotional depth and intensity |
| 2. Motivation to learn | 2. Unusual sensitivity to feelings and expectations of others |
| 3. Personality | 3. Leadership |
| 4. Learning style | 4. Conceptualization of solutions to problems |
| 5. Native language proficiency (single most important predictor of success) | 5. Unusual capacity for processing information. |
| 6. Verbal intelligence | 6. High verbal ability levels |

tion parents have a long-standing history in the education of their own children and of being involved with the schools that serve them. Any successful school-based program typically has a strong level of parental involvement.

Effective programs also have high standards. Dual language programs have clearly defined, well articulated, and challenging standards in all curriculum areas, as well as for second language learning and cultural domains (Teachers of English to Speakers of Other Languages, 1997). The National Association for Gifted Children (NAGC) promotes gifted education program standards and encourages schools that offer a gifted program to aim for excellence by connecting theory with practice. High standards promote equity and excellence and challenge all stakeholders to be the best they can be (Landrum, Callahan, & Shaklee, 2001).

This is essential for the principals of dual language programs who provide the critical leadership that is necessary for the adoption and rigorous implementation of challenging standards in all curriculum domains. Classroom teachers can also demonstrate their leadership by supporting the program by emphasizing the importance of challenging language and content standards so that parents and others are assured that the program is sacrificing nothing (Thomas & Collier, 2001). For administrators and teachers of gifted education programs the same is true. Support is demonstrated for a school's most able, gifted students by allocating the necessary resources and materials that encourage individual academic and cognitive development. In gifted education, this leadership and support is critical because these programs receive no federal categorical funding.

Dual language programs are developmental in nature. That is, they extend and broaden their students' skills and knowledge in developmentally meaningful ways throughout the school years. From the teacher's point of view, instruction that is linked to students' existing development, knowledge, and experiences provides a solid foundation for extending their skills and knowledge in new directions (Cloud et al., 2000; Richard-Amato, 1996). In gifted education the process is generally the same. A gifted student's readiness level allows the teacher to target the curriculum and instruction to meet their individual needs. This information is formally provided in the student's gifted education individual program plan. The services that are provided are supported with resources and materials that are responsive to the readiness abilities of able learners.

One of the most important characteristics of an effective dual language program is that instruction is student centered. In other words, an important starting point for planning instruction is the individual student. Students are different from one another because of differences in their experiential background. Teachers who acknowledge and accept this fact are successfully able to tailor curriculum and instruction that is appropriate for each student. This line of thinking is also a foundation of effective gifted education programs, and is especially important as it impacts those gifted students who are culturally and linguistically diverse, poor, and who have been historically under-represented. A strategy often employed by teachers of the gifted is the administration of an in interest inventory. Information gathered from this exercise allows teachers to recognize areas of personal interest and strengths, thus creating a nurturing instructional environment that is student-centered (Granada, 2003).

Historically, language instruction in dual language programs has been integrated with challenging academic instruction. A basic tenet of language acquisition theory is that a child's cognitive and social development is linked with other areas of development (Howard, Sugarman, & Christian, 2003). For example, as children's cognitive capacities develop, they become increasingly able to use longer utterances and refer to abstract concepts and events that are remote in time and place. At the same time, language development contributes to the developing child's ability to think in abstract term (Cloud, Genesee, & Hamayan, 2000; Howard et al., 2003). In gifted education, challenging academic instruction serves as a program anchor and is reflected in the pace, complexity, and depth of the curriculum. A student's learning needs and the task at hand determine pacing of instruction. Complexity, or difficulty level differs according to individual readiness levels, and depth speaks to the degree of involvement in a topic that the student has a profound interest. Promoting challenging academic instruction helps prepare students to be a successful consumer and participant in today's complex society.

Teachers in effective dual language programs are also reflective. They have a repertoire of assessment techniques they use to obtain feedback about the effectiveness of the teaching and about student learning. Teachers who reflect on their behavior are engaging in a healthy process that allows them to further enhance their skill and ability (Bernal, Perez, & Rode, 1997). "What if?" is a question that teachers of the gifted often contemplate about what they do and the impact they have on the teaching and learning process. Working with academically gifted students is a challenge. Reflection allows teachers to analyze, synthesize, and evaluate their performance with the idea of improving the processes by which they engage their students.

The whole premise of this article is to advocate for integration of programs. The collaboration between dual language programs and gifted education makes sense because they are so compatible. Bridge building of programs in today's public school arena strengthens the foundation of each. It makes them less susceptible to budget cuts and a reallocation of resources.

Finally, dual language bilingual programs foster an additive learning environment. Students are viewed as clever, intelligent, and such an environment supports high expectations and standards for what children can and should learn. An additive bilingual approach is fundamental to the success of dual language programs because it confirms the belief that all children are capable of acquiring proficiency in more than one language if given appropriate learning environment (Cloud, et al., 2000). In gifted education, this same premise is demonstrated through the implementation of lessons that enrich and accelerate students' learning experiences. This instruction is provided in an environment that is nurturing and considers the individual gifts and talents of each student.

## CHARACTERISTICS OF STUDENTS IN DUAL LANGUAGE
## AND GIFTED EDUCATION PROGRAMS

It is not surprising that the characteristics of students participating in dual language and gifted education programs are very similar. Both programs attract our country's best and brightest students. Cloud and collaborators (2000) suggested that individual characteristics that influence success in second language learning include attitudes toward language, motivation to learn, personality, learning style, native language proficiency (which is the single most important predictor of success), and verbal intelligence. Similarly, the characteristics required by gifted students that make them viable participants to receive an advanced education includes an emotional depth and intensity, as well as an unusual sensitivity to feelings and expectations to others. These characteristics speak to their individuality, attitudes, motivation, and personality, are linked to how well they perform in the classroom. Furthermore, gifted students have an unusual capacity for processing information and have developed a more advanced ability to conceptualize solutions to problems. In a program where academic content is presented in a second language the application of these skills would serve them well. Students participating in a gifted program also tend to have high verbal ability levels. Because heir English language proficiency is well beyond their age and grade level, and serves as an important predictor of success, deduction would conclude that they would be good candidates for a dual language program.

## Challenges

As undeserved as it may seem, both dual language and gifted education programs are often perceived as elitist, serving only the most able of students. The challenge presented to administrators, teachers, and parents, as a result, is how to best combat this negative stereotype. To ignore this perception would only perpetuate the problem. Education through a proactive approach would serve to accurately inform others of the need for these school-based program options. Connecting both programs allows schools to successfully account for all students, which is a federal mandate of the No Child Left Behind legislation.

Another challenge facing district and school-based administrators is that of scheduling students to participate in both categorical programs. Elementary schools who offer both programs often require students to choose one over the other, particularly when the gifted education program is a full-time, self-contained classroom model. The conundrum that exists is how to offer the "Best of both worlds" to interested parents and their children. Appropriate and challenging resources and materials is an additional consideration that must be made.

A third challenge that must be addressed centers on training that is necessary for teachers of dual language programs on how to best meet the individual needs of gifted students in both languages. The instructional program of gifted students is dictated by their individual education plans and may reference specific goals, objectives, and strategies. Additional training is the best answer to this challenge. Effective dual language programs often require their teachers to be endorsed in both bilingual education and ESL, and gifted education.

## SUMMARY AND CONCLUSIONS

Kogan (2001) maintained there is no one right way to teach gifted children. No single approach to meeting the needs of the gifted can possibly be right for all schools and communities. The decision as to which scheduled or group strategy, or teaching–learning model, i.e., dual language, are most appropriate should be determined by the characteristics and special education needs as well as upon the availability of specially trained staff, the number of gifted students identified, the physical facilities, and the philosophy of the school district, among others. Although the challenges of educating the gifted bilingual child are numerous, the benefits are many. An educational system that can meet the needs of this population can facilitate the development of a society that is enriched by the linguistic and cultural heritage of all citizens participating in an equitable educational basis.

Dual language and gifted education programs challenge students academically and linguistically, and the outcomes of each prepare these students to successfully participate in a global society that is culturally, ethnically, and linguistically diverse. Programs for gifted, or potentially gifted children, among cultural and/or linguistic groups should be designed to nurture the strengths of students and provide a classroom climate that encourages them to use their skill and talents in productive ways.

## REFERENCES

Bernal, E. M. (2002). Recruiting teachers for bilingual gifted and talented programs. In J. A. Castellano & E. I. Diaz (Eds.), *Reaching new horizons: Gifted and talented education for culturally and linguistically diverse students.* Boston, MA: Allyn and Bacon.

Bernal, E. M., Perez, R. I., & Rode, R. (1997). *Project EXCEL: An elementary school bilingual program for gifted English language learners.* Unpublished manuscript.

Castellano, J. A. (2004). *Connecting dual language programs with gifted education: It just makes sense.* Paper presented at the 33rd Annual International Bilingual Education Conference (NABE): Albuquerque, NM.

Castellano, J. A. (2002). Re-navigating the waters: The identification and assessment of culturally and linguistically diverse students for gifted and talented education. In J. A. Castellano & E. I. Diaz

(Eds.) *Reaching new horizons: Gifted and talented education for culturally and linguistically diverse students*. Boston, MA: Allyn and Bacon.

Castellano, J. A. (2002). Gifted education program options: Connections to English language learners. In J. A. Castellano & E. I. Diaz (Eds.), *Reaching new horizons: Gifted and talented education for culturally and linguistically diverse students*. Boston, MA: Allyn & Bacon.

Castellano, J. A., Faivus, A., & White, W. (2003). Serving the economically disadvantaged in gifted education: The Palm Beach County story. In J. A. Castellano (Ed.), *Special populations in gifted education: Working with diverse gifted learners*. Boston, MA: Allyn and Bacon.

Cenoz, J., & Genesee, F. (1998). Psycholinguistic perspectives on multilingualism and multilingual education. In J. Cenoz & F. Genesee (Eds.), *Beyond bilingualism: Multilingualism and multilingual education* (pp. 16–34). Clevedon, England: Multilingual Matters.

Christian, D., & Genesee, F. (2001). *Bilingual education*. Alexandria, VA: Teachers of English to Speakers of Other Languages (TESOL).

Clark, B. (1992). *Growing up gifted*. New York, NY: Merrill.

Cloud, N., Genesee, F., & Hamayan, E. (2000). *Dual language instruction: A handbook for enriched education*. Boston, MA: Heinle.

Crawford, J. (1997). *Best evidence: Research foundations of the Bilingual Education Act*. Washington, DC: National Clearinghouse on Bilingual Education (NCBE).

Diaz, E. I. (2002). Introduction. In J. A. Castellano & E. I. Diaz (Eds.), *Reaching new horizons: Gifted and talented education for culturally and linguistically diverse students*. Boston, MA: Allyn and Bacon.

Duncan, S. E, & De Avila, E. A. (1986). *Language Assessment Scales (LAS)*. Monterey, CA: CTB/McGraw-Hill.

Gallagher, R. M. (2002). A parent-family involvement model to serve gifted Hispanic English language learners in urban public school settings. In J. A. Castellano & E. I. Diaz (Eds.), *Reaching new horizons: Gifted and talented education for culturally and linguistically diverse students*. Boston, MA: Allyn and Bacon.

Granada, J. (2003). Casting a wider net: Linking bilingual and gifted education. In J. A. Castellano (Ed.), *Special populations in gifted education: Working with diverse gifted learners*. Boston, MA: Allyn and Bacon.

Hakuta, K. (1990). *Bilingualism and bilingual education: A research perspective*. [NCBE Occasional Papers in Bilingual Education, No. 1]. National Clearinghouse on Bilingual Education, Washington, DC.

Howard, E. R., Sugarman, J., & Christian, D. (2003). *Trends in two-way immersion education: A review of the literature. Report 66*. Baltimore, MD: Center for Research on the Education of Students Placed at Risk.

Henderson, A. T., & Berla, N. (1995). *A new generation of evidence: The family is critical to student achievement*. Washington, DC: The Center for Law and Education.

Kogan, E. (2001). *Gifted bilingual students*. New York, NY: Peter Lang Publishing.

Landrum, M. S., Callahan, C. M., & Shaklee, B. D. (2001). *Aiming for excellence: Gifted program standards*. Waco, TX: Prufrock Press.

Lessow-Hurley, J. (2000). *The foundations of dual language instruction*. New York, NY: Longman Press.

Lockwood, A. T. (1997). *Conversations with educational leaders: Contemporary viewpoints on education in America*. Albany, NY: State University of New York Press.

Lindholm, K. (1992). Two-way bilingual/immersion education: Theory, conceptual issues, and pedagogical implications. In R. Padilla & A. Benavides (Eds.), *Critical perspectives on bilingual education research*. Tucson, AZ: Bilingual Review Press.

Richard-Amato, P. (1996). *Making it happen: Interaction in the second language classroom from theory to practice* (2nd edition). White Plains, NY: Pearson Education.

School District of Palm Beach County, Florida (2004). *Limited English proficient students: District plan 2004–05 to 2007–08.* West Palm Beach, FL: Department of Multicultural Education.

Slavin, R. E., & Cheung, A. (2003). Effective reading programs for English language learners: A best-evidence synthesis. *Center for Research on the Education of Students Placed at Risk. Report 66.* http://www.csos.jhu.edu.

Teachers of English to Speakers of Other Languages. (1997). *ESL standards for Pre-K–12 Grade students.* Alexandria, VA: TESOL.

Thomas, W. P., & Collier, V. (2001). *A national study of school effectiveness for language minority students' long-term academic achievement.* Center for Research on Education, Diversity, and Excellence. http://www.crede.ucsc.edu/research/llaa/1.1_final.html.

Thomas, W. P., & Collier, V. (1998). *School effectiveness for language minority students.* Clevedon, England: Multilingual Matters.

United States Department of Education, Office of Educational Research and Improvement. (1993). *National excellence: A case for developing America's talent.* Washington, DC.

United States Department of Education, Office of Educational Research and Improvement. (1998). *Talent and diversity: The emerging world of limited English proficient students in gifted education.* Washington, DC.

# 6

# Educational Challenges and Sociocultural Experiences of Somali Students in an Urban High School

Afra Ahmed Hersi
*Boston College*

## ABSTRACT

As a descriptive cultural case study, the author examined the educational challenges and sociocultural experiences of Somali students in an urban high school. The case study data consisted of in-depth interviews with three participants. Results showed that Somali students had a tremendous need for native language literacy development as well as English language literacy in order to access academic learning. A significant implication for practice suggested by the study was the importance of creating extra academic and psycho-social support for Somali students so that they succeed in the era of high-stakes testing. Schools and educational communities that serve these students must provide professional development for teachers and work collaboratively with organizations and institutions within the Somali community. Additionally, the theoretical implication of the study supported the use of a sociocultural perspective in order to gain insight into the schooling experiences of Somali students.

## INTRODUCTION

Many Somali students in the U.S. have come from war-torn regions in East Africa and have spent many years in refugee camps in Kenya or Ethiopia. As a result of the ongoing civil war in Somalia, many of these students received little or no formal education prior to their arrival in the U.S. (Farah, 2002). Others received some schooling in refugee camps; however, their education was often interrupted

(Friedman, 2002). Once they arrived in the United States, many Somali students and their families experienced a great deal of stress in adjusting to their new country. Towns and cities with large concentrations of Somali residents have struggled to provide educational and social services for students and their families. How schools respond to this tremendous challenge will have a significant impact on the educational and economic achievement of Somali students (August & Hakuta, 1998). For this reason, it is critically important for educators and policy makers to understand the complex factors that affect the educational achievement of these students.

This case study sought to explore the perceptions of three adults with extensive experience working with Somali students. Joseph Sanchez (pseudonym) was a principal of East City High School[1] (ECHS) an urban high school with a large enrollment of Somali students. Ali Nurdin (pseudonym) was a Somali bilingual teacher who had worked with Somali students in the district for eight years. Amina Seynib (pseudonym) was a Somali social worker with experience with a number of state and city agencies that served immigrant and refugee communities. For the past four years, Amina had been working with Somali teens and their families at ECHS.

As a descriptive cultural case study, this research project hoped to describe the participants' understanding of the educational and social issues that confronted Somali students in an urban high school. In addition, the study hoped to identify steps that schools could take to improve the way they serve these students. The following research questions were examined:

- What has been the experience of Somali students in a large urban high school context?
- How has the process of acculturation impacted students?
- What might schools do to improve how they serve Somali students?

## IMMIGRANT CHILDREN IN THE UNITED STATES

According to the 2000 Census, approximately 30 million people in the U.S. were foreign-born (U.S. Census, 2000). In some states, one in five students came from a home in which a language other than English was spoken (Beykont, 2002). Demographic statistics for urban schools, such as in New York City show that more than a hundred different languages are spoken by the student population. In California, nearly 1.5 million students were classified as limited English Proficient (LEP) (Suarez-Orozco & Suarez-Orozco, 2001). This increased in linguistic diversity was not only felt in urban and western parts of the country. Even in rural

---

[1]The name of the school as well its identifying features had been changed.

communities like Dodge City, Kansas, more than 30% of the students enrolled in public schools were the children of immigrants (Suarez-Orozco & Suarez-Orozco, 2001).

Several researchers had highlighted the vast differences in background and experience between the largely white, middle class female teaching force and many students of color, who had a greater chance of living in poverty, and/or speaking a first language other than English (Beykont, 2002; Cochran-Smith, Davis, & Fries, 2003; Ladson-Billings, 1995). In addition, teachers unfamiliar with the experiences of their diverse student population felt unprepared to face the challenges of teaching those whose cultural and linguistic backgrounds were different from their own (Beykont, 2002; Gay, 2002; Ladson-Billings, 1995; Nieto, 1999).

According to the 2000 U.S. Census, nearly 14 million people had limited English proficiency; among these were 3.2 million school age children (5–17 years) (Beykont, 2002). James Crawford (1998), an educational historian and policy researcher, highlighted the enormous educational and economic underachievement of language minorities in the U.S. He noted that culturally and linguistically diverse students were "12 times as likely to have completed less than five years of schooling and were half as likely to have graduated from high school, as compared to native English speakers. In addition, children from such households were 50 percent more likely to live in poverty" (Crawford, 1998, p. 44).

## Refugees in America

Many Somalis entered the U.S. as refugees, escaping their country because, in the words of the Geneva Convention of 1951, "of a well-founded fear of persecution" (Suarez-Orozco & Suarez-Orozco, 2001, p. 25–26). The most fundamental difference between refugees seeking asylum and immigrants coming to a new country is their motivation for migration. Refugees, uprooted from one society and culture to another, migrated in order to flee persecution, imminent violence, and torture and death (Breton, 1999; Haines, 1985). Carola Suarez-Orozco and Marcelo Suarez-Orozco (2001) noted that immigrants who sought "asylum cannot carefully plan their move in the way most immigrants do. Often, when the threat becomes imminent, families must . . . move [to safety] at once."

Immigrants and refugees who were Black often experienced the racism and discrimination that long-term involuntary minorities in the U.S. faced (Suarez-Orozco & Suarez-Orozco, 2001). While such immigrants continue to hold optimistic views about American society and to believe in education as a key to social progress, research involving second-generation immigrants of color suggested that this might be different for the second and third generations (Portes & Rumbaut, 2001). As immigrants transitioned into the larger American society, they often had to deal with ethnic, racial, or language biases that operated within the U.S. (Suarez-Orozco & Suarez-Orozco, 2001). While all immigrants may face structural obstacles, not all groups generated the same attitudes from the dominant culture. For example, immigrants from religious and racial minority communities encountered more inequities and barriers than immigrants from Europe or Asia (Brisk, Hamerla, & Burgos, 2003; Haines, 1985; Nieto, 1999; Rutter & Jones, 1998).

## The Somali Context

According to figures from the 1990's, the East African nation of Somalia had an estimated population of 7.3 million people (Metz, 1992). Early in 1991, the Somali civil war started with the ouster of the Siad Barre regime; plunging the nation into twelve years of turmoil, factional fighting, and anarchy (Lewis, 1965, 2002; Metz, 1992). Since this upheaval, a large number of Somalis, many of them refugee women and children migrated to the U.S., Canada, and Western Europe. Estimates were that nearly 1.5 million Somalis lived outside their country (Farah, 2000). In the U.S., most of the Somali population was concentrated in five major cities: Boston, MA; Columbus, OH; Atlanta, GA; Minneapolis, MN; and San Diego, CA.

Most sources reported that 95% to 98% of the Somali population is Sunni Muslim, the largest denomination of the Islamic religion (Lewis, 1965, 2002; Metz, 1992). The Somali culture was deeply rooted in Islamic culture and had a patriarchal social structure (Farah, 2000). The basis of Somali social structure was the clan–family system, which was traced through patrilineal descent. Social identity in Somali society was tied to clan differentiation rather than race or religion (Farah, 2000). Somalis deeply valued the family; the strength of family ties provided a safety net in times of need. Thus, racial categories were not part of the social meaning and everyday interaction in Somali culture (Lewis, 1965, 2002). Somalis often struggled with labels such as African-American which were applied to them in the U.S. They struggled to maintain their cultural, linguistic and religious identities as they also dealt with the labels, stereotypes, and structural inequities that people of color encountered in the U.S. (MacQuarrie, 2002; Zehr, 2001).

Education was highly valued in Somali society. The Somali language had no written form until 1972 when a Somali script was adopted based on the Roman alphabet. Until that time, English and Italian served as the languages of government and education (Lewis, 1965, 2002). Twelve years of civil war had greatly disrupted the education of an entire generation of Somali children (Farah, 2000; Lewis, 1965, 2002). While some had access to school in refugee camps, parents and family members often had to pay to send their children to school. As a result, boys were more likely than girls to have been exposed to some schooling in the refugee camps (Farah, 2000). These major interruptions in education required school districts serving Somali students to develop programs and strategies for meeting their needs. In order to facilitate the academic achievement of Somali students, educators and community members had to understand the issues and challenges these students faced. This study was undertaken to examine the factors that affected the educational experience of Somali students.

## METHODS

### Setting

Located in a renovated five-story building that used to house a gas company, East City High School was a large urban high school serving 1,156 students. According to state-wide standardized tests, ECHS was a low-performing school. In 2002, 43% of its students failed the English Language Arts section of the exam, while 72% failed the mathematics[2] portion. Like many schools in America's urban centers, East City High's student population was mostly African American (51%) and Hispanic (38%), with a few White (7.2%) and Asian (1.7%) students. A large percentage of the student population came from families with low socioeconomic status, with 75% of the students qualifying for free or reduced lunches.[3] The entire school received Federal Title I funding due to the concentration of poverty.

ECHS, home to the district's multilingual English as a second language (ESL) program and the Somali bilingual program, was one of the more linguistically diverse schools in the city. For example, 60% of the student population spoke a language other than English as its first language. According to Joseph Sanchez, the principal of ECHS, over 28 different languages were spoken in the school. Forty flags, representing the countries of origin of ECHS students, hung from the ceiling of the school's main lobby. According to figures kept by the school, roughly 15% of the student population was made up of Somali immigrants whose families came to the U.S. within the past ten to 12 years.

### Participants

There were three participants in this study: (a) Joseph Sanchez, a high school principal; (b) Ali Nurdin, a Somali bilingual teacher; (c) and Amina Seynib, a Somali social worker. The informants were selected based on their extensive experience of working with Somali students. At the age of 16, Joseph immigrated to the U.S. from Cape Verde with his family. He finished high school in the same city school district in which he was currently employed. After graduating from college and a

---

[2]Data based on the school report card prepared by the state department of education. For the purposes of this article, the name of the school and the school district were kept confidential to protect the anonymity of the participants.

[3]Data based on the school report card prepared by the state department of education.

period of service in the Army National Gaurd, Joseph began teaching in mathematics in middle school. For most of his professional experience, Joseph had
worked in middle schools; first as a math teacher, then as an assistant administrator and finally as a principal. As a middle school administrator, Joseph was recognized for his leadership and his commitment to student achievement. In 2000, the
superintendent of the school district appointed Joseph as principal of ECSH. This
was a very challenging assignment. The State Department of Education (DOE)
was considering taking over the management of the school do to poor performance on the state standardized test.

Amina Seynib was a Somali social worker who worked at the school as part of a
collaboration between Oak Street Health Clinic (pseudonym), a family health clinic
operated by a major medical school in the city, and ECHS. She worked as an adjustment counselor for all of the African refugee students, who were mostly Somali,
Sudanese, and Liberian. She described herself as a Kenyan Somali and was fluent
in Somali, Swahili, Arabic, and English. As a member of a wealthy Somali mer-
chant family living in Nairobi, Kenya, Amina did not describe herself as a refugee.
After the war, she worked with the United Nations High Commissioner for Refugees, helping to settle Somali refugees that had fled to safety in Northern Kenya.
In 1996, Amina immigrated to the U.S. with her husband and five children.

Ali Nurdin was a bilingual teacher who had been working with the Somali bilingual program at ECHS for eight years. Ali was a graduate student in the U.S.
when the Somali civil war broke out. During the early days of the war, his wife
and son were in the northern Somali city of Hargaso when it was bombed. He explained that after weeks of shelling, they were able to leave on the second to the
last plane to depart the city. Reunited with his family, Ali finished his Masters degree in international development and began to seek employment. Fairly quickly,
he found employment with the public schools because there was a great need for
bilingual teachers. He returned to school for a second Masters degree in education
with a concentration in secondary history. Ali was one of the first Somali teachers
brought in to help construct the Somali bilingual program in the district. After two
years working with the program, Ali returned to school for a certification in ESL,
and for his third Masters degree. Because of the lack of educational resources in
Somali, Ali found himself creating and translating much of the materials used in
the program. For example, he designed a test to assess native language proficiency of Somali students when they entered the building. Because of his service
to students in the school, Ali was respected and well liked by his colleagues and
the Somali community.

## Reflexivity

Social science researchers have long understood that the qualitative researcher
who describes, interprets, or explains human behavior brings certain assumptions,
lenses, and biases to the task. To minimize researcher bias, the participants were

encouraged to voice their thoughts and beliefs, and every effort by the researcher to adhere as closely as possible to the participants' own words (Knafl & Webster, 1988). I assumed a reflective research stance, making explicit my experiences and assumptions and how they might have impacted my approach to this study.

As a Somali immigrant, an educator, and a researcher, I have a very personal connection to this topic and a unique insider perspective. First, as a nine-year old immigrant, I experienced the stress, confusion, excitement, and, the anger of leaving behind everything that was familiar in order to come to a country and culture profoundly different from my own. Second, the informants in this study were perhaps more open and willing to share their insights with me due to my insider status as a Somali immigrant and as an educator. Finally, prior to this study, I spent one year working as a tutor for the Somali bilingual program at the school site; therefore, I had the opportunity to learn about the school culture and get to know many of the school staff that work with Somali students. For example, as one of the few Somali adults in the school, I would often act as a translator for Somali parents, students and administrators. By working at ECHS, I learned a great deal about the school culture, built good relationships with teachers and administrators, and was able to provide a service to the school, parents and students.

## Data Collection Procedure

Each of the participants agreed to participate in the study through an informed consent process. The participants were each interviewed twice in a semi-structured interview format for approximately 40 minutes. The interviews took place in the participants' place of work. A general interview protocols was used during the first interview, and after the tapes were transcribed verbatim, follow-up interview questions were generated. The interview data from the three participants were triangulated with field notes from class observations and visits to ECHS' after-school program. Data collection took place between February and May 2002.

## Data Analysis

A descriptive cultural case study design was used to explore the complex issues surrounding educators' perceptions about schooling experience of Somali students. As Sandelowsky noted "qualitative descriptive studies offer a comprehensive summary of events in everyday terms" (p. 336). A case study design allows for greater understanding through a close examination of a particular incident or case (Rossman & Rallis, 1998). Content analysis method was used to analyze data, providing "a systematic and objective means to make valid inferences from verbal, visual, or written data in order to describe and quantify specific phenomena" (Downe-Wamboldt, 1992, p. 314). To begin the content analysis, I listened to and carefully transcribed the interviews of the three participants (Easton, McComish, & Greenberg, 2000). I followed Downe-Wamboldt's (1992) steps for

content analysis research as a general guide (p. 315) during the analysis procedure. The interview transcripts and the field notes were entered into a Windows
Word document, and Morse's (1991) procedures for conducting data analysis
with a word processor was used as a guide to prepare interview transcripts, to
code, and to sort ideas into categories. The unit of analysis was set as a phrase,
consisting of one or more words that convey a complete thought or meaning. In
order to achieve reliability coded data was refined and tested until the text was ex-
hausted. Additionally, reliability was improved by coding the data twice (Downe-
Wamboldt, 1992; Knafl & Webster, 1988). Initially I developed 25 codes from
the data, and as further analysis was carried out, the initial 25 codes were col-
lapsed into ten categories. Finally, I relied on the work of Brisk and collaborators
(2003) and Suarez-Orozco and Suarez-Orozco (2001) frame the final five categories: (1) educational challenges, (2) acculturation and the struggle for belonging,
(3) navigating the sociocultural contexts, (4) confronting cultural and religious
bias, and (5) meeting the challenge by providing possible solutions.

## FINDINGS

### The Educational Challenge

Somali students confronted overwhelming educational challenges in the classrooms and hall corridors of ECHS. The educational challenges could be organized
into two major areas of need: the need for native language literacy and the need
for English language literacy. The first area of need focused on students' educational background, whether or not they had schooling experience prior to coming
to the U.S. While many Somali students entered American schools with major interruptions in their education, others had not attended school at all. Along with native language literacy, the second area of need Somali students had was the need
to develop the English language proficiency in order to access academic learning.
For Somali students who arrived as adolescents, state standardized testing created
an intense pressure to acquire English and grade-level content knowledge in order
to graduate high school.

### Native Language Literacy

Many Somali students had little access to education because of the civil war in
Somalia and the time they spent in refugee camps in Kenya and Ethiopia. Amina,
who worked as an adjustment counselor with many of the schools' refugee students, noted that some students from Africa, which included Somalis, Liberians,
and Sudanese, faced a unique challenge because "they were in refugee camps . . .
they have never been to school." As was the case for many immigrants, when Somali students arrived in the U.S., they were placed in classes that were age appro-

priate, rather than academically appropriate. Ali, who taught a Somali literacy class, explained that some of his students had "never held a pencil . . . [or] learned to write their name in Somali." ECHS's Somali bilingual program, which served as many as 170 students, offered such students literacy and content instruction in Somali. However, as a Transitional Bilingual Education Program (TBE), students were expected to enter mainstream classes within two or three years.

## English Language Proficiency

Somali students' lack of native language literacy had a profound impact on the acquisition of English language proficiency and the development of content knowledge, such as science, math, and history. Therefore, for many Somali students, native language coupled with English language instruction was critical. As Ali explained,

> Lack of English language proficiency was a problem [for students]. Even if the student had a good educational background, still he would not be able to follow along in many of the mainstream classes because of language [issue]. Language was a key factor. . . . it was of no help to throw him in a class without giving him [solid] language support.

While Somali students made enormous gains in the bilingual program, many consistently remained years behind their classmates. According to Amina, many Somali students were discouraged by the linguistic and academic difficulties they encountered in these mainstream classes. For example, she noted that students "suddenly hit a wall" after they entered mainstream classes. Despite working hard in school for 5 years, many Somali students' academic and English development remained behind their peers. These students struggled to pass the state graduation test and were at risk for dropping out. Joseph noted that students who had been in the U.S. for two to three years experienced the highest rates of failure in the state graduation test. Although students may repeat the test as often as five times before they achieve a passing score, it is not uncommon for students become discouraged and drop out of school.

## High-Stakes High School Diplomas

For Somali adolescents, the dream of a high school diploma was particularly difficult to achieve during the age of national and state standards. Students faced the enormous challenge of learning a second language, and studying subject matter content, in language not yet mastered. This challenge was complicated by state and national school reform effort, which mandated that students' pass a standardized test in order to receive a high school diploma. Joseph noted that the state standardized graduation test was an ever present and a constant pressure [on everyone]. Students [had] to pass [the test to graduate]. [This was] huge pressure on us, [and] pressure on the kids and their families. A lot of things [were] at stake, our jobs, [and] how we conduct things in school.

Students and the school officials faced tremendous pressure to produce passing scores on these standardized tests. This pressure was felt as "ever present", resulting in "high stakes"; if a student does not pass the MCAS he or she would not get a high school diploma. The stakes were also high for educators, with "jobs" on the line. In this high stakes context, progress was not enough. As more and more of these students struggled to pass the graduation test, the school sent them a subtle message that making progress and learning was not enough. Both Joseph and Amina expressed concern about the possibility of increased school drop out among Somali students.

## Acculturation and the Struggle for Belonging

Each of the participants in the study expressed concern about Somali students' acculturation or the "process of learning new cultural rules and interpersonal expectations" (Suarez-Orozco & Suarez-Orozco, 2001, p. 73). Somali students experienced alienation and dislocation as a result of being in a different culture and society while at the same time adjusting to the challenge of going to high school. The sociocultural transitions of immigration to the United States were complicated by Somali students' experience of loss and displacement as a result of the civil war and famine. Ali noted that for many of his students, the flight for safety and "displacement and refugee status started long before they arrived" in the U.S. Ali explained their desperate journey to safety

> Many of my students [told] stories of how they ran away from Mogadisho . . . to Merca, then went to Kismayo . . . then [they went] back to Mogadisho, And then go back to Kismayo . . . then . . . all the way to the Kenyan border, . . . then [they] crosseds the Kenyan border. [They stayed] in Kenya [for] three to four years, and finally, [they were] resettled in [U.S.]

Indeed, many of the students and their families might have spent six to seven years displaced within Somalia and/or living in a refugee camp in Kenya or Ethiopia. Thus, Somali students' transition into American society and schools were complicated by the distance between the American and Somali cultures. Joseph notes that for "Somali students, the biggest challenge was . . . 'culture shock'. That is, the shock of coming to a new culture and new country, [the] struggle . . . between . . . home [culture] and . . . the school" [culture]. He explained that Somali students were "from . . . very traditional, structured, Muslim families. [Once they left] home, [Somali students entered a] . . . commercial world [dominated by] peer pressure, and the [popular] culture." They struggled to forge new identities, and negotiate their roles in both their home and new culture. As Joseph noted, students struggled with central questions such as

Who am I? Who do I follow? . . . Do I continue to wear my traditional garments, or do I look [more] American . . . jeans, and bagging pants. Do I get involved with the culture of drugs, drinking, not [going] to school, or do I to try my best?

There was a real concern about Somali students' possibly taking-up the negative attitudes and risky behavior. Drugs and teen pregnancy were a real risk for Somalis adolescents. Most Somali teens respected the Islamic religion's prohibition against drugs and alcohol, but some students fell into serious drug and alcohol abuse use. Although cultural prohibitions limited pre-marital sex, peer-pressure and the desire to fit in might lead some students to engage in risky sexual behavior.

Ali noted that the young adjusted much faster in "to the new culture" than Somali adults. The different rates of acculturation resulted in a situation in which the children acted as translators and interpreted for their families. Amina explained that "sometimes only the children speak English" which meant that they often "spoke for their parents." She noted this was a great source of trouble in some families, especially when, "teenagers and the parents disagreed." According to Amina, parents worried that their children would "lose" their culture, language, and religion by becoming "too American." This stress of acculturation and tension associated with children fitting in to the American culture created a "real crisis" for many Somali families.

## Navigating the Sociocultural School Context

Another factor that contributed to the educational challenges and problems experienced by Somali students was related to the cultural norms and expectations in the school. Both Ali and Amina noted that certain behaviors were acceptable in American schools, yet were unacceptable in Somali homes, such as making eye contact with elders. Likewise, some behaviors that were rewarded in Somali homes were viewed negatively in American school context. For example, Amina counseled three girls who had attempted to use the girl's restroom sink to wash their feet in an effort to carry out *wudu*, ritual of washing before prayer. The girls' efforts to adhere to their Islamic faith would be a great source of pride for their parents and families. However, in the school context, such a behavior violated American socially accepted behavior.

In addition to differences in cultural norms and expectations, many Somali students also faced linguistic and cultural barriers when they interact with teachers and school officials. Somali students and parents were unfamiliar with the American educational system. Amina noted that sometimes Somali students and their parents did not understand that the school must be "notified if a child was absent from school". A child may get a number of unexcused absences resulting in a failure in class before it was determined that the parents did not understand they had to call or send a note to school if their child was absent. Both Amina and Ali noted the lack of experience with the American education system and the language barrier were major challenges to parents as they interacted with schools. Ali noted that "many parents did not speak English", and they were not able to "help" their children with homework.

Moreover, students encountered difficulties in school when they did not understand school policies or class expectations. For example, a bright Somali eleventh-grade student complained about zeros on his math homework, despite working with a tutor. A meeting with the math teacher revealed that the student was getting zeros on his homework because he failed to label his assignment in the specific way the teacher required. The teacher continued to mark his assignments as zeros, expecting the student to ask why and the student to take corrective measures. Respectful of elders, and ashamed for doing poorly in class, the student felt he could not question the teacher. Clearly in this situation, the teacher and the student were affected by cultural and educational miscommunication. After giving the direction two or three times, the teacher felt the student should have "gotten it" while the student had no idea why his assignment continued to receive zeros. It was not until Amina and Ali intervened by setting up a meeting with the student and the teacher that steps were taken to resolve the issue.

## Confronting Cultural and Religious Bias

Another problem facing Somali students in school was related to the issue of cultural and religious bias. There have been a number of fights involving Somali and African American students in the school. In the fall of 2001, shortly after the September 11th bombing of New York City and Washington, D.C., tension between African American and Somali students at ECH erupted into violence. According to Joseph, the conflict began "over an earring" and led to the "arrest of five girls and one boy." He explained that the fight began in the gym when a group of African American boys and girls taunted four Somali girls about their traditional Muslim scarves and ankle length-skirts. From the gym, the conflict made its way to the fifth floor, where the fight eventually erupted. While Joseph and Ali both attributed much of the fighting to personal issues involving a handful of girls, Amina called the fight a "hate crime" and "major display of intolerance."

The tensions at East City High reflected the overall tension and apprehension felt by members of the Somali community in the city. During the same week of the fight at the school, local and national media were filled with stories about alleged Somali connections to Osama bin Laden and Al-Qaida. Muslim women, wearing the *hijab* reported being harassed on the trains and in their neighborhoods. Although it began in the fall of 2001, this tension could still be felt in the school during the spring of 2002. While I was visiting the school, the police were called twice to break-up fighting between Somali students and African-American students.

## Meeting the Challenge: Possible Solutions

East City High School was fortunate to have a partnership with three organizations that serve the immigrant and refugee community: Refugee Settlement Agency, Somali Community Agency, and the Chestnut Street Clinic. The three non-profit organizations provided social, psychological, and educational adjustment support for refugees. This collaboration resulted in the creation of the Somali Teen Program (STP) (pseudonym), which operates out of the ECHS. STP was a drop-in program, which meant that students did not have to make an extensive commitment. With volunteer tutors from colleges across the city and retired teachers, Somali students received reading and math remediation, preparation for the state standardized test, and help with their homework assignments. In addition to the tutoring support, the Refugee Settlement Agency and the Somali Community Agency held workshops on health and social issues. In the past two years, Ali noted that the non-Somali immigrant and refugee "students were using the tutoring services of the after-school program."

In addition to the academic support provided through STP, Chestnut Street Clinic offered medical and mental health services for Somali students and their families. Amina has been coming to the school three times a week for three years, as an social adjustment counselor. She met with students one-one-one, ran group counseling sessions, and worked with teachers and school student support team meetings. Amina explained that a major goal of the collaboration was to provide social and psychosocial services for those who need it. She stated that the collaborative team "helped the youth with counseling . . . [provide] support groups . . . to teach them [to cope with] low self-esteem . . . communication, and conflict solutions." This unique collaboration offers innovative solutions to the complex psycho-social and educational problems that Somali students encounter.

## DISCUSSION

The educational experience and performance of Somali students was affected by a number of educational, sociocultural, and political factors (Brisk et al., 2003; Suarez-Orozco & Suarez-Orozco, 2001). As with most immigrant students, Somali students' academic achievement depended on the quality of the education they received in school, and the sociocultural and political contexts they encountered within the school and the larger society (Brisk et al., 2003).

## Educational Factors

The quality of a school impacted the educational achievement and social integration of immigrant students. Research had demonstrated that when students were placed in effective schools with well-prepared teachers who were knowledgeable about effective instruction, those from cultural and linguistically diverse backgrounds performed well in school (Farstrup & Samuels, 2002; Pressley, 2000; Snow, Burns, & Griffin, 1998). However, urban schools such as ECHS were often unprepared to meet the educational needs of immigrant children (Suarez-Orozco & Suarez-Orozco, 2001). These students were often taught by teachers with little experience or professional development in providing effective instruction and support for immigrant students (August & Hakuta, 1998; Beykont, 2002). In the past, the responsibility for educating immigrant students was assigned to specialists, e.g. ESL teachers or bilingual teachers like Ali (August & Hakuta, 1998). However, the rapidly increasing population of culturally and linguistically diverse students and a shortage of trained ESL/bilingual teachers have created a situation for teachers with little or no professional training to serve second language learners (August & Hakuta, 1998; Henke, Chen, & Goldman, 1999).

Somali students faced tremendous challenges as they acquired the language, academic skills, and knowledge necessary to succeed in school. Many of these students entered school with significant gaps in their educational backgrounds. They had a great need for literacy and content instruction in their native language. Over a decade of war and displacement had meant that Somali students were often illiterate in their native language. Researchers had stated that students with limited or interrupted education often struggled academically (Beykont, 2002; Henke et al., 1999). As Thomas and Collier (2002) noted "the strongest predictor of [second language] achievement [was] the amount of formal [native language] schooling" (p. 9). Many Somali students entered school in the U.S. never having "learned to write their name in Somali." For these students, the linguistic and academic support provided in the Somali bilingual program at ECHS was invaluable.

Second language proficiency must be considered in terms of relative development (Birch, 2002; Brisk et al., 2003). Language proficiency included the ability to function in school both socially and academically (Brisk et al., 2003). Regardless of grade-level or age, Somali students' English language proficiency had to be seen developmentally; it was necessary to determine whether a student was a beginner, or at an intermediate, or advanced level in his or her knowledge of the English language. More often, school districts used inappropriate assessment instruments that did not consider the length of students exposure to English (Brisk et al., 2003). Thus, Somali students were placed in certain grade levels or in mainstreamed classes despite their limited English proficiency and content knowledge. Researchers noted that it took five to seven years to develop the proficiency necessary for academic learning in a second language (Brisk et al., 2003; Cummins, 2003; Gass & Selinker, 2001). Students with limited English proficiency lagged behind academically and experienced difficulties with reading and writing (August & Hakuta, 1998; Gersten, 1999; Jimenez, 2002). Moreover, these students were at a greater risk for academic failure and dropping out of school (August & Hakuta, 1998; Hodgkinson, 2000; Jimenez, 2002).

## Sociocultural Factors

The educational achievement of Somali students was supported or constrained by sociocultural factors they encountered living in the U.S. While these sociocultural transitions challenged most immigrants, research has found that the sociocultural distance between cultural of origin and host culture was one of the factors that influenced the degree of successful integration of refugee students (Suarez-Orozco & Suarez-Orozco, 2001). As Portes and Rumbaut (2001) noted, "the more similar new minorities [were] in terms of physical appearance, class background, language, and religion to society's mainstream, the more favorable their reception and the more rapid their integration" (p.47). The marginalization of immigrant students of color, particularly those living in urban communities, often lead to the adoption of an oppositional stance that viewed schooling as an instrument of oppression (Portes & Rumbaut, 2001). In essence, these students "learned to not learn" (Suarez-Orozco & Suarez-Orozco, 2001).

As a whole, the three participants in the study expressed a great deal of compassion for Somali students who faced tremendous difficulties in American schools. It was not uncommon to find that the Somali parents of these students were also undergoing difficulties: adjusting to the mainstream culture, finding employment, and learning the language. Exacerbating the situation, were the intergenerational conflicts between Somali students, who were acculturating to American society, and their parents, who were more traditional in their values. Portes and Rambaut (2001) referred to this phenomenon as "role reversal . . . , when children's acculturation moved so far ahead of their parents' that key family decisions become dependent on the children's knowledge" (p. 53). Successful integration was "associated with a relative lack of intergenerational conflict, the presence of many co-ethnics among children's friends, and the achievement of full bilingualism" (Portes & Rambaut, 2001, p. 54).

Somali students wanted and needed to understand the American system of schooling. For example, Somali students needed to understand how to keep safe by developing the cultural and interpersonal skills to avoid conflict and solve problems. According to Amina, sometimes Somali students and their parents did not understand that the school must be notified if a child was absent. Because many Somali parents struggled with English and with understanding American institutions, they often lacked the human and social capital necessary to help their children with homework or to interact with school officials on behalf their children (Portes & Rumbaut, 2001). School officials needed to take proactive steps to make school rules and policies explicit for parents and their children. The Somali non-profit organization, Somali Women and Children, one of East City High

School's collaborating partners, often helped the school to communicate with parents and students.

## Political Factors

Research had found that the level of acceptance some immigrants received from the host culture impacted their experience (Haines, 1985; Suarez-Orozco & Suarez-Orozco, 2001). Issues of religious and cultural discrimination were of great concern for Somali students. In the post 9–11 context, Somali students experienced harassment and discrimination in school. Suarez-Orozco and Suarez-Orozco (2001) argued that immigrant children have a critical need for a culture of acceptance and tolerance in schools, particularly from their teachers. Fights between Somali students and African American students at East City High School were dismissed by school officials as conflict between a "few girls", so it was not clear if there were genuine steps taken to create a better culture in the school. Clearly, Somali students, as well as other students in the school, would benefit from such a move.

The national accountability movement created an additional challenge for Somali students. This politically motivated policy initiative narrowly defined academic success as passing a standardized test. In the era of standards and high-stakes testing, significant educational progress still may not amount to passing scores. Students with only two to three years of schooling were required to pass the state graduation test in order to receive a high school diploma. This type of unfair policy illustrated the need for advocacy. Clearly, Somali students with interrupted or limited educational experiences would encounter tremendous difficulty with standardized tests measuring content and literacy knowledge and skills in English.

Overall, a majority of the student population at ECHS was not passing the state graduation test. In 2002, a staggering percentage of students did not pass the gradation test: 43% failed and 44% needed improvement in English language arts, while 72% failed and 23% needed improvement in mathematics. School districts and in particular, building administrators were under pressure to raise student scores. As Joseph noted, school officials "jobs were on the line"; the stakes were high for both students and educators. As students struggled to pass the graduation test, there were valid concerns among teachers and parents that Somali students and other at-risk students might drop-out of school after repeatedly failing the graduation test.

## CONCLUSIONS

Somali young people in urban schools struggled with past experiences of war, chaos, and flight, in addition to the ongoing challenges of acculturation and second language acquisition. At the same time, Somali teenagers faced the same adolescent pressures as American born counterparts: street violence, drug and alcohol abuse, teen pregnancy and gangs. The Somali Teen Program, its collaborating partners, staff and volunteers, kept young people safe, healthy and provided tremendous educational and psycho-social support. With the right kind of support, Somali students developed strategies for succeeding in school and making better choices as they built a new life in America. The after-school program was a safe zone for many Somali students, a place for them to be with other Somali students who might be going through similar transitions. It is also a place to work with adults and interact with fellow students from other cultures.

## SIGNIFICANCE AND IMPLICATIONS OF THE STUDY

As an initial exploration of the topic, this case study has implications for theory and practice. First, there is little available research on the educational and sociocultural experiences of Somali students. As more research involving Somali students is generated, it is important to develop a theoretical framework to understand the concepts and issues involved. A potential theoretical implication of this case study is the use of a sociocultural perspective to examine Somali students' educational and sociocultural experiences. Such a theoretical orientation has the potential to generate insight into specific issues and challenges Somali students encounter.

The study has several implications for schools that serve Somali students. First, as students with interrupted education, Somali high school students have needs that may not be addressed by traditional approaches to educating immigrant students. While some immigrant students might only need English language instruction and support, Somali students may have significant gaps in their content knowledge. For these students, extra academic and psychosocial support was critical if they were to succeed in the era of high-stakes testing. Second, the challenges facing schools with Somali students were many, thus the efforts to meet them must be multileveled and collaborative. While the schools had ethical and moral obligations to educate all students, the responsibility should not fall only upon the schools. Schools should work in collaboration with community organizations and institutions that serve the Somali community. These organizations could contribute much needed resources and knowledge to the school.

## LIMITATIONS OF THE STUDY

The qualitative data used in this descriptive cultural case study only included the perceptions of three adults who have worked with Somali students in an urban high school. Thus, the findings cannot be generalized beyond the case studied. Additionally, the type of data analysis used in this study (content analysis), can only reveal low inference categories. A further exploration of this topic, involving Somali students and parents would provide better insight into their lived experience.

## REFERENCES

August, D., & Hakuta (Eds.). (1998). *Educating language-minority children.* Washington, D.C.: National Academy Press.

Beykont, Z. F. (Ed.). (2002). *The power of culture: Teaching across language difference.* Cambridge, MA: Harvard Educational Publishing Group.

Birch, B. M. (2002). *English L2 reading.* Mahwah, NJ: Lawrence Erlbaum Associates.

Breton, M. (1999). The Relevance of the structural approach to group work with immigrant and refugee women. *Social Work with Groups, 22*(2), 11–29.

Brisk, M. E., Hamerla, S. R., & Burgos, A. (2003). *Situational context of education: A window into the world of bilingual learners.* Mahwah, NJ: Lawrence Erlbaum Associates.

Cochran-Smith, M., Davis, D., & Fries, M. K. (2003). Multicultural teacher education research practice and policy. In J. Banks & C. M. Banks (Eds.), *The handbook of research on multicultural education* (2nd ed.). San Francisco: Jossey Bass.

Crawford, J. (1998). *Best evidence: Research foundations of the bilingual education act.* Washington D.C.: National Clearinghouse for Bilingual Education.

Cummins, J. (2003). BICS and CALP: Origins and rationale for the distinction. In C. B. Paulston & G. R. Tucker (Eds.), *Sociolinguistics: The essential readings* (pp. 322–328). Malden, MA: Blackwell.

Downe-Wamboldt, B. (1992). Content analysis: Method, applications, and issues. *Health Care for Women International, 13*, 313–321.

Easton, K. L., McComish, J. F., & Greenberg, R. (2000). Avoiding common pitfalls in qualitative data collection and transcription. *Qualitative Health Research, 10*(5), 703–707.

Farah, M. H. (2002). Reaping the benefits of bilingualism: The case of Somali refugee students. In Z. F. Beykont (Ed.), *Lifting every voice: Pedagogy and politics of bilingualism.* Cambridge: Harvard Educational Publishing Group.

Farah, N. (2000). *Yesterday, tomorrow: Voices from the Somali diaspora.* New York: Cassell.

Farstrup, A. E., & Samuels, S. J. (Eds.). (2002). *What research has to say about reading instruction* (3rd ed.). Newark, Delaware: International Reading Association.

Friedman, A. A. (2002). Agents of literacy change: working with Somali students in an urban middle school. In Z. F. Beykont (Ed.), *The Power of culture: Teaching across language difference.* Cambridge: Harvard Educational Publishing Group.

Gass, S. M., & Selinker, L. (Eds.). (2001). *Second language acquisition: An introductory course.* Mahwah, NJ: Lawrence Erlbaum Associates.

Gay, F. (2002). Preparing for culturally responsive teaching. *Journal of Teacher Education, 53*, 106–116.

Gersten, R. (1999). Lost opportunities: Challenges confronting four teachers of English-language learners. *The Elementary School Journal, 100*(1), 37–56.

Haines, D. W. (Ed.). (1985). *Refugees in the United States: A reference handbook.* London: Greenwood Press.

Henke, R. R., Chen, X., & Goldman, G. (1999). *What happens in classrooms? Instructional practices in elementary and secondary schools, 1994–1995.* Washington D.C.: National Center for Educational Statistics, U.S. Department of Education, Office of Educational Research and Improvement.

Hodgkinson, H. (2000). *Secondary schools in a new millennium: Demographic certainties, social realities.* Reston, VA: National Association of Secondary School Principals.

Jimenez, R. T. (2002). Fostering the literacy development of Latino students. *Focus on Exceptional Children, 34*(6), 1–10.

Knafl, K., & Webster, D. (1988). Managing and analyzing qualitative data: A description of tasks, techniques, and materials. *Western Journal of Nursing Research.*

Ladson-Billings, G. (1995). Toward a theory of culturally relevant pedagogy. *American Educational Research Journal,* (32), 465–491.

Lewis, I. M. (1965, 2002). *A modern history of the Somali: Revised, updated and expanded.* Oxford: James Curry.

MacQuarrie, B. (2002). New Arrivals put strain on Lewiston. *Boston Globe,* 1–3.

Metz, H. C. (1992). *Somalia: A country study* (Report). Washington DC: Library of Congress.

Morse, J. (1991). Analyzing unstructured, interactive interviews using the MacIntosh computer. *Qualitative Health Research, 1,* 117–122.

Nieto, S. (1999). *The Light in their eyes: Creating multicultural learning communities.* New York: Teachers College Press.

Portes, A., & Rumbaut, R. G. (2001). *The story of the immigrant second generation.* Berkeley: University of California Press.

Pressley, M. (2000). What should comprehension instruction be the instruction of? In R. Barr (Ed.), *Handbook of reading research* (Vol. III, pp. 545–561). Mahwah, NJ: Lawrence Erlbaum Associates.

Rossman, G. B., & Rallis, S. F. (1998). *Learning in the field: An introduction to qualitative research.* Thousand Oaks: Sage Publications.

Rutter, J., & Jones, C. (Eds.). (1998). *Refugee education: mapping the field.* Staffordshire: Trentham Books Limited.

Snow, C. E., Burns, S. M., & Griffin, P. (Eds.). (1998). *Preventing reading difficulties.* Washington, D.C.: National Academy Press.

Suarez-Orozco, C., & Suarez-Orozco, M. (2001). *Children of Immigrants.* Cambridge, MA: Harvard University Press.

Thomas, W. P., & Collier, V. P. (2002). *A national study of school effectiveness for language minority students' long-term academic achievement.* Santa Cruz: Center for Research on Educational, Diversity and Excellence, University of California, Santa Cruz.

Zehr, M. A. (2001). Out of Africa. *Education Week,* 30–40.

# 7

# A Model for Training
# Bilingual School Counselors

Rick A. Bruhn, Beverly J. Irby,
Mei Luo, and W. Tom Thweatt, III
*Sam Houston State University*

Rafael Lara-Alecio
*Texas A&M University*

## ABSTRACT

Bilingual counselors are needed as essential school staff who speak the "emotional language" of English language learners and their parents. In a project funded by the United States Department of Education, a model was created for adapting a school counseling master's program to train bilingual counselors. The curriculum emphasized collaboration between the school district and the university, action research, developing guidance and parent involvement programs, field-based instruction, mentor training, and post-degree induction supervision to maximize practical application and effectiveness. Through the project, Spanish-speaking teachers learned and practiced school counselor roles and functions focused toward helping Spanish-speaking students and their parents succeed in the education process.

## A MODEL PROGRAM FOR TRAINING
## BILINGUAL COUNSELORS

When a school counselor enters the building on any given day, he/she may be asked to (a) respond to crises in classrooms or the halls, (b) provide individual and guidance counseling, (c) disseminate information on career opportunities or test results, (d) plan schedules for middle and high school students; (e) deliver developmental guidance materials and in-service training, coordinated with the priorities of the school and district, (f) serve as a mediator (or teach students and teachers to serve as peer mediators), (g) offer consultation, (h) develop crisis intervention, (i) network with the community and agencies, (k) communicate empathetically with students, teachers, administrators, and parents, and (l) offer group counseling to angry children, depressed teens, or to students from homes where there has been a recent divorce (Texas Education Agency, 1998). School counselors may do those activities and even more on any given day (Blum, 1998; Gysbers & Henderson, 2000; Texas Education Agency, 1998). Otwell and Mullis (1997) indicated that the "purpose of school counseling is to facilitate the instructional process and students' academic success" (p. 343).

## Counselors, Student Outcomes, and Cultural Considerations

The literature reports a number of outcomes from having a counselor on the school campus. A review of professional literature covering 30 years led Borders and Drury (1992) to conclude, "School counseling interventions have a substantial impact on students' educational and personal development" (p. 495). A more conservative view was taken by Whitson and Sexton (1998) in their review of school counseling outcome research from 1988 to 1995. They suggested that, while school counseling activities often result in positive outcomes for students, methodological problems and the omission of some common activities performed by school counselors prevented more definitive statements about the outcomes produced.

In order to provide positive outcomes for English language learner (ELL) students due to school counseling activities, it is important to consider the impact of changing population demographics, and the growing recognition of how a dominant male European American worldview permeates many aspects of counseling practice (Katz, 1985; Sue & Zane, 1987). There appear to be cultural biases of theory that would impact practice of counselors (Hall, 1997; Harris, 1996; Pedersen, 1997; Sue & Sue, 1990; Sue & Zane, 1987). According to Behring and Ingraham (1998), most counseling studies, particularly those including consultation, between 1988 and 1998 were authored by European Americans and conducted primarily with European American clients. They indicated it was very likely that European American values also were embedded throughout the counseling field. Furthermore, they expressed concern of not knowing if current counseling consultation theories and techniques are equally effective or appropriate for other culturally distinctive groups. A challenge for counselor educators is to prepare prospective counselors to effectively serve ELL students.

The growing, distinctive group of ELL students comes from the 34 million Hispanics in the U.S., accounting for 12% of the total population (U. S. Census Bureau, 2004). Both the increase in immigration (Santiago-Rivera, 1995) and the high birth rate (Cofresi & Gorman, 2004) make the Hispanic population the fastest growing minority group in the United States. Future projections indicate that by the year 2050, one in every five Americans will be Hispanic (U. S. Census Bureau, 2004).

These population projections give credence to the notion that school counselors will be more and more frequently called on to intervene with Hispanic children (Baruth & Manning, 1992), and that the Hispanic children and other "people of color deserve adequate, effective, and sensitively attuned treatment" (Jacobs & Bowles, 1988, p. x). According to Mokuou and Shimizu (1991) school counselors have ethical mandates to address effective services to ethnically diverse groups. For example, in 1999, the American School Counselor Association (ASCA) revised its position statement for multicultural counseling to read: "School counselors take action to ensure students of culturally diverse backgrounds have access to appropriate services and opportunities promoting the individual's maximum development" (ASCA, 2004).

School counselors need to provide support to Hispanic students including those who are also ELL. Hispanic children raised in families that speak primarily Spanish are vulnerable to many of the challenges associated with being a numerical and racial/ethnic minority. They struggle to negotiate competing cultural value systems. According to Yeh (2001), cultural differences may contribute to "depression, social isolation, low self-concept, relationship problems, and academic and career concerns" (p. 350). Meanwhile, the psychological adaptation of children from minority groups to their surroundings has been the subject of increasing focus in the fields of mental health and psychology (Baruth & Manning, 1992; Constantine & Gushue, 2003; Fuertes, 1999; Seinrach & Thomas, 1998; Yeh, 2001). A growing number of studies recently have focused on examining aspects of multicultural counseling competencies in school counseling preparation and have begun to expand the literature (Ancis, 1998; Arthur & Achenbach, 2002; Constantine, 2001; Constantine, et al., 2001).

## Need for Training of Bilingual School Counselors

Several arguments can be made in favor of training bilingual school counselors. Burgeoning Hispanic ELL populations in school districts have needs for services that only bilingual counselors can provide. Children and parents are more likely to engage in the expression of feelings and personal concerns when they speak in their native language (Cano, 1986); they are simply more comfortable communicating in their native language, which is the foundation of their emotional language.

Counselors should not rely on interpreters because of legal requirements for confidentiality. Compared to bilingual counselors, monolingual, English-speaking school counselors cannot adequately and as effectively provide the essential academic and personal connections to students and families where Spanish is the language spoken at home.

Another argument in favor of training certified personnel in this area is that effective school counselors, as indicated earlier, support academic achievement (Dahir & Stone, 2003; Hadley, 1988; Lapan, 2001; Lapan, Gysbers & Sun, 1997; Lee, 1993; Otwell & Mullis, 1997; Sink & Stroh, 2003). Sink and Stroh (2003) found that third and fourth graders had significant increases in achievement scores in direct relation to the number of years they were in elementary schools using comprehensive school counseling programs. Another study showed that academic achievement in mathematics was positively influenced by classroom guidance lessons (Lee, 1993). Lapan, Gysbers and Sun (1997) published the results of a study examining the relationship between the implementation of comprehensive guidance programs in the state of Missouri and the perceptions of high school students. "Students who felt that there was more career information available in their school were more likely to report earning higher grades" (Lapan, et al., 1997, p. 75). These students were also more likely to report earning higher grades than students in schools without comprehensive guidance programs. Lapan et. al. (1997) concluded, "It appears that schools that were spending time with students to more fully implement comprehensive guidance programs did not detract from student academic progress but may, in fact, have played a positive role in enhancing student achievement" (p. 75).

## The Case of Need Established for the Model Training Program

In 2000, the primary author conducted a needs assessment with six school districts in the Houston area, serving a total of 442,518 students. With nearly 100,000 ELL students and 2,343 certified bilingual teachers, the six directors of counseling and guidance programs in those districts identified a total current need for 102 bilingual (Spanish/English) school counselors. When asked to project the needs over the five years, the directors estimated 145–175 bilingual school counselors would need to be employed. This would indicate that in 2005, for the six districts included in the survey, the need for bilingual school counselors would have almost doubled over five years. The Texas Developmental Guidance Model (1998) suggested a ratio of one school counselor for every 350 students. However, assuming that these six districts have 102 bilingual counselors, there is at best an average of one bilingual school counselor for every 979 ELL students. While not all of the ELL students are concentrated where they can be served in a statistically balanced way, any shortfall of qualified bilingual counselors diminishes the potential for fulfilling a free and appropriate education for ELL students. These districts are constantly recruiting bilingual and English-as-a-Second-Language (ESL) teachers to meet district needs. Like other teachers who seek additional certification as counselors, administrators, and diagnosticians, a portion of bilingual and ESL teachers may seek graduate education in the field of school counseling.

## A Model Program for Training Bilingual School Counselors in Collaboration with School Districts

The model program that is described herein was developed through a grant, "The Nontraditional Field-Based Inservice Preparation Program for Bilingual Counselors: ¡Entrenando Consejeros para los Niños!" a Title VII, Teachers and Personnel Grant funded by the United States Department of Education, Office of Bilingual Education and Minority Language Affairs. The program was offered through the Department of Educational Leadership and Counseling at Sam Houston State University (SHSU). SHSU is located 30 minutes north of the northernmost suburb of Houston, Texas; SHSU brings its counseling program to school districts in cohort groups to several districts in Houston. Over the five-year span of the grant, four cohorts from six Houston school districts totaling 43 teachers progressed from being graduate students to serving as school counseling interns. The school-counseling interns, along with their mentor/supervisors, had an impact on an estimated 40,000 ELL students. The grant focused on field-based instruction, developing parent involvement programs, classroom guidance units, and staff development programs. A second focus was conducting action research.

We describe the components of the training program in terms of (a) changes to the existing program of study, (b) school district partners, (c) resources for the students, (d) curriculum infusion and bilingual counselor competencies, (e) parent involvement, (f) staff development, (g) staff development, (h) action research, (i) program evaluation, (j) field-based internship, and (k) mentors.

*Changes to the program.* To educate Spanish-speaking school counselors, the SHSU Counseling Program made adaptations to an existing 36 semester-hour Master of Education program. To facilitate taking classes after teaching all day, 11 out of 12 required graduate classes were offered in sites near or in six participating school districts. Curriculum included the history and professional practice of counseling, ethical issues, study of human development over the lifespan, research methods, practice in basic counseling skills, counseling theories, effective and abnormal behavior, career counseling, group counseling, assessment, school counseling methods, cross-cultural issues in counseling, and supervised practice in counseling (with real clients—the students and parents in the schools). The conscious effort was made to focus the curriculum and dialogue in each class on service to the ELL population. Cohorts of 10 or more students were formed in the first four years of the grant, with each cohort scheduled for five semesters to earn the M.Ed., and were endorsed to take the state examination for school counselor certification. A supervised "induction" semester immediately followed graduation. The courses could also be applied to meet academic requirements for licensure for private mental health practice (Texas State Board of Examiners of Professional Counselors, 2004), which require 48 graduate semester-hours.

*School district partners.*   The six school district partners were from the greater Houston area. Each district had a limited number of teachers to recommend for enrollment in the program. Districts also identified mentor counselors who later provided on-site supervision during the practicum and post-degree induction semesters. The districts had unique procedures for assessing an applicant's level of proficiency in Spanish, although certified bilingual teachers were automatically considered to meet the requirement. Applicants were then required to meet specific SHSU and Counseling Program admissions criteria which included an acceptable Graduate Record Examination score, three letters of recommendation, an interview, an endorsement by the district, and a 2.5 undergraduate grade point average.

*Resources for the students.*   Students received a full scholarship for tuition and fees, as well as $300 toward books and $250 toward conference travel during each calendar year for two years. Laptop computers were purchased and made available for student use. Distance learning connections between the SHSU campus and two districts were used to deliver a didactic class, Introduction to Counseling and Guidance.

*Curriculum infusion and bilingual school counselor competencies.*   The Counseling faculty worked to infuse multiculturalism and bilingualism throughout the curriculum. The faculty had staff development time bi-monthly to discuss ways to address the needs of ELL students and their families into the curriculum. Three faculty members were reassigned to work on multicultural assessment of the curriculum. A mini-library related to ELL student counseling was purchased for faculty and student use. Following discussions of ways to improve the curriculum at faculty meetings, research and special focus on components of the grant led to the development of workshops presented at conferences (such as: National Association of Bilingual Education, American Counseling Association, American Education Research Association, and Texas Counseling Association) on various aspects of the process of training bilingual school counselors. While at the conferences, faculty attended sessions that helped them relate the needs of ELL students to school counseling.

The faculty met to discuss ways to increase the amount of multicultural and bilingual focused field-based experiences throughout the curriculum. For example, students in the Assessment in Counseling and Career Counseling classes were required to conduct achievement and vocational assessments, respectively, with individuals in the community. In the Introduction to Counseling and Guidance course, students interviewed active professionals in the counseling field. Students in the Methods of Research class conducted action research with bilingual student populations in their schools. Students in the Pre-Practicum, Group Counseling, and Supervised Practice in Counseling classes worked with "live" counseling clients. Supervised Practice in Counseling interns conducted individual and group counseling as well as developmental guidance activities in a public school setting.

A set of competencies for bilingual school counselors were adapted and created based on literature in counselor education and experiences of the faculty working in the field with ELL students and their counselors. These competencies had their origins in proficiencies and competencies that are outlined by the State Board of Educator Certification (SBEC) (2004). While the SBEC competencies and proficiencies were already being addressed throughout the curriculum, the impact of the bilingual/multicultural infusion process led to the development of the bilingual school counselor competencies as indicated in Table 7.1. Due to this work with the competencies, faculty members found that they became increasingly aware of multicultural issues and bilingual education issues as the grant moved into its second year. The professors built in class activities to highlight the impact of bilingual students on the process of school counseling. For example, in the Methods of Consultation, Coordination, and Counseling class, participants of the grant were required to research and create developmental guidance programs to be delivered to bilingual students. Faculty supervisors visited schools to watch interns deliver the guidance lessons in Spanish (Bruhn, et al., 2000). A report of the infusion process was delivered at the annual conference of the American Counseling Association (Bruhn, DeTrude, Robles-Piña, Nichter, & Geyen, 2001).

TABLE 7.1
Sam Houston State University Bilingual Counselor Competencies

*Ten Bilingual Counselor Competencies*

1. Have an understanding of human development in order to provide a comprehensive developmental guidance and counseling program

2. Be aware of the impact of environmental, cultural, and linguistic influences on learners' development and achievement

3. Have an understanding of ELL students' self-efficacy levels and reasons for a lack of high self-efficacy among these students, as well as how to alter these levels

4. Appreciate human diversity by providing equitable guidance and counseling services for all learners, including effectively communicating with ELL students and parents

5. Be able to use effective leadership skills to plan, implement, and evaluate a comprehensive developmental guidance and counseling program for ELL student

6. Be able to provide responsive services that address immediate concerns of ELL learners with their academic, personal, social, and career planning

7. Be able to use formal and informal assessment in the native language to provide information about ELL learners, to monitor student progress, and recommend modifications to the educational environment

8. Be able to provide expertise in counseling with parents of ELL students, bilingual teachers, regular teachers, special ed. and gifted ed. teachers, and administrators and to establish collaborative relationships between the school and community

9. Be able to establish strong positive ties between the school and community

10. Have an understanding and be able to comply with legal, ethical, and professional standards for Texas public school educators, engage in self-reflection and professional growth, and work with colleagues to advance the counseling profession and work with the LEP populations.

*Parent involvement component.* The faculty believed that bilingual school counselors provide an effective bridge to parents, thus facilitating increased parent involvement in their children's education both at home and at school. Further, they felt that the involvement of language minority parents in their children's education is necessary for the reinforcement of native language development, as well as to communicate high expectations and emotional support for academic achievement. To further these goals, students were required to either develop their own or expand the districts' parent involvement projects in the Methods of Consultation class. Participants presented the programs in class or to parents on the school campus during their internship. Graduates employed as school counselors participated in and delivered components of parent education programs as part of a school's guidance program. In Supervised Practice in Counseling, students were required to conduct counseling program needs assessments and surveys of parents, teachers, and students, thus increasing the level of contact with and between each group.

*Staff development programs.* Staff development programs were also developed by the students in Methods of Consultation. The goal was for the bilingual school counselor to assist new teachers (bilingual and regular) to understand and work with LEP students and parents. Graduates conducted staff development programs in their schools as well as providing individual consultation to teachers on effective ways to understand and respond to the needs of LEP children and parents.

*Action research.* Each student was required to complete an "action research" project in the Methods of Research class. The goals of action research are to define problems, formulate research questions, collect data, draw conclusions, make changes accordingly, and measure outcomes. The outcomes of some of these projects were presented at two National Association of Bilingual Education (NABE) conferences (Robles-Piña & Bruhn, 2000; Robles-Piña & Bruhn, 2001; Robles-Piña, Cavazos, Morales, & Bruhn, 2000; Robles-Piña, et al., 2000) and published in a NABE Research and Evaluation SIG newsletter (Robles-Piña, Bruhn, & Irby, 2001).

*Program evaluation.* Participants were also taught to evaluate their programs and their professional behavior, and to make data-based changes accordingly. Meetings with cohort members were held yearly, and the grant evaluator collected programmatic feedback yearly. The principal investigator and faculty made adjustments to the program, such as recommending that school districts use the emergency certification process to hire the counseling interns as school counselors during the Supervised Practice in Counseling internship. Another example was to increase the depth and specificity of in-service training for the mentor counselors.

*Field-based internship and induction semesters.* During the Supervised Practice in Counseling class, interns were provided avenues to demonstrate their capacity for meeting the competencies listed above. Interns counseled clients from the community in SHSU's on-campus Counseling Practicum under faculty supervision. Each intern also had a mentor counselor in the school district to supervise field-based activities. The mentor was involved for one academic year (the practicum and induction semesters) with the school district receiving a $3,000 stipend for each intern to help defray costs and support school and district counseling programs. A few principals released the teachers part of the day in order to serve in the role of counseling intern.

*Mentors.* Mentors, selected by the districts to supervise interns in field-based activities during the internship and post-graduation induction semesters, attended an orientation/supervision training meeting. Since interns were encouraged to use reflective thinking strategies to gain the most from field experiences, journaling and e-mail communication were highly successful means for mentors to provide support. The project evaluator thought that engaging the interns in an ongoing mentorship relationship with a practicing professional in the field was one of the most successful elements of the grant. The process of developing and supporting the relationships between interns and mentors was presented as a workshop at the Texas Counseling Association Professional Development Conference (Bruhn, et al., 2001).

Faculty conducted yearly training for the mentors, delivered either at a site in one of the participating districts or at an on-campus workshop to train supervisors for all interns, whether involved with the grant or not. The mentor training evolved from only one hour into a three-hour process to include instruction on ethical issues, supervision theory and techniques, and specific requirements for each internship course.

Mid-year meetings were scheduled for the mentor counselors and the interns at an off-campus site to encourage reflection and to collect recommendations for program improvement. Mentors learned from comparing their activities with those of other mentors and used the opportunity to interface with university faculty to solve issues in counseling both students and parents. Both mentors and interns rated the program's curriculum as successful in meeting the standards for school counselors as set forth by the State Board of Educator Certification. Faculty visited interns and mentors on their campuses to observe internship activities and discuss the pragmatic and theoretical issues that arose during the internship and mentoring experience.

## Outcomes of the Model Program

There were several positive outcomes of the model program. First, it was determined that districts profited from hiring bilingual counselor graduate students in their last semester to serve in the role of the school counselor. Secondly, the structure developed in this program serves as a model for developing additional university/school collaborative cohorts.

Several districts hired interns through emergency certification prior to or during the practicum semester. Those interns completing the practicum semester employed as school counselors seemed to gain more from the experience than colleagues who were employed full-time as teachers. When employed as teachers, interns found they needed to use lunch hours, preparation periods, and before and after school time to complete the practicum and induction semester requirements. On the other hand, the interns hired as school counselors found that they could focus their entire efforts on practicing the role of school counselor.

The relationship between the graduate program and school districts was enhanced to the point that six school districts, including three not involved in the grant, have invited the university to develop cohorts to train school counselors with teachers from the districts. One district has already started three cohorts and has developed a child and family referral network to provide real clients for the Supervised Practice in Counseling offered at the school district. A description of the collaboration of two districts and the university was presented at the annual conference of the Texas Counseling Association (Bruhn, Malone, DeTrude, Nichter, & Kutka, 2003).

## CONCLUSIONS AND RECOMMENDATIONS

There were many lessons learned in the development and implementation of the model bilingual counselor training program. First, we determined that collaboration is essential between the university graduate program and participating school districts for such a program to be successful. Additionally, we determined that there were lessons learned related to (a) collaboration, (b) cohorts, (c) students themselves, (d) program-courses, (e) field-based internship and induction, (f) employment, (g) directors of programs, (h) faculty reactions, and (i) continued relationships.

### Collaboration

We recommend first the development of relationships with the school district directors of counseling and guidance. Initial meetings prior to setting up such a program clarify district, university, and student needs. Early meetings facilitate trust-building and goal-oriented activities by all. Clear university expectations of the district need to be provided to the district in writing, while university personnel must strive to understand and accommodate to district needs. Clear statements of program goals, curriculum, facility needs, location of classes, and establishing plans for ongoing, yearly review through advisory committee meetings must be provided. Advisory committees should include stakeholders from the school districts, the community and the university. A short contractual agreement would be advisable. In Table 7.2, the elements and suggestions for development of a bilingual counselor training program with collaboration are outlined.

TABLE 7.2

Sam Houston State University Model for Training Graduate
Level Bilingual School Counselors Suggestions for the University
and School District Partners

| *Suggestions for the University* | |
| --- | --- |
| Program guidelines | Use existing program |
| | Infuse focus on multiculturalism and bilingualism |
| | Provide professional development for the faculty |
| | Use bilingual school counselor competencies |
| | Maintain program and university admissions rules e.g., writing samples, interviews |
| | On campus program orientation, advisement for cohort |
| Didactic classes | Research: Study action research |
| | School Counseling |
| | Developmental Guidance Units |
| | Parent involvement programs |
| | Needs assessment |
| | In-service unit on needs of LEP students and parents |
| | Offer all didactic classes off-campus |
| | Distance learning techniques, such as ITV, Blackboard |
| Practicum | On campus for direct observation and training |
| | Orientation for Supervisors |
| | Minimum of 2 off-campus visits |
| Mentors from school district | Provide supervision for practicum and post-degree induction semester |
| | On-campus Supervisor training workshop |
| | Mid-year feedback meeting |
| | Visited 2 times each semester |
| Program maintenance | Yearly meetings with district directors of counseling and guidance |
| | Financial support may be necessary e.g. tuition and fees, books |
| | Evaluate and collect data yearly |

| *Suggestions for Collaborating School Districts* | |
| --- | --- |
| Student recruiting | Determine own recruiting standards |
| | Determine standard of writing/reading/speaking proficiency in second language |
| | References from principal and school counselor |
| | Recommend top candidates |
| Communicate program value to district administrators and principals | |
| Hire students at 21 semester hours as Counselor Interns or emergency certification | |
| Place students in full-time counseling role during practicum and induction semesters | |

## Cohorts

Participants cited the formation of cohort groups that took all classes together, in sequence, as a major factor in their success and satisfaction in the program. Cohort members worked on class projects together and provided each other with academic, psychological, and social support throughout and after the program. They relied on each other and learned from each other's experiences. Faculty members liked the support cohort members gave each other and the cohesiveness that developed. The cohorts still get together, in one case monthly, for fellowship and professional sharing. The cohort model is highly recommended.

## Student Feedback

Based on student feedback, we recommend that district consider a financial incentive for bilingual teachers to seek school counselor certification. As one student emphatically stated, "Most Hispanic Spanish-speaking teachers are going to put their energies after work into their families, unless there is a strong financial incentive or opportunity that will outweigh the sacrifices needed to be made with and for the family."

Other recommendations are based students' expressed appreciation in the following areas: (a) It was effectively planned— "It's quick, already planned for you, and free; " (b) We had responsive professors— "I like the group of professors; they are there for you when you are stressed out; we talk it over with each other;" (c) This was an outreach program— "I feel a sincere attempt is being made to try to help in an area, reaching out to Hispanic students, families and teachers, where much help is needed;" (d) This program met many needs of the population served— "I feel this program will help the LEP population and their parents;" and (e) This program was delivered conveniently— "We like that the coursework is delivered in the districts where we work instead of driving to the university campus."

## Program-Courses

We suggest that the minimum graduate program should take at least six semesters for a 36 semester-hour program. Our students were so fatigued through the combination of graduate coursework and full-time employment in a five-semester timeframe that we recommend decreasing the number of courses required in the summer sessions from four to three. To provide a much stronger foundation, our graduate program has moved to provide a 48-semester hour program following the standards for school counseling programs outlined by the Council on Accreditation for Counseling and Related Educational Programs (CACREP, 2004).

*Related to courses.* Students' experienced the immediate relevance of practical research impacting highly concentrated ELL classes and schools through completing action research projects that positively impacted their own practice.

Action research for professional development is recommended. Students were required to create and deliver classroom guidance units in the ELL students' first language. Practice of curriculum development and implementation is important for prospective bilingual counselors. Students were required to develop and implement parent involvement programs with the parents and caretakers of ELL students. Working with parents within the ELL population is critical to the success of the students; therefore, a parent involvement component is needed in such a program. Graduate students developed competence in providing in-service training and informal support to colleagues to understand the unique needs and strengths of ELL students; this experience is desired for prospective bilingual counselors as they are advocates on the campus for the ELLs. Finally, school counselor interns were required to implement needs assessments and program evaluations for school counseling programs. The understanding of how to have ongoing evaluation of the program on the campus the bilingual counselor serves is critical to the continuous improvement.

## Field-based Internship and Induction

Field-based internship opportunities are essential. We recommend that practicum interns meet weekly with district selected mentors. When bilingual teachers are serving as counseling interns and teaching at the same time, it is an exhausting process. Initially, one district hired participants as Counselor Interns after the completion of seven courses, and two other districts reassigned teachers in a way that freed them to serve in the role of school counseling interns. As Directors of Counseling and Guidance learned of their colleague's success, several other districts hired interns through emergency certification or other programs. Programmatically, we recommend that school districts make bilingual counselor internship positions available, e.g. through emergency certification or reassignment from teaching duties.

On-going support in the "induction" semester following graduation was acclaimed as a particularly effective outcome of the grant. Graduates hired as school counselors were quickly guided into effective participation in the overall district effort to provide school counseling services. Directors of Counseling and Guidance commented on the energy and enthusiasm of the new school counselors during the induction semester. We recommend an induction semester supported by a district mentor (practicing school counselor with experience with ELLs).

Mentors function best when university faculty prepare clear guidelines for supervision activities, grant objectives, and course requirements. We recommend a three-hour supervision workshop provided by university faculty. This should include two hours of instruction on supervision ethics, theories, and techniques. The third hour, interns and mentors need to meet with university faculty to talk about specific course expectations. Continuing education credit for licensure should be offered for the mentors.

## Post-Graduation Employment

Thirty-seven of the graduates moved into counseling positions. However, several of the participants used the program and master's degree as a springboard to further their careers. For example, three graduates have already moved into principal and assistant principal positions. Two graduates have chosen to stay in the classroom at this point and one retired from the profession to stay home with her baby.

## Directors of District Counseling and Guidance Programs

The district directors believed the program to be positive. "This program will improve the quality of delivery of services for the school." "This will assist us in better communicating with students and their parents . . . (when) because parents don't speak English, he/she can be the bridge of communication between the parent and the school. I am talking about more than a translator." We recommend yearly feedback meetings with the district directors to assist with continuous improvement efforts in the program.

## Faculty Reactions

While standard school counselor certification programs meet the basic needs of students, we recommend that faculty be provided workshops and work together to infuse issues relevant to bilingualism and multiculturalism throughout the graduate curriculum. We recommend that other university programs wishing to introduce a similar model use the Bilingual Counselor Competencies included in Table 7.1 as we found that they provide the faculty in each class with a clear direction for preparing effective bilingual school counselors. The competencies were actually a piece of development work from the faculty in the program and helped to situate the state competencies for school counselors.

The faculty enjoyed the fact that the vast majority of students in the program are minorities and they liked the students' sensitivity to ELL student needs. Faculty learned more about the emerging ELL populations and increased the focus on bilingual and multicultural issues into courses. The cohort model is strongly endorsed by the faculty.

## SUMMARY

We found that a clearly articulated, well-planned, collaborative approach between the university and school district(s) supports the development of competent bilingual counselors. We recommend that other universities place an intentional focus on developing field-based and bilingually-oriented curriculum for programs training bilingual school counselors.

# REFERENCES

American School Counseling Association, Position Statement on Multicultural Counseling (revised 1999). *American School Counselor Association position.* Retrieved June 21, 2004, from http://www.schoolcounselor.org

Ancis, J. R. (1998). Cultural competency training at a distance: Challenges and strategies. *Journal of Counseling & Development, 76*(2), 134–143.

Arthur, N., & Achenbach, K. (2002). Developing multicultural counseling competencies through experiential learning. *Counselor Education & Supervision, 42,* 2–14.

Baruth, L. G., & Manning, M. L. (1992). Understanding and counseling Hispanic American children. *Elementary School Guidance & Counseling, 27*(2), 113–122.

Behring, S. T., & Ingraham, C. L. (1998). Culture as a central component of consultation: A call to the field. *Journal of Educational and Psychological Consultation, 9,* 57–72.

Borders, L. D., & Drury, S. M. (1992). Comprehensive school counseling programs: A review for policymakers and practitioners. *Journal of Counseling & Development, 70*(4), 487–498.

Blum, D. J. (Ed.). (1998). *The school counselor's book of lists.* West Nyack, NY: The Center for Applied Research in Education.

Bruhn, R., DeTrude, J., Robles-Piña, R., Nichter, M., & Geyen, D. (2001, March). *Infusing bilingualism into the counselor education curriculum.* Workshop presented at the meeting of the American Counseling Association, San Antonio, TX.

Bruhn, R., Malone, B., DeTrude, J., Nichter, M., & Kutka, T. (2003, November). *A tale of two districts (and one university): School district-based training for school counselors.* Workshop presented at the meeting of the Texas Counseling Association, Galveston, TX.

Bruhn, R., Robles-Piña, R., Nichter, M., Beimgraben, E., Molina, D., Gonzales, E., & Martinez, C. (2000, November). *"Mision-Bilingue": Blending classroom guidance and bilingualism.* Workshop presented at the meeting of the Texas Counseling Association, Houston, TX.

Bruhn, R., Robles-Piña, R., Nichter, M., Trevino, J., Restivo, M., Beimgraben, E., & Shasteen, E. (2001, November). *Mentoring school counselors: Soaring to new heights.* Workshop presented at the meeting of the Texas Counseling Association, Dallas, TX.

Cano, J., Jr. (1986). *Hypnotic responsiveness among bilingual Mexican-Americans to English and Spanish litanies.* Unpublished doctoral dissertation, East Texas State University.

Cofresi, N. I., & Gorman, A. (2004). Testing and assessment issues with Spanish-English bilingual Latinos. *Journal of Counseling & Development, 82*(1), 99–106.

Constantine, M. G., & Gushue, G. V. (2003). School counselors' ethnic tolerance attitudes and racism attitudes as predictors of their multicultural case conceptualization of an immigrant student. *Journal of Counseling & Development, 81*(2), 185–190.

Constantine, M. G. (2001). Theoretical orientation, empathy, and multicultural counseling competence in school counselor trainees. *Professional School Counseling, 4*(5), 342–348.

Constantine, M. G., Arorgah, J. J., Basakett, M. D., Blackman, S. M., Donnelly, P. C., & Edles, P. A. (2001). School counselors' universal-diverse orientation and aspects of their multicultural counseling competence. *Professional School Counseling, 5*(1), 13–18.

Council on Accreditation for Counseling and Related Educational Programs (CACREP). *2001 Standards.* Retrieved December 6, 2004 http://www.cacrep.org/2001Standards.html

Estrada, A. U., Durlak, J. A., & Juarez, S. C. (2002). Developing multicultural counseling competencies in undergraduate students. *Journal of Multicultural Counseling and Development, 30,* 110–123.

Fuertes, J. N. (1999). Asian Americans' and African Americans' initial perceptions of Hispanic counselors. *Journal of Multicultural Counseling and Development, 27*(3), 122–135.

Dahir, C. A., & Stone, C. B. (2003). Accountability: A M.E.A.S.U.R.E. of the impact school counselors have on student achievement. *Professional School Counseling, 6*(3), 214–221.

Gloria, A. M., & Rodriguez, E. R. (2000). Counseling Latino university students: Psychosociocultural issues for consideration. *Journal of Counseling Development, 78*(2), 145–154.

Gysbers, N. C., & Henderson, P. (2000). *Developing and managing your school guidance program* (3rd ed.). Alexandria, VA: American Counseling Association.

Hadley, H. R. (1988). Improving reading scores through a self-esteem prevention program. *Elementary School Guidance & Counseling, 22,* 248–252.

Hall C. (1997). Cultural malpractice: The growing obsolescence of psychology with the changing U. S. population. *American Psychologist, 52,* 642–651.

Harris, K. C. (1996). Collaboration within a multicultural society. *Remedial and Special Education, 17,* 2–10.

Jacobs, C., & Bowles, D. D. (1988). *Ethnicity and race: Critical concepts in social work.* Silver Spring, Md.: National Association of Social Workers, Inc.

Katz, J. H. (1985). The sociopolitical nature of counseling. *The Counseling Psychologist, 13,* 613–624.

Lapan, R. T. (2001). Results-based comprehensive guidance and counseling programs: A framework for planning and evaluation. *Professional School Counseling, 4*(4), 289–299.

Lapan, R. T., Gysbers, N. C., & Sun, Y. (1997). The impact of more fully implemented guidance programs on the school experiences of high school students: A statewide evaluation study. *Journal of Counseling & Development, 75,* 292–302.

Lee, R. S. (1993). Effects of classroom guidance on student achievement. *Elementary School Guidance & Counseling, 27,* 163–171.

Mokuau, N., & Shumizu, D. (1991). Conceptual framework for social services for Asian and Pacific Islander Americans. In N. Mokuau (Ed.) *Handbook for social services for Asian and Pacific Islanders* (pp. 12–34). New York: Greenwood Press.

Otwell, P. S., & Mullis, F. (1997). Academic achievement and counselor accountability. *Elementary School Guidance & Counseling, 31*(4), 343–349.

Pedersen, P. (1997, March). *Learning to hear the voices as a cross-cultural competency.* Keynote presentation at the "Cross-Cultural Competencies for Interactive Diversity" Western regional conference of the Association for Multicultural Counseling and Development, San Diego, CA.

Robles-Piña, R., & Bruhn, R. (2000, February). *Professional development through action research.* Workshop presentation at the Office of Bilingual Education and Minority Affairs pre-conference institute, 29th Annual International Bilingual/Multicultural Education Conference, San Antonio, TX.

Robles-Piña, R., & Bruhn, R. (2001, February). *Action research: Measuring change in achievement for bilingual learners.* Round Table presentation at the Research andEvaluation SIG Institute at the meeting of the National Association for Bilingual Education, AZ.

Robles-Piña, R., Bruhn, R., & Irby, B. (2001, Winter). Training bilingual school counselors in action research. *Research and Evaluation Special Interest Group of the National Association for Bilingual Education,* 4–5.

Robles-Piña, R., Cavazos, V., Morales, C., & Bruhn, R. (2000, February). *Through action research: A correlational study investigating the effects of parental involvement factors on APRENDA scores* and *through action research: The effects of role-playing on the self-esteem of third grade bilingual students.* Round Table presentation at the Research and Evaluation SIG Institute at the 29th Annual International Bilingual/Multicultural Education Conference, San Antonio.

Robles-Piña, R., Vasquez, N., Morales, C., Hinojosa, R., Molina, D., Trevino, J., Lopez, N., Cavazos, V., & Bruhn, R. (2000, February). *Professional development through action research.* Round Table presentation at the Research and Evaluation SIG Institute at the 29th Annual International Bilingual/Multicultural Education Conference, San Antonio.

Santiago-Rivera, A. L. (1995). Developing a culturally sensitive treatment modality for bilingual Spanish-speaking clients: Incorporating language and culture in counseling. *Journal of Counseling & Development, 74*(1), 12–17.

Sink, C. A., & Stroh, H. R. (2003). Raising achievement test scores of early elementary school students through comprehensive school counseling programs. *Professional School Counseling, 6*(5), 350–364.

State Board of Educator Certification, Texas. *Rules for the school counselor certificate.* Retrieved June 11, 2004, from http://www.sbec.state.tx.us/SBECOnline.

Sue, D. W., & Sue, D. (1990). *Counseling the culturally different: Theory and practice.* New York: Wiley.

Sue, S., & Zane, N. (1987). The role of culture and cultural techniques in psychotherapy: A critique and reformation. *American Psychologist, 42,* 37–45.

Texas Education Agency. (1998). *A model developmental guidance and counseling program for Texas public schools.* Austin, TX: Author.

Texas State Board of Professional Counselors. Rules of the Texas State Board of Examiners of Professional Counselors. http://www.tdh.state.tx.us/hcqs/plc/lpc/lpc_def.htm

U. S. Census Bureau. (2004). U.S. Interim Projection, by Age, Sex, Race, and Hispanic Origin. Retrieved June 21, 2004, from http://www.census.gov/:pc/www/usinterimproj/natprojtab01a.pdf

Weinrach, S. G., & Thomas, K. R. (1998). Diversity-sensitive counseling today: A postmodern clash of values. *Journal of Counseling & Development, 76,* 115–122.

Whitson, S., & Sexton, L. (1998). A review of school counseling outcome research: Implications for practice. *Journal of Counseling & Development, 76,* 412–426.

Yeh, C. J. (2001). An exploratory study of school counselors' experiences with and perceptions of Asian-American students. *Professional School Counseling, 4*(5), 349–356.

# III

## POSITION PAPERS
## AND REFLECTIONS

# 8

# Let's Tell the Public the Truth About Bilingual Education

### Stephen Krashen
*University of Southern California*

*"In the intellectual battle over bilingual education, the campaigns opposing Ron Unz surrendered without firing a shot."*

—Crawford (2003)

## ABSTRACT

Bilingual education has been dismantled in three states, and is slowly dissolving in several others. This is a major attack: The three states that passed anti-bilingual education initiatives enroll 43% of the English language learners in the United States (Crawford, 2003). This should never have happened. The case for bilingual education is very strong, but somehow this information has never reached the public. I will briefly review the strong case for bilingual education, discuss what went wrong, and suggest what could be done about this in the future. I will suggest that the cure is better public relations (but not necessarily from public relations professionals), and even better programs.

## THE STRONG CASE FOR BILINGUAL EDUCATION

Bilingual education has two independent goals, and both are worthy, but they are independent. One goal I term "learning English," and by this I mean what Jim Cummins means, academic English, the language of school, coupled with academic success. A second goal can be termed the "Heritage Language" goal, the

165

maintenance and development of the heritage language and an appreciation of the heritage culture.

## The Research Is Impressive

In terms of the first goal, English, bilingual education has done well. The research is consistent: Students in bilingual programs typically do at least as well on tests of English reading as comparison students in all-English programs, and often do better (for reviews, see Willig, 1985; Greene, 1997; for a current exemplary study, see Oller & Eilers, 2002).

## The Two Pillars of Bilingual Education

There are two ways in which bilingual education helps English language development and contributes to academic success: The two pillars of bilingual education. The first pillar ("background knowledge") is the fact that when students have a good education in their first language, they get background knowledge, and this knowledge helps make the English they hear and read more comprehensible. The second pillar ("literacy transfers") is that developing literacy in the first language is a short cut to developing literacy in the second language. These two pillars are consistent with a number of psycholinguistic research findings, which I discuss in detail elsewhere (Krashen, 1996).

## The Pillars Make Sense

A series of studies by Fay Shin and associates has shown that the two pillars appear to be reasonable to many people (see Shin, 2000; Krashen, 2003a, for reviews). Shin asked various groups if they agreed that having background knowledge makes subject matter in another language more comprehensible and whether they felt that those who were literate in one language had an easier time developing literacy in a second language. There was widespread agreement, with some "do not know" responses and few disagreements. This was true of teachers, administrators, parents, graduate students (Lao, 2003), and student teachers in Spain (Ramos, 2003).

## The Public Was Not Anti-Bilingual Education

Before 1998 and the anti-bilingual education initiatives, the public was not anti-bilingual education (for a review of poll results, see Krashen, 1996, 1999). I will mention only one poll here, because it is of special interest: The Los Angeles Times (April 13, 1998) reported that only 1/3 of those polled preferred English-only; 2/3 approved either of use of the first language with no constraints (25%) or approved of short-term use of the first language (39%). The Dallas Morning News did a similar poll with nearly identical results.

Let us summarize: The research supports bilingual education, the underlying principles are consistent with other research results, many people find the underlying principles reasonable, and public opinion was, at least at one time: Mildly favorable to bilingual education. So why did bilingual education lose in three states, with all these factors going for it?

## Why We Lost: Not Xenophobism

There is no doubt that some people oppose bilingual education because of xenophobic, anti-immigrant attitudes. But there is no evidence that this was a deciding factor in the recent elections. Huddy and Sears (1990) reported that in their study, anti-immigrant and xenophobic attitudes accounted for less than 26% of the variance in attitudes toward bilingual education.

Even more convincing is the fact that according to polls, attitudes toward bilingual education were once fairly positive and have shifted. As noted above, in polls done before the Unz initiatives, the public was at least moderately in favor of the use of the first language in school. That is no longer so. In my view, we have lost the middle third in the last few years: Now about 2/3 favor English-only (Krashen, 2002). The middle third did not become xenophobes so rapidly. The reasonable conclusion is that most people are not xenophobes and sincerely want all children to succeed.

## Why We Lost: Ignorance

I think that the problem is ignorance, not racism. Consider this astounding fact: Some of the same people who approved of the use of the first language in school also supported anti-bilingual education initiatives. The same Los Angeles Times poll in which 2/3 supported at least some use of the first language also showed approximately 2/3 support for Proposition 227. Amazingly, the Los Angeles Times did not notice the contradiction.

The Los Angeles Times Web-site had data that helps us understand this strange result: They asked those who said they would support Proposition 227 why they would do so: 63% said it was because of the importance of English. Only 9% said it was because they felt bilingual education was not effective, and only 6% said it was because they preferred immersion. In other words, supporters of Proposition 227 thought they were supporting English.

My view is that most people have no idea of what bilingual education is. They do not know that bilingual education is based on the principles they would find reasonable. They do not know that bilingual education has been successful in helping children acquire English. In fact, I suspect that many do not know that bilingual education even has English as a central goal. Tragically, the profession has not tried very hard to inform them.

## The Frustration of Dealing With the Media

One reason not to try, of course, is the well-known difficulty of dealing with the press. While there are some very competent and patient reporters, many are neither. But bilingual educators must keep trying. Yes, it is frustrating to be ignored or misquoted, but if supporters of bilingual education continue to say nothing they will certainly be continued to be ignored and not be quoted at all. There is good evidence that information makes a difference: A. Garcia (2001) found that parents who applied for waivers for their children after Proposition 227 were significantly better informed about program options and language acquisition than those who did not.

## Aim at the Core

When supporters of bilingual education communicate with the public, I think it is important to focus on the core message: What bilingual education is, how it works, and how successful it is. Only a few important links need to be made: The public is already sympathetic to the underlying principles, as Shin (2000) and others have noted.

The Unz campaigns were a wonderful chance to do this, a potential platform to explain bilingual education, but supporters blew their big chance. The anti-Unz initiative organizations aimed at the periphery and not the core, with disastrous results. In the campaigns, the focus was only on issues such as not suing teachers and allowing only one year of special help, while actually refusing to discuss bilingual education itself.

Such a strategy, even if it had helped turn back the initiatives, puts bilingual education in long-term danger: At a minimum, we failed to educate the public about bilingual education, which gives us less protection against the next attack. Even worse, it is an implicit concession that we do not believe in bilingual education. Unz quickly discovered that opponents of Proposition 227 in California were refusing to defend bilingual education in California (this advice was even posted on the No on 227 Web-site) and took advantage of it, pointing out that even the professional bilingual education organizations would not defend bilingual education. All Unz and his allies have to do now is propose anti-bilingual initiatives that do not impose a one-year limit on special help and do not sue teachers. Bilingual education would be defenseless. This is not to say that these issues should be ignored. What I am saying is that we must emphasize the core issues.

The official advocacy groups were persuaded to follow this path because of advice from professional Public Relations firms, advisors who told them that the public would never understand our abstract, intellectual arguments. But polls showed modest support for bilingual education already, and the Shin studies (2000) showed that many people understood the underlying principles. What needed to be done was to make the missing connections: Bilingual education is based on these reasonable principles, and the research supports it. Instead, the advocacy groups did not try. The campaigns lost, as Crawford (2003) has pointed out, without firing a shot.

We should also bear in mind the possibility that some Public Relations firms are interested in only the short-term, in winning the one campaign they are hired to help win, and do not consider the potential long-term damage their tactics might cause.

The failure to explain bilingual education and the failure to respond to attacks on bilingual education has, undoubtedly, been the cause of the decline in attitudes. Unz' mantra of failed programs became received wisdom.

## THE SKYROCKET MYTH

The situation was not helped at all when California test scores appeared to rise after Proposition 227 was passed, an event that was publicized by the New York Times ("test scores skyrocket") and carried in stories throughout the United States (Thompson, DiCerbo, Mahoney, & MacSwan, 2002). Once again, the facts were on the side of bilingual education, and the explanation was not too complex. Test scores rose for several reasons that had nothing to do with the dismantling of bilingual education or improved learning in general: A new test, the SAT9, was introduced at the same time Proposition 227 was passed. The first time a new test is given, scores seem low, but in the following years, as students and teachers become more familiar with the test, scores rise until the test needs to be recalibrated (Linn, Graue, & Sanders, 1990). SAT9 scores for 1998 were interpreted as a measure of the effectiveness of bilingual education. The normal increase one sees with subsequent administrations of the test was misinterpreted as evidence that Proposition 227 was working.

Test inflation was especially pronounced in California because there was very strong pressure to raise test scores, including bribes (cash rewards) and punishments (threats of being closed down). This encouraged what must be considered a bogus means of raising test scores (i.e., certain kinds of test preparation, selective testing).

In addition, there was no evidence that schools that dumped bilingual education showed higher gains. A study conducted by WestEd (Parrish, Linquanti, Merickel, Quick, Laird, & Esra, 2002) in fact, showed no difference in improvement in English reading for English learners between Grades 2 and 5 between schools that kept and schools that dropped bilingual education. But once again, this information did not penetrate the public consciousness, nor was there any organized effort to get the word out.

## Another Error

Before turning to possible strategies, I need to point out one more error: Campaigners for bilingual education consistently confused the two goals of bilingual education. Advocates pointed out the advantages of being bilingual and understanding one's heritage ("two languages are better than one"), and sometimes insisted that everybody in the United States should be bilingual. The public interpreted this as enforced bilingualism for English-speakers, and was wondering when language-minority children were going to learn English.

## WHAT TO DO? EXPLAIN BILINGUAL EDUCATION

There are several possible paths, and we can easily take all of them.

### Better Communication With the Public

Clearly bilingual educators must make greater efforts to communicate with the media and the public in general, to use both traditional means (e.g., letters to the editor, magazine articles) and more recent, innovative means (the Internet). Reporters generally contact official organizations for comments on issues; it is crucial that professional organizations be ready with clear and concise answers to frequently asked questions, and that they respond to *all* attacks on bilingual education. Failure to answer an attack is perceived as conceding the point. When advocates do answer, they can use the space provided as another opportunity to educate the public, whenever possible repeating the core arguments: Bilingual education is successful in helping children acquire English, and there are good reasons why it is successful.

### Focused Efforts From the Academic Community

The professional organizations cannot do this alone. They need more help from the only segment of the population that has the time and expertise to deal with some of the issues in detail: University-level researchers.

Bilingual education is now in a state of all-out war, one we are losing. Researchers can no longer devote their time to peripheral issues and academic subtleties. They must focus their energies and abilities to studying the impact of bilingual education, studying different models and innovations, and responding to attacks with empirical evidence. Each attack is a research opportunity, an opportunity to see if in fact the bilingual education approach has been deficient, and to extend our knowledge. Is it true that bilingual education causes dropouts? Is it true that children "languish" in bilingual programs for years? Is it true that current immersion programs are getting better results than bilingual education? The studies and analyses need to be done, and need to be reported in clear and concise language. Opponents of bilingual education have kept up a steady stream of attacks; researchers should regard these as research opportunities. (Note that I am not recommending that researchers simply become a cheering section for bilingual education). As Jim Crawford has noted (personal communication), bilingual education supporters need to apply the same high level of scrutiny to apparently positive results for bilingual education as they apply to what appear to be negative results.)

## Improve Existing Programs

A third path is probably the most effective of all: Currently existing bilingual programs need to be made so good that there is no doubt. As noted earlier, bilingual education has done well, but, like most things, it can improve. Moreover, simply showing that bilingual education is as good or better than alternatives may satisfy the academic community, but it will not satisfy a critical public who has been convinced that it is a failure. The absolute achievement of students in bilingual education must be higher.

There is an easy way to do this: Improve the print-environment. Research supports the common-sense view that children with more access to print read more, and it also supports the common-sense view that children who read more read better (e.g. Krashen, 1993; McQuillan, 1998). Thus, improved access to books means improved reading, a conclusion consistent with research on the positive impact of school libraries (Lance, 1994, 2001; McQuillan, 1998).

It is also very well established that children from low-income backgrounds have little access to books: They live in communities with inferior public libraries, few bookstores, come from homes with few books, and attend schools with inferior school libraries (DiLoreto & Tse, 1999; Neuman & Celano, 2001; Smith, Constantino & Krashen, 1997).

A large percentage of children in bilingual education come from low-income families. A true book flood in the form of vastly improved school and classroom libraries would have a dramatic effect.

I suggest a three-step plan (see Krashen, 2003b):

1. Early reading in the first language, which provides a short cut to English reading. Of course, many programs are doing this already, but they are hampered by the fact that books in the primary language are not plentiful (Pucci, 1994). This needs to change.
2. Something we are not emphasizing: Massive recreational reading in both languages as soon as students can read independently, as soon as they reach the "Goosebumps Threshold." This will provide a huge boost in test scores; it is test preparation the legitimate way.
3. Continued reading in the heritage language, to insure continued growth in the heritage language and the lasting benefits of true bilingualism (Tse, 2001).

Thanks to the anti-bilingual education initiatives, however, this path is harder to take. In California, access to books in Spanish in communities where English learners live has been reduced (Pucci & Ulanoff, 2004), and despite lip-service on the importance of libraries (e.g. the Laura Bush Foundation) library funding has not improved. In California, in fact, the state with the lowest reading scores, library funding has dropped from insufficient to absolutely dismal. In 1992, California's fourth Graders ranked last in the United States in reading. At that time, California was spending half of what other states spent on school libraries. Today, in 2004, California is still ranked last among the states in the United States, despite the huge push for increased skills in language arts classes. And next year California is planning to spend only 3% of the national average on school libraries, ignoring the considerable research showing that better school libraries are related to higher reading scores.

## SUGGESTIONS

Here are my "radical" suggestions:

1. A vigorous attempt to explain bilingual education to the public, why it works to help children acquire English as well as the fact that it works. In other words, let's tell the public the truth about bilingual education.

2. University-level researchers and scholars devote their efforts to core issues in bilingual education.

3. Improved school libraries, providing more to read in both languages. This will result in more recreational reading and more language acquisition and literacy development, and even better results from our bilingual programs.

## REFERENCES

Crawford, J. (2003). *Hard sell: Why is bilingual education so unpopular with the American public?* Arizona State University: Language Policy Research Unit. http://www.asu.edu/educ/epsl/LPRU/features/brief8.htm

Di Loreto, C. & Tse, L. (1999). Seeing is believing: Disparity of books in two Los Angeles area public libraries. *Public Library Quarterly, 17*(3), 31–36.

Garcia, A. (2000). Informed parent consent and Proposition 227. *Bilingual Research Journal, 24,* (1,2), 57–74

Greene, J. (1999). A meta-analysis of the Rossell and Baker review of bilingual education research. *Bilingual Research Journal, 21*(2,3): 103–122.

Huddy, L., & Sears, D. (1990). Qualified public support for bilingual education: Some policy implications. *Annals of the American Academy of Political and Social Science, 508,*119–134.

Krashen, S. (1993). *The power of reading.* Westport, CT: Libraries Unlimited.

Krashen, S. (1996). *Under attack: The case against bilingual education.* Culver City: Language Education Associates.

Krashen, S. (1999). *Condemned without a trial: Bogus arguments against bilingual education.* Portsmouth, NH: Heinemann.

Krashen, S. (2002). *Evidence suggesting that public opinion is becoming more negative: A discussion of the reasons, and what we can do about it.* http://ourworld.compuserve.com/homepages/JWCRAWFORD/Krash11.htm

Krashen, S. (2003a). The amazing case of bilingual education. *Mosaic, 8*(1), 3–6.

Krashen, S. (2003b). Three roles for reading for language-minority students. In G. Garcia (Ed.) *English learners: Reaching the highest level of English proficiency* (pp. 55–70). Newark, Delaware: International Reading Association.

Lance, K. C. (1994). The impact of school library media centers on academic achievement. *School Library Media Quarterly, 22*(3), 167–170, 172.

Lance, K. C. (2001). Proof of the power: Recent research on the impact of school library Media programs on the academic achievement of U.S. public school students. *ERIC Digest.* ED45686.

Lao, C. (2003). A study of graduate students' attitudes toward bilingual education. *Mosaic, 8*(1), 10–15.

Linn, R. L., Graue, M. E., & Sanders, N. M. (1990). Comparing state and district test results to national norms: The validity of claims that everyone is above average. *Educational Measurement: Issues and Practice, 9*(3), 5–14.

McQuillan, J. (1998). *The literacy crisis: False claims and real solutions.* Portsmouth, NH: Heinemann.

Neuman, S., & Celano, D. (2001). Access to print in low-income and middle-income communities: An ecological study of four neighborhoods. *Reading Research Quarterly, 36*, 8–26.

Oller, D. K., & Eilers, R. (2002) *Language and literacy in bilingual children.* Clevedon, UK: Multilingual Matters.

Parrish, T. B., Linquanti, R., Merickel, A., Quick, H.E., Laird, J., & Esra, P. (2002). *Effects of the implementation of Proposition 227 on the education of English learners, K–12: Year 2 report.* Palo Alto, CA: American Institutes for Research, and San Francisco: WestEd.

Pucci, S. (1994). Supporting Spanish language literacy: Latino children and free reading resources in schools. *Bilingual Research Journal, 18*, 67–82.

Pucci, S., & Ulanoff, S. (2004). *Where are the books? The evolution of the Spanish print environment in one Los Angeles community.* Paper presented at NABE, 2004, Albuquerque, New Mexico, February 5, 2004.

Ramos, F. (2003). Pre-service teachers' attitudes toward theoretical and practical aspects of native language instruction in the schooling of language-minority students. *Mosaic, 8*(1), 16–20.

Shin, F. (2000). Parent attitudes toward the principles of bilingual education and children's participation in bilingual programs. *Journal of Intercultural Studies, 21*(1), 93–99.

Smith, C., Constantino, R., & Krashen, S. (1997). Difference in print environment for children in Beverly Hills, Compton and Watts. *Emergency Librarian, 24*(4), 8–9.

Tse, L. (2001). Heritage language literacy: A study of US biliterates. *Language, Culture and Curriculum, 14*(3), 256–268

Thompson, M.S., DiCerbo, K.E., Mahoney, K., & MacSwan, J. (2002) Exito en California? A validity critique of language program evaluations and analysis of English learner test scores. *Education Policy Analysis Archives*, 10(7). www.epaa.asu.edu/epaa/v10n7

Willig, A. (1985). A meta-analysis of selected studies on the effectiveness of bilingual education. *Review of Educational Research, 55*(3), 269–317.

# Biographical Notes
# of Contributing Authors
# to the NRRP Volume 3

**Ilana Alanís** is an Assistant Professor in Curriculum and Instruction at The University of Texas at Brownsville. Her research interests include early childhood biliteracy, two-way bilingual programs, and oral language development. She is the Co- Principle Investigator for the Training for All Teachers Project; a grant designed to work with teachers in bilingual and English as a second language (ESL) settings. She has a Doctoral Degree in Multilingual Studies from the University of Texas at Austin.

**Rafael Lara-Alecio** is a Professor in the Department of Educational Psychology and Director of Bilingual Programs at Texas A&M University. His research is focused in program evaluation assessment and methodologies for Hispanic/Latino students and their parents.

**Genevieve Brown** is Dean of Education at Sam Houston State University. A former public school administrator, she has experience and expertise in curriculum development, literacy development and assessment for second language learners, and in developmental and cognitive psychology and emergent language skills.

**Rick Bruhn** is a Professor of Counselor Education in the Department of Educational Leadership and Counseling at Sam Houston State University in Huntsville, Texas. He directed a five-year grant to train bilingual school counselors, funded by the US Department of Education. He also presents at conferences and writes about marriage and family therapy.

**Jaime A. Castellano** is a gifted education program administrator with the School District of Palm Beach County, Florida. He is also an Adjunct Professor in bilingual education, gifted education, English to speakers of other languages, and educational leadership for Florida Atlantic University, Lynn University, and Arizona State University. He is also a nationally recognized leader in the field of gifted education culturally and linguistically diverse students and consults across the country on this topic.

**Martha Galloway** is an Assistant Professor and Coordinator of Bilingual Undergraduate Programs in the Department of Educational Psychology at Texas A&M University. Her research is focused on bilingual and biliteracy methodologies for culturally and linguistically diverse students.

**Virginia Gonzalez** is an Associate Professor and Coordinator at the Teaching English as a Second Language (TESL) Program, College of Education, University of Cincinnati. Her major expertise and extensive publication record centers on the development of innovative models and assessment and instructional applications for ESL children and adults. She holds a Doctoral Degree in Educational Psychology from The University of Texas At Austin.

**Afra Ahmed Hersi** is a doctorial student in the Lynch School of Education at Boston College. Her research is primarily in the areas of bilingual education, adolescent literacy, multicultural education, and teacher education. A former secondary social studies teacher, she currently teaches courses at Boston College and Brandeis University.

**Beverly J. Irby** is a Professor and Chair of the Department of Education Leadership and Counseling at Sam Houston State University in Huntsville, Texas. Her research focuses on social justice issues related to bilingual and English as a second language teachers and administrators within the school context.

**Stephen Krashen** is Professor Emeritus, Rossier School of Education, at the University of Southern California. His research interests include literacy, bilingual education, second language education, and language acquisition theory. He holds a black belt in Tae Kwon Do and was the 1978 Incline Bench Press Champion of Venice Beach California.

**Mei Lou** is an international student from China. She attended Sam Houston State University where she was awarded the Master's of Educational Leadership degree. She is currently a student at Columbia University Teacher's College, pursuing her doctorate degree in Educational Leadership. Her main focus of research is comparative education.

**Margarita Pinkos** is currently the Director for the Department of Multicultural Education for the School District of Palm Beach County, Florida. She was instrumental in initiating dual language programs in her district.

**Linda Rodríguez** is the Principal in the Aldine Independent School District in Houston, Texas, and an Adjunct Professor at Sam Houston State University in Huntsville, Texas. She teaches research to pre-service bilingual administrators, and is engaged in research for the improvement of academic achievement of Pre- and-Kindergarten students and their parents.

**Tom Thweatt, III** is a master's student in the Counseling Program at Sam Houston State University. He developed an interest in program management while completing Texas A&M University's Master of Business Administration degree. Mr. Thweatt's career goals include increasing the sharing of information and management within university systems.

**Josefina Villamil Tinajero** is the Dean of the College of Education and Professor of Teacher Education at The University of Texas at El Paso. She has served as President and Vice-President for the National Association for Bilingual Education (NABE). She has published extensively and is a noted speaker and researcher in the area of bilingual education.

Janet Y. Gutiérrez